CHIKAMONEKA!

Published by
Mzuni Press
P/Bag 201 Luwinga
Mzuzu 2

ISBN   978-99960-76-02-2
eISBN   978-99960-76-03-9

The Mzuni Press is represented outside Malawi by:
African Books Collective Oxford
(order@africanbookscollective.com)

www.mzunipress.blogspot.com
www.africanbookscollective.com

Editorial assistance: Hope Kaombe

CHIKAMONEKA!

Gender and Empire in Religion and Public Life

Edited by
Lilian Cheelo Siwila
Sylvia Mukuka
Nelly Mwale

MZUNI PRESS

Mzuzu 2022

Acknowledgements

The production of this book is the effort of the women of the Circle of Concerned African Women Theologians, Zambia Chapter. Special thanks go to the executive for their initiative to organize a conference that brought together the contributors of this volume. We are also grateful for the support of the elders of the Circle as such Dr Elizabeth Nkumbula, for her unwavering support and participation in all the Circle meetings, Dr Inonge Mbikusita Lewanika, Mama Lucy Kasanga, Mama Omega Bula, and the late Rev Sampa-Bredt. We honour you as the pioneers of the Circle work in Zambia. We also want to thank our sponsors, the United Methodist Church of Canada and the Council for World Mission through the support of Dr Collin Cowan. And finally, to the publishers for accepting to put the work of Zambian Women scholars on the world map.

Contents

Foreword

For centuries, women have been struggling to find means of
addressing oppressive structures both in religious and secular spaces.
The exclusion of women from participating in what are known as
male dominated spaces as a historical factor continues to haunt our
societies especially when such moves are viewed as normative in the
name of culture and religion. The influence of colonialism and
mission work in most African countries did not make things any
better for women, while our own African cultures also continue to
contribute to the silencing and subjugating of women as they have
done over the centuries. Musimbi Kanyoro is right to say that African
culture is like a double-edged sword - while we embrace our culture
as something that informs our identity, there are some aspects of our
cultures that require critical scrutiny.[1] This unique volume, the first
edited volume to be written in Zambia by *The Circle of Concerned African
Women Theologians*, presents the experiences of women in religion,
culture and other empires around and within such as patriarchy,
colonialism and globalization. Informed by narratives of their own
experiences and those of other women drawn from various contexts,
these authors have produced a volume that is worth celebrating. As
members of the Circle of Concerned African Women Theologians'
Zambian chapter, they have become the pioneers of an academic
volume focused on gender and religion from a Zambian perspective.
This is a historical event in that even those of us who were the
pioneers of the birthing of the Circle were not able to produce a book
volume bred in Zambia.

Mercy Amba Oduyoye argues that "for a long time African women's
experiences were written by others and those 'others' spoke on our

---

[1] Musimbi Kanyoro, "Introducing Feminist Cultural Hermeneutics: An African
Perspective," *Introductions in Feminist Theology,"* Cleveland: Pilgrim Press, 2002.

behalf and wrote on our behalf as though we were dead."[2] But time has come for Women Theologians in our country to begin to publish what emerges from their own research and experience as women to bring gender issues from a religious perspective to the academic space. In his book *Orientalism*, Edward Said observes that colonialism involves political, economic, and cultural hegemony and military domination when it comes to the production of knowledge about the "other" who in this case is the colonized.[3] The era we are in is an era of empire whose attitude to those on the margins is no different from that of the colonial systems. Hence the need for local knowledge that will speak to the realities of our contexts.

I want to congratulate the authors of this volume who have accepted the challenge to break the void on gender and religion academic work in our context. The volume comes as an asset both in academic institutions, religious and secular society. As Gayatri Spivak asks when speaking about the Dalit women of India: "Can the Subaltern Speak?" I confidently respond to her question; "Yes, the Subaltern has Spoken![4]

By bringing out the diverse voices and experiences, the authors recount and expose the negative practices that are retrogressive to human development. The book also demonstrates the power of narrative theory as a tool for academic discourse analysis. The stories in this book are not just any other form of narrative but are stories that stimulate the reader's consciousness. As Sarojini Nadar argues,

---

[2] Mercy Amba Oduyoye, *Hearing and Knowing: Theological Reflections on Christianity in Africa*, Maryknoll: Orbis, 1986.

[3] Edward W. Said, *Orientalism*, New York: Vintage, 1978.

[4] Gayatri Chakravorti Spivat, "Can the Subaltern Speak?" (1993), since then reprintted in various forms.

"stories are data with a soul"[5] and as these stories unfold, they unmask the positions of power and how these spaces have become sites of struggle for women who have been subjugated and pushed to the periphery of society. Speaking of women's resistance to empire, this book adopted the theme: *Chikamoneka,* which literally translates, *"it shall be seen."* The book borrowed this metaphor from the famous narrative of Mama Julia Chikamoneka to illustrate the need for women to resist all forms of injustice imposed on humanity that are not life giving. The word *Chikamoneka* provides an affirmation of the position of women and how society should value their potential when presented with appropriate opportunities.

Lastly, I will not do justice to the volume if I don't relate it to where it all began! The Circle of Concerned African Women Theologians, where this work is located, began in 1989. Prior to that a number of women across the continent and those in the diaspora participated in the birthing of this work, whose aim is to bring together women and men who are passionate in transforming spaces that are oppressive to both men and women. The Zambia chapter of the Circle began in 1999 with pioneers such as Inonge Mbikusita Lewanika, Violet Sampa-Bredt, Lucy Kasanga and many others. This book is also honouring these Circle veterans as it emerges as the first of its kind in Zambia reflecting the objectives of these women. We look forward to more work of this nature, especially from the young generation who are to carry the work of the Circle on.

Dr Inonge Mbikusita Lewanika (Ambassador, Diplomat and Peace Community Activist)

---

[5] Sarojini Nadar, "Stories are Data with Soul: Lessons from Black Feminist Epistemology," *Agenda*, 28(1), 2014, 18-28.

Contributors

Petronella Bweupe Bwalya is an MA student in Catholic Theology at the University of KwaZulu Natal. She is a religious sister in the congregation of the Sisters of Mercy in Mansa Diocese of Zambia. She is also a member of the Circle of Concerned African Women Theologians, Zambia Chapter.

Helen Chisanga has a BA in Education from Solusi University in Zimbabwe and a Diploma in Theology. She is an ordained minister in the United Church of Zambia and a member of the Circle of Concerned African Women Theologians.

Judith Lubasi Ilubala-Ziwa (PhD) is a Lecturer in Religious Studies at the University of Zambia. She is a member of the Circle of Concerned African Women Theologians, Zambia Chapter.

Cynthia Kabanda (Bachelor of Theology candidate) United Church of Zambia University. She is a member of the Circle of Concerned African Women Theologians.

Sylvia Mukuka (PhD) in Practical Theology is a Lecturer in Practical Theology at the United Church of Zambia University. She is also serving as a pastor in a local congregation. She is a member of the Circle of Concerned African Women Theologians, Zambia Chapter.

Charity Chali Mulalami (PhD) candidate in Gender Studies at the University of KwaZulu Natal. She is also a nurse by profession and an ordained minister. She is a member of the Circle of Concerned African Women Theologians.

Peggy Mulambya-Kabonde (PhD) in Gender Studies. She is the General Secretary of the United Church of Zambia and the current Circle Regional Coordinator for Southern Africa. She is also a gender activist and reference group member of the World Communion of Reformed Churches.

Rose Mulowa PhD candidate in Systematic Theology at the University of the Free State, South Africa. She is an ordained minister in the Reformed Church in Zambia.

Nelly Mwale (PhD) in Religious Studies. She is a Lecturer at the University of Zambia in the Department of Religious Studies. She is also a member of the Circle of Concerned African Women Theologians, the African Association for the Study of Religions (AASR), and the Association for the Study of Religion in Southern Africa (ASRSA).

Mary Mwiche Zulu (PhD) in Practical Theology at the University of KwaZulu Natal. She is also a lecturer at United Church of Zambia Theological College. She is the National Coordinator for the Circle of Concerned African Women Theologians, Zambian Chapter.

Maligelita J. Njobvu (Masters) in Religious Education is a lecturer at the University of Zambia in the Department of Religious Studies. She is also a member of the African Association for the Study of Religions (AASR).

Lungowe Sinjwala (Masters) in Religious Studies is currently a Secondary School teacher in Kabwe, Zambia and a member of the Circle, Zambia Chapter.

Lilian Cheelo Siwila (PhD) Associate Professor and Head of Department in Systematic Theology and Gender Studies at the University of KwaZulu Natal. She is also a member of the Circle of Concerned African Women Theologians.

Introduction

African Women Speak out in the Face of Empire

Lilian Cheelo Siwila

During the conference that led to the production of this volume, one thing that became very clear was the way in which most of the women in Zambia have been oppressed by different structures and yet remain silent. The themes associated with this silence were culture, patriarchy, religion, mission and colonial influence in the form of empire. All these were seen as tools for the silencing and subjugation of women to the periphery of society. According to Omolara Ogundipe-Leslie, an African woman carries six mountains on her back namely; external oppression through colonialism, oppression from traditional structures, her backwardness, man, her colour or race and herself.[1] Reading the chapters presented in this volume, one is able to identify with the authors that all these six mountains are reflected by the voices of women in this volume. The mountains presented by Ogundipe-Leslie are sometimes so intertwined that they end up forming a vicious circle in the lives of women which require women to seek ways of being liberated from these mountains. This raises the need for women to theologically reflect on their work and begin to tell their stories differently. As Musa Dube would say, African women need to arise and call for justice against the oppressor. For a long time, women's stories have been told through pulpits and lecture rooms.[2] As African women emerged through the birth of the Circle,

---

[1] Omolara Ogundipe-Leslie, *Re-claiming Ourselves: African Women and Critical Transformation*, Trenton, New Jersey: Africa World Press, 1994, 28.

[2] Musa Dube, "Grant Me Justice: Towards Gender Sensitive Multisectoral HIV/AIDS Reading of the Bible," in Musa Dube & Musimbi Kanyoro (eds), *Grant*

they began to see the need to join the global body of feminist scholars and other gender activists to speak out against gender injustices.

As part of the project of the Circle of Concerned African Women Theologians, whose main objective is to write and publish, this volume emerges as the first kind of work undertaken solely by Circle women in Zambia. The authors are academics, church workers and those working in secular organizations. The book is presented as an academic resource within the field of Humanities, especially useful to those working in the field of Gender and Religion. The uniqueness of this volume lies not only in its being the first Circle publication solely written by Zambian women, but also in the rich variety of themes knit around the central theme of the volume, which is a call to transform religious and public spaces that oppress women in our society. Hence, naming these structures as African Women Theologians also meant creating safe spaces for us to tell our stories and the stories of other women. As Brigalia Bam would say when she reflects on the road to the formation of the Circle, "the time had come when women needed to move from being spoken for to speaking for themselves."[3] The author further argues, women were not satisfied even with the "speaking with" paradigm though it was better than being spoken for, being spoken about and being spoken at.[4] Telling their stories and the stories of others then becomes a healing process for women. Narrative theory is also a main focus for African Women Theologians' ways of doing theology. Hence, the aim of this volume is to encourage women from Zambia to research and write about

---

Me Justice: HIV/AIDS and Gender Readings of the Bible, Pietermaritzburg: Cluster, 2004, 3-27.

[3] Brigalia Bam, "Women and the Church in (South) Africa: Women are the Church in (South) Africa," in Isabel Phiri & Sarojini Nadar (eds), _On Being Church: African Women's Voices and Visions_, Geneva: WCC, 2005, 8.

[4] Ibid, 8.

their own stories and experiences and those of other women that have not been told for too long.

The What and the Why of the Circle of Concerned African Women Theologians

The Circle of Concerned African Women Theologians, hereafter the Circle, is an academic body that grew out of women's concerns on how religion, culture, patriarchy and society have treated women over the centuries. The Circle emerged through women such as Mercy Amba Oduyoye, Brigalia Bam, Musimbi Kanyoro, Nyambura Njoroge, Inonge Lewanika, Violet Sampa-Bredt and others in their different meetings, especially at a predominantly male dominated conference of the Ecumenical Association of Third World Theologians (EATWOT) in 1988. The lack of women presence in these conferences and in theological colleges provoked debates among these women that led to the founding of the Circle in 1989 under the leadership of Mercy Amba Oduyoye.[5] It was in this contested male space that these African women theologians began to question their embodiment in a theological academic debate that speaks with a voice of patriarchal discourse. Among the topics that are prominent in the work of the Circle is the need to strengthen women's participation in theological and public discourses and to make their contributions visible in both the church and the public space through publications. Since then, the work of the Circle has grown in presence and publications both locally and globally. Much of the publishing is done in regions such as Southern Africa, West Africa and East Africa, with limited books from other parts of the continent. Although Zambian women scholars are acknowledged elsewhere in these contexts, the

---

[5] For its overall history see: Rachel NyaGondwe Fiedler, *The History of the Circle of Concerned African Women Theologians, 1989-2007*, Mzuzu: Mzuni Press, 2016.

lack of published work that is located within the country by Zambian women is what promoted this book.

Transforming Religio-cultural and Gender Ideologies

In the title of this chapter, I am calling for African women to speak out in the face of empire. One may wonder as to whether this is a noble call since for a long time now, women are said to have been _'making a lot of noise about their issues'_. Although this seems to be the common narrative, the noise made by women has not produced much change in any way, mainly because injustice still prevails on women and girls. Women and girls are still being raped and killed, domestic violence is still rampant and gender inequalities both in religious and secular society are still being condoned. Therefore, the six mountains that women carry[6] are still weighing on women's backs, and hence the need for women to keep speaking out against all forms of injustice in our societies cannot be overemphasized. Transforming religio-cultural and gender ideologies that are oppressive to women should be on the agenda of both men and women who are passionate about the ordering of a just society. Some of the main structures that need to be transformed are the religio-cultural spaces that embody women's lived experience. As Musimbi Kanyoro argues, in the African context, religion and culture are bedfellows and both are key factors for women's oppression.[7] This is a hard fact to grasp, especially for those of us who grew up within Christian traditions where the Biblical and cultural interpretations were not to be questioned. Nyambura Njoroge in her quest for women's resistance to oppressive structures argues that Biblical narratives have presented

---

[6] Leslie M. Ogundipe, _Re-claiming Ourselves: African Women and Critical Transformation_, Trenton, New Jersey: Africa World Press, 1994, 28.

[7] Musimbi Kanyoro, "Introducing Feminist Cultural Hermeneutics – An African Perspective," _Introductions in Feminist Theology,"_ Cleveland: Pilgrim Press, 2002; John S. Mbiti, _African Religions and Philosophy_, 2nd ed, London: Heinemann, 1969.

us with stories of women who were muted and silenced in the quest for their rights. She further contends that for many years, African women have been spoken for and commented on while they remained faceless and voiceless. When Africa's new institutions such as hospitals, churches and schools were introduced by missionaries and colonial powers, the low position of women in the social, religious and cultural life of African women was taken for granted.[8]

The doctrine of *"women be silent,"* as I would call it, is one teaching that has not been well addressed by feminist scholars and yet it remains one of the main contributing factors to domestic violence because it disempowers women from speaking out. Both the Bible and African culture place much emphasis on *'women being silent'*. In the Zambian context, as a girl is growing up, one of the key lessons she is taught to embrace is the culture of respecting the husband by being silent. African culture teaches that a good wife should learn in silence as a sign of obedience. This patriarchal narrative is also emphasized in 1 Timothy 2:11-14 where Paul is telling women to learn in silence. Worthy as the teaching may be in its essence to bring about mutuality in marriages and to make good Christian wives, in many cases the teaching has contributed to the perpetuation of gender-based violence and subjection of women to all sorts of oppression and dehumanization. Keeping silent disempowers the person who is silenced for he/she is not given an opportunity to express their views or to speak out about their struggles. Zambia, like many other African countries, has a number of cultural practices that are life denying to women. Teachings like *"when your husband is shouting at you, you should not answer back but rather put water in your mouth to keep you silent, never speak about marital issues outside the home"* are harmful to women just like

---

[8] Nyambura Njoroge, "A Spirituality of Resistance and Transformation," in Nyambura Njoroge & Musa Dube (eds), *Talitha Cum! Theologies of African Women*, Pietermaritzburg: Cluster, 2001, 66-68.

all the silences around incest, which is rampant in the country. Associated with such teachings are proverbs and songs that teach women to be silent even before the oppressor. These are some of the mountains women are carrying in the name of preserving their culture. Musimbi Kanyoro argues:

> Women in Africa are custodians of cultural practices. For generations, African women have guarded cultural prescriptions that are strictly governed by the fear of breaking taboos. Many practices that diminish women continue to be practiced to various degrees, often making women objects of cultural preservation. Harmful traditional practices are passed on as 'cultural values' and therefore are not to be discussed, challenged or changed.[9]

The fear to question or challenge these taboos has in some cases led to some women's death. From a theological perspective, the Pauline Theology of '*women should learn in silence*' is in many cases interpreted out of context for the benefit of those behind this teaching, mostly men. Hence, Musimbi Kanyoro would argue that whether from church pews or among theologically trained women, there are only a handful that are comfortable with challenging the texts of the Bible by subjecting them to hermeneutics of critical biblical analysis.[10] As a result of this, both the Bible and Christian tradition have continued to be used as weapons for women's subjection through interpretations that are not life affirming. It is these kinds of teachings that prompted the authors in this volume to speak out and name some of the oppressive structures in their societies. As Musimbi Kanyoro

---

[9] Musimbi Kanyoro, "Engendering Communal Theology," in Nyambura Njoroge & Musa Dube (eds), "*Talitha Cum! Theologies of African Women,*" Pietermaritzburg: Cluster, 2001, 158-180 [161].

[10] Ibid. – For such recent challenging voices see: Rachel NyaGondwe Fiedler, Johannes Hofmeyr & Klaus Fiedler, *African Feminist Hermeneutics. An Evangelical Reflection*, Mzuzu: Mzuni Press, 2016 (esp 97ff) and Lazarus Chilenje, *Paul's Gender Theology and the Ordained Women's Ministry in the CCAP in Zambia*, Mzuzu: Mzuni Press, 2021.

would argue; feminist cultural hermeneutics conditions how women understand their realities.[11]

Besides transforming religio-cultural ideologies, gender ideologies also need to be analyzed and transformed through a feminist lens. Ursula King alludes that although gender issues are the concern for both men and women, there is always a bias to pay more attention on women's issues when talking about gender because, of the two genders, women tend to be more vulnerable to sexism and abuse. That's why in most of the societies, when people talk about gender, they just think of issues that relate to women, and only issues that relate to experiences of women are interpreted through the lens of gender.[12] In this volume, the authors are more concerned with gender ideologies that are related to the unequal distribution of power between men and women. Both Musa Dube and Lilian Siwila call for a multi-sectoral transformative approach to discussions on gender justice especially for women.[13] Such an approach would accord women an opportunity to find liberating tools to speak out about their concerns. This also calls for a need to transform peoples' perceptions about the understanding of gender. Terms such as gender and feminism have not been well received; especially in the church their usage is mostly perceived negatively. The negative perception of these terms also contributes to the need for women to

---

[11] Musimbi Kanyoro, "Engendering Communal Theology," in Nyambura Njoroge & Musa Dube (eds), *"Talitha Cum! Theologies of African Women,"* Pietermaritzburg: Cluster, 2001, 158-180 [161].

[12] Ursula King, *Introduction: Gender in the Study of Religion*, Oxford: Blackwell, 1995.

[13] Musa Dube, "Grant Me Justice: Towards Gender Sensitive Multisectoral HIV/AIDS Reading of the Bible," Pietermaritzburg: Cluster, 2004, 3-27; Lilian Cheelo Siwila, "Gender Trouble: Navigating Distorted Gender Discourses in Faith Communities," in Herbert Moyo (ed), *Pastoral Care in a Globalised World: African and European Perspectives*, Pietermaritzburg: Cluster, 2015, 243-256.

speak out about gender injustice. A study by Lilian Siwila on distorted discourses in the conceptualizing of gender in faith communities has shown that although some churches have developed programmes that focus on gender justice, the reality on the ground is different. In these same spaces women who wish to speak out are ridiculed and silenced in the name of religion and culture. The solution to this kind of dilemma is for women to create their own path to liberation.[14]

Finding our own Path to a Feminist Liberation Praxis

While a great amount of literature written about women speaks of how they have been abused by patriarchy throughout history, there is also a need to find liberating ways of speaking about women's emancipation. Historically, we also see a situation where women's presence in religion and public life meant that women were left out of the lecture rooms, political positions and pulpits, as these were seen as spaces only for men. That's why, even when these spaces have now become inclusive of both genders, they still operate under androcentric frameworks which favour the male gender. Both secular and religious institutions still struggle to open the space for women in top leadership positions and even when they do, it becomes a milestone that calls for publicity and awe, and yet, if a man holds the same position, it is viewed as the norm. This is the power of patriarchy that African women are trying to resist. The birth of the Circle of Concerned African Women Theologians was one way of helping women to find their own path to liberation. In her book titled *Daughters of Anowa,* Mercy Amba Oduyoye calls for a feminist

---

[14] Lilian Cheelo Siwila, "Gender Trouble: Navigating Distorted Gender Discourses in Faith Communities," in Herbert Moyo (ed), *Pastoral Care in a Globalised World: African and European Perspectives*, Pietermaritzburg: Cluster, 2015, 243-256.

liberation praxis when she calls for women to account for and stand up against their abusers.[15] Rosemary Radford-Ruether contends that:

> The key to the erasure of women in religious history as in all of the patriarchal history is not that women were inactive, but that they have not been able to shape the tradition by which the story of what they have done is remembered and carried on. Although the Israel exodus and prophetic traditions define key elements of the identity of Israel as God's chosen people in the Hebrew scripture and of the church in the New Testament, the memory of women's participation in the liberating movements is continuously erased or reinterpreted according to the male interests.[16]

Following the statement of Rosemary Radford-Ruether, it is evident that although women like Miriam, the sister of Moses, were part of the leaders in the Exodus journey of the Israelites, we hear very little about her role in this journey and even when she is mentioned, she is mostly reflected on in a negative way. The common discourse of overlooking women when they do exploits is what makes the feminist liberation movement critical to the recognition of women's work in society. Some of the stories presented in this book speak of this kind of concern of skipping women's narratives as presented by Rosemary Radford-Ruether.[17] For example, the Zambian political history has significant female figures such as *Mama* Julia Chama Chikamoneka, who played a significant role in uniting women to fight against the dehumanizing effects of colonial rule. As an icon of the pre-independence liberation movement in Zambia, *Mama* Julia Mulenga Nsofwa with other women demonstrated a strong spirit of resistance to imperial powers. Her history records an incident when she and other women marched to the district commissioner's office as a way

---

[15] Mercy Amba Oduyoye, *Daughters of Anowa: African Women and Patriarchy*, Maryknoll: Orbis, 1995.

[16] Rosemary Radford-Ruether, *Women-Church. Theology and Practice of Feminist Liturgical Communities*, Eugene: Wipf & Stock, 1985, 43.

[17] Ibid.

of protest and while there, she slapped the white district commissioner in the face in anger due to the evil treatment of black people. This was the highest form of postcolonial feminist resistance to empire and yet it is not as well recorded in the political history of Zambia compared to the history of her male counterparts. Despite this milestone, her story has fallen through the cracks of history like many other stories of African women who stood against the political empire of the day and fought for the liberation of African nations. Amina Mama states that:

> During the nationalist era it was very common to see women throw their support behind male-led struggles than to organize their own parties and fight against these gender relations. During the 1950s Ghanaian women rallied behind Kwame Nkrumah while the Kenyan women took to the bush as fighters and played a key role in support of the Land and Freedom Army and many others. Women's involvement in African liberation struggles became a favoured subject for feminist scholars during the 1970s and 1980s, hence the documentation of numerous historical female militancy move-ments.[18]

Within the Zambian context the work of women such as Julia Chama Chikamoneka becomes a significant point of departure to our rewriting the struggles and the resistance of African women to colonial influence in their pursuit of liberation. Their stories are not only political stories but are also stories of faith. This is because for countries such as Zambia the road to national liberation was also embodied with religions such as Christianity and African Traditional Religion. Women's resistance to empire needs to be celebrated as a feminist liberation paradigm. Conclusively, we can also argue that colonial masters who colonized most African states excluded African women from playing important roles in the politics of their nations.

Therefore, in our attempt to find our own path to a feminist liberation praxis, we cannot just end at telling our stories but write

---

[18] Amina Mama, *Women's Studies and Studies of Women in Africa during the 1990s,* Dakar: CODESRIA, 1996, 6.

them so that the coming generation may find liberative elements in these stories. Mercy Amba Oduyoye, when talking about the need for African women to write their own theology, urges that:

> In doing theology as women of Africa we shall have the advantage of knowing the methods our brothers have used and the results that emanate from them … if we are to be part of the team of midwives assisting the rebirth of African theology and the resurrection of the human in Africa, we have to operate from the standpoint that westernizing Africa is not our road to liberation.[19]

Oduyoye's plea for women to find their own liberation path through publications should be understood in two ways. First, she is provoking women to find the will to arise and embody their own methodological frameworks that are relevant to their African realities and context.[20] This kind of liberation does not, however, mean the oppression of men as Susan Rakoczy would argue, but rather a need to create a theology of inclusivity and partnership of equals.[21] The second reason alluded to by Mercy Amba Oduyoye is the need for African female scholars to move away from a Eurocentric approach of scholarship that does not promote nor speak to their experiences as Africans. The best way to avoid this trap of using western frameworks to speak about our struggles as African people is to be deliberate in promoting our own literature. John Mbiti argues that the African soil is not ineffective and that it can produce its own new ideas. Not until we, as African women, realize the wealth of untapped knowledge that we have, will we cease being epistemologically

---

[19]   Mercy Amba Oduyoye, "The Search for a Two-winged Theology," in Mercy Amba Oduyoye & Musimbi Kanyoro (eds), *Talitha Cum! Proceedings of the Convocation of African Women Theologians*, 1989, Ibadan: Daystar, 53.

[20]   Ibid.

[21]   Susan Rakoczy, *In Her Name: Women Doing Theology*, Pietermaritzburg: Cluster, 2004.

colonized, continuing to depend on western frameworks to name our work.[22] Feminist liberation praxis also means being liberated from the historical oppression embedded in colonial and missional influence as identified by a number of authors in this volume.

Towards a Spirit of Resistance

A common thread that runs through this volume is the naming of the oppressive structures and the calling for a spirituality of resistance as proposed by Nyambura Njoroge.[23] Remembering the past is not just for the sake of critical inquiry, but rather to encourage introspection and reflection of our experiences.[24] This helps us to see the past in a new way and thereafter reshape our future and identity.[25] In this volume, stories that have been told have not only provided a critical inquiry but have also helped us to create a shift from being "observers and victims to participants and actors in the history."[26] The best way to participate in creating a history is to move together as a partnership of equals and to become a community of sisterhood that celebrates unity in diversity. As Rosemary Radford-Ruether puts it:

> Women's movement does not create its own alternative expression of community. Women bond together in support groups and coalitions for action. They gather mainly outside the formal structures of church and society to share experiences and analysis. Sometimes, the church, which is

---

[22] John S. Mbiti, _African Religions and Philosophy_, 2nd ed, London: Heinemann, 1969.

[23] Nyambura Njoroge, "A Spirituality of Resistance and Transformation," in Nyambura Njoroge & Musa Dube (eds), _Talitha Cum! Theologies of African Women_, Pietermaritzburg: Cluster, 2001, 66-88.

[24] Isabel Apawo Phiri et al, _Her-Stories. Hidden Stories of Women of Faith in Africa_, Pietermaritzburg: Cluster, 2002, 6.

[25] Ibid.

[26] Ibid, 7.

the great symbol making institution, of women's traditions operates as countersign to their hopes.[27]

Developing a spirit of resistance as women is a complex issue which requires careful reflection on the consequences thereof. However, unless women learn to resist empires both external and internal within their communities, their oppressors will continue to enjoy their privileged positions. As power is a complex term with personal, social and religious connotations, religious leaders have the right to choose to either be sanctioning agents of abuse of power or to be prophetic critics of the way power is used,[28] and even though church and society claim to be concerned about human suffering and injustice, society is ineffective in dealing with gender-based violence and the church has kept a deadly silence in spite of its ethics and concern for all humanity.[29] As a result of this, women and girls continue to suffer while church and society create 'blind zones' that keep overlooking women's issues.

Another form of resistance is the need to address the unfinished business of the struggles of the girl child in Zambia. Although Zambia is praised by many international bodies to have responded positively to practices such as child marriage, the reality on the ground is different. The girl child is still trapped in gender role discrepancies and other forms of injustices including sexual violence. When one speaks of resisting empires that perpetuate the oppression of women and girls and thereafter hinder the speaking out on these

---

[27] Rosemary Radford Ruether, _Women-Church. Theology and Practice of Feminist Liturgical Communities_, Eugene: Wipf & Stock, 1985

[28] James N. Poling, _The Abuse of Power: A Theological Problem_, Nashville: Abingdon, 1991, 13.

[29] Ibid, 14.

oppressions, it is these kinds of struggles that would provoke women not to be 'silent any longer'. Rosemary Radford Ruether argues that

> in the story of the Exodus, we find that the first acts of rebellion against the empire Pharaoh are those of women. The Mother of Moses refuses to obey the decree to kill her new-born son and hides him in the bulrushes. The sister of Moses sizes the opportunity to save him by presenting him to the daughter of Pharaoh who takes him as her own child. Thus, a conspiracy of women takes place across class and ethnic lines to save a child who will be the liberator of Israel.[30]

What the Book is all about

This volume presents experiences of Zambian women of faith on religion, empire, culture and patriarchy. Scholars, some of whom tell their own stories, present us with narratives of lived experiences of African women. The book is divided into 15 chapters, and each of these chapters presents us with a unique theme and topic that is related to gender and religion in church and public life. **Chapter One** opens the debate on issues of masculinity as it relates to gender and religion in public life. The chapter is developed around three concepts of masculinity that are seen to be very prevalent in Zambia namely; culture masculinity, white collar masculinity and clerical hero masculinity. Lilian Siwila argues that in our attempt to address gender issues and their effects on women, we cannot avoid the topic of masculinity because most of the negative attitudes displayed by men towards women are manifestations of different forms of masculinities that are nurtured by men. The chapter concludes by calling for a form of masculinity that will help to transform some of the negative religio-cultural, colonial and missional trends of masculinity found among some of the men in Zambia.

---

[30] Rosemary Radford Ruether, _Women-Church. Theology and Practice of Feminist Liturgical Communities_, Eugene: Wipf & Stock, 1985, 44.

Chapter Two interrogates the representations of women's experiences of prophecy for prayer and profit in the media in the context of the prophetic empire. The chapter draws on narrative research that is informed by the content analysis of the media portrayal of women, prayer and prophets in Zambia through a mediatization lens. The chapter demonstrates how women are made to be vulnerable in their quest for prayer and prophecy at the hands of the new prophets. This vulnerability ranges from sexual abuse to financial exploitation. Nelly Mwale argues that the boom of neo-Pentecostal Christianity in Zambia after the 1990s, where prophets were popularized in the media, with women being at the centre of the prophecy for prayer and profit discourse, have attracted media attention without much scholarly engagement, because scholarship on prophecy has been preoccupied with the historical study of the growth of Pentecostal Christianity in Zambia.

Chapter Three focuses on clerical sexual scandals revealed within the Catholic Church. Although Sr Petronella Bweupe does not focus this study within the Zambian context, suffice it to say that the experiences of the western context also affect the global church. Using Philippians 2:5-7 as the point of departure, she draws on extracts of research findings from the United States of America (USA), the Netherlands and Australia on the sexual violence scandal in the Catholic Church to inform her discussions on the subject matter. Chapters Four and Five continue the debate on gender-based violence.

Chapter Four focuses on a rarely discussed aspect of gender-based violence, namely sexual violence on women with disabilities. Lilian Cheelo Siwila and Charity Mulalami contend that this is one of the key population groups that are normally silenced and sidelined when it comes to discussions of gender-based violence. The authors of this chapter analyze how the Zambian society conceptualizes disability through the use of words such as _ishilu_ and how that leads to the negative perceptions of disability. Through the lens of social construction, the chapter concludes that although there seems to be some positive response to addressing gender-based violence in the country, little or no attention is paid to women with mental disabilities who are victims of sexual abuse because of society's social construction of disability.

Chapter Five summarizes the theme of gender-based violence arguing that the problem of gender-based violence continues to affect all sections of family and social life. The chapter demonstrates that sexual violence has today become a global issue that continues to draw the attention of the public as well as of the church. As such, it has led to the _Thursdays in Black_ campaign, which Cynthia Kabanda and Sylvia Mukuka propose as a model that can be emulated in Zambia in the fight against gender-based violence.

The next section of the book deals with stories of women and their experience of patriarchy both in the church and in society. In **Chapter Six**, Peggy Mulambya-Kabonde focuses on the challenges of gender equity and leadership in the church. The author argues that, while there is an acknowledgement of the church to be inclusive, there is a deep concern of the fact that policies and strategies used to call for inclusivity are determined by men. In most cases, women are only required to implement these policies and strategies. The author calls for a revision of these gender discrepancies in policies and strategies in order to create a church that is all inclusive.

Chapter Seven provides us with a historical account of the first significant woman in the Zambian struggle for independence, Mama Betty Kaunda who also became the first lady of the nation. In writing her story Judith Lubasi Ziwa also demonstrates the forgotten role of women in political spaces. **Chapter Eight** presents us with experiences of women in patriarchal male dominated spaces. Sylvia Mukuka presents her journey in ministry as the first female Bishop, arguing that in as much as the battle against the ordination of women in the church has been won, the reality on the ground is different. This can be argued from the point of the pain and the struggles that women have endured in their journey of faith. The author challenges women to tell their story as a form of therapy and as a tool for interpreting their experiences.

Chapter Nine presents another narrative of a single woman's experience in ministry, Helen Chisanga. She looks at the challenges that a single female clergy goes through in terms of discrimination from those who are married and the society at large. The author argues that in many African societies, it is not recommended for a woman to remain as a single mother even after having two or more children outside marriage. This article argues, on the contrary, being a single mother and clergy should not be associated negatively with the calling of God to ministry. The author concludes that God's call knows neither gender nor marital status.

Chapter Ten is yet another personal narrative of a women's journey to ordination. Speaking from a gender perspective Rose Mulowa presents her life struggles with theological training and thereafter, ordination in the Reformed Church of Zambia. Being the first woman to be enrolled for theological education, Rose Mulowa presents us with a narrative of her experience of patriarchy and of the extent to which women have to strive in order to be accepted in the ministry of word and sacrament.

As compared to their male colleagues, the female exclusion from theological education negatively influenced the progression of women in leadership roles, and consequently women remained in the minority in leadership positions. Even today the problem of women's presence in theological education is still a big challenge in the church.

This is reflected in **Chapter Eleven** where Nelly Mwale and Maligelita Njobvu explore women's representation in theological education through an engendered theological education lens. The chapter reveals the underrepresentation of women in faculties of Theology in Christian universities in Zambia. The inquiry is premised on the fact that despite calls for the advancement of women through their active participation in all spheres of public and private life, including theological education, women continue to be underrepresented and issues of gender continue being addressed from a policy level with little or no practical action. The chapter proposes a move beyond verbalizing women's access to theological education to implementation.

Chapter Twelve discusses the patriarchal tendencies of Theological Colleges especially those that have become universities. Mary Zulu Mwiche reviews how these theological universities are significant to her experiences of spaces that informed her understanding of theological education from a gendered/feminist perspective. She argues that patriarchy is deeply rooted in the theological education institutions of Zambia. She does this by drawing on the structuration approach to analyze the primary foundations of education which have perpetuated an endemic system that frowns upon women in theological education. The author concludes that patriarchy is systematically entrenched in the schooling system, a primary foundation of all formal education, including theological education. The chapter advances that theological educators ought to consider system reforms by implementing gender transformative approaches.

The last two chapters focus on women's empowerment and its effect on women and society. The chapters both argue that while women's subjugation is a reality in our society, women too have managed to rise to positions of power. **Chapter Thirteen** uses the story of Jezebel to demonstrate the power behind women and its influence on society. Charity Mulalami uses 1 Kings 21 to demonstrate how

Jezebel, representing the female empire, exhibits leadership and power. Since the United Nations' Fourth World Conference on Women in 1995, better known as the Beijing Conference, which discussed issues of equality, there has been improvement on women's empowerment both in the area of academics and secular society. Zambia is not exceptional to this experience which was clearly seen when the late President Mr Michael Chilufya Sata publicly announced in 2011, that his government will also focus on women empowerment. This presidential vision saw several women in the government positions. The chapter reflects on how women have performed in these previously male dominated positions. The last chapter (**Chapter Fourteen**) of this volume addresses yet another key theme, women's participation in seemingly male dominated traditional ceremonies. In this empirical study Lungowe Sinjwala and Judith Ilabula-Ziwa focus on the *Kuomboka kwa Likomu* (KKL) ceremony in the Munyama area of the Kalabo district in Zambia. The findings of the study show that historically, traditional beliefs and stringent taboos did not allow women to participate in this ceremony. However, women's participation is now gradually being accepted. The chapter concludes that although positive strides have been made to involve women, a number of traditional beliefs and taboos still excludes women from full participation in the KKL, so that women's self-identity in society still requires reconstruction.

In concluding this introduction, I wish to point out the need to recognize and appreciate women's experience in addressing issues of gender injustice, because the lack of appeal to women's experiences undermines the credibility of women's stories of struggles against all forms of injustice. The experiences of women presented in this book through narratives or otherwise, need to be acknowledged as a legitimate source of knowledge and a norm for theological reflection. The book also emphasizes the need to realize the historical ills of patriarchy and gender injustice and how they have influenced the way in which issues of gender are still being addressed even today both in religion and in public life. Therefore, a call from feminist scholars to address the historical past cannot be undermined in the fight against women's struggles to attain full humanity. The empire spirit that silences women in the name of culture and religion as addressed in this chapter and the book at large needs to be critically analyzed through a feminist liberation lens. Hence, as Beverly Haddad argues, women cannot afford to choose to remain silent amidst society's injustices.[31]

---

[31] Beverley Haddad, "Choosing to Remain Silent: Links between Gender Violence, HIV/AIDS and the South African Church," in Isabel Phiri, Beverly Haddad & Madipoane Masenya (eds), *African Women, HIV/AIDS and Faith Communities*, Pietermaritzburg: Cluster, 2003.

Chapter One

Masculinity and Empire in Religion and Public Life: Social Construction of a 'Real Man' in Zambia

Lillian Cheelo Siwila

Introduction

This chapter emerges from much of the research that I have conducted in Zambia mainly on gender-based violence. The chapter is influenced by the responses from some of the workshops conducted which revealed that, although Zambia like other countries is trying to address issues of gender-based violence, the approach is seemingly focused on one gender. There isn't much said about men, who in most cases are the perpetrators of gender-based violence. In my response to the need to involve men I opted to work in the field of masculinity. My focus is an attempt to understand how masculinity influences behaviour that leads to violence against women and children. This is because in Zambia the religio-cultural and Missional-Victorian model of what it means to be a man is rarely challenged. Instead, the concept is nurtured and men are elevated to the status of empire. Hence, in this context, there is a need to challenge masculinity as a form of empire both in religion and in public life. Through the title of this chapter, I ask the question *"where are the real men?"* This question is to demonstrate how the power of assigning a naming has been used to promote dangerous masculinities through cultural or religious beliefs. I begin the chapter by providing a brief overview of masculinity and thereafter discuss the intersection between gender and masculinity and then I look at ways through which masculinities are nurtured and condoned at the expense of women's bodies, both in religion and public life, and I conclude the chapter by proposing a transformative kind of masculinity as a route through which discussions on the need for 'real men' in Zambia should be focused.

Why a Two-winged Theology? The Need to Involve Men in the Fight against Gender Based Violence

Gender-based violence is one of the most researched topics worldwide, both from a religious and secular perspective. Scholars across the world are working hard to find ways to stop this form of violence, especially on women and children. Although the response to this call seems to be positive, what is surprising is the way in which both scholars and activists tend to focus their research on women and the girl child, who are the victims of the practice. When men are involved, it is usually at the level of perpetrator or, on rare occasions, as partners in the fight against the practice. In their fight against women's oppression, African Women Theologians started their work by inviting men to partner with them. Mercy Amba Oduyoye, the founder of the Circle noted:

> Africa cannot continue with the strategy of apportioning blame. All of us women and men have to observe, analyze, think and create liberating alternatives. It is this joint responsibility that the African Women Theologians want recognized thus a plea for a "Two-Winged Theology." As it is, both our vision and practice are lopsided.[1]

This call by African Women Theologians is significant to this study in that my discussion of masculinity is to recognize the value of partnership in our fight against gender-based violence. This is only possible once we recognize the different forms of masculinities that are at play in the battle against gender-based violence. Hence, as

---

[1] Mercy Amba Oduyoye, "The Search for a Two-winged Theology," in Mercy Amba Oduyoye & Musimbi Kanyoro (eds), _Talitha Cum! Proceedings of the Convocation of African Women Theologians_, 1989, Ibadan: Daystar, 43.

African Women Theologians indicate in their work, there is need to value the presence of men in addressing women's struggles both in the church and in society. Adriaan van Klinken's research on African Women Theology and masculinity has further highlighted that African Women Theologian' (Circle) have realized that it takes both women and men to empower women and to transform gender relations.[2] He further quotes African Women Theologians arguing that a critical analysis and transformation of masculinities is required in order to understand and overcome destructive male behaviour. This kind of reflection resulted in the invitation of a number of African male theologians to do research on the work of the Circle with the aim of "Liberating Masculinities."[3] Scholars such as Tinyiko Maluleke, Gerald West, Kä Mana and Ezra Chitando became pioneers of men working with African Women Theologians in the field of gender, masculinities and HIV and AIDS. The arrival of HIV and AIDS made it very clear that in order for society to effectively fight this pandemic, there was a need for a gendered approach where men and women work together as partners in the struggle. Hence, the need for men to partner with women in the fight against the oppression of women is emphasized by Maluleke who argues that male theologians should not just join the struggle with women theologians but that they need to be 'born again and again'.[4] This special rebirth that is proposed by Maluleke is required in contexts

---

[2] Adriaan S. van Klinken, "Theology, Gender Ideology and Masculinity Politics: A Discussion on the Transformation of Masculinities as Envisioned by African Theologians and a Local Pentecostal Church," _Journal of Theology for Southern Africa_, 138, 2 November 1985, 2-18.

[3] Ibid.

[4] Tinyiko S. Maluleke, "The 'Smoke Screens' Called Black and African Liberation Theologies - The Challenge of African Women Theology," in _Journal of Constructive Theology_, 3:2, 1997, 39-63.

such as Zambia where there is so much talk around gender issues by men, but very little has been done to address these issues. Hence, a need for regenerated hearts and minds leading to positive actions towards all forms of violence against women is what this chapter is trying to promote. Being sensitive to gender issues as men means leaning towards liberative theologies for both men and women. This demands ethical choices that will inform transformation that leads to respect of all humanity. It is from this background that the Circle's writings on masculinity, theology and HIV and AIDS became more vivid.

Brief Overview on Masculinity and Manhood

Robert Morrel defines masculinity as a collective gender identity which is fluid and socially constructed. The author demonstrates that there is no one form of masculinity. Instead, there are multiple forms of masculinities that are generated in particular situations and contexts.[5] In respect to Morrel's definition, this study will selectively address particular forms of masculinity and show how they are generated at each particular period in life and context. Kopano Ratele states that masculinities are produced both socially and psychologically.[6] For him, men can choose which kind of masculinity to perform and at what occasion. He further argues that masculinities can also be defined as traits or behaviours associated with what it means to be a man. It is also about ideologies that constitute 'being a man' and how men should live and perform in society.[7] Hence for the author, masculinity is about manhood, manliness or maleness.

---

[5] Robert Morrel, *Journal of Southern African Studies*, vol. 24, no. 4, December 1998, 607, www.tandfonline.com/loi/cjss20 [22.6.2020].

[6] Kopano Ratele, "Analysing Males in Africa: Certain Useful Elements in Considering Ruling Masculinities," *African and Asian Studies* 7, 2008, 515-536, www.brill.nl/aas.

[7] Ibid.

While we appreciate the many definitions of masculinity, this chapter will be limited to definitions of masculinity by the scholars stated above. Another thing to consider is that the concept of masculinity is always associated with power; either power to conquer or power to be conquered by the other. It is also a field of study that engages the experiences and identities of men. Masculinity also refers to patterns of social practices associated with men's positions as distinguished from those of women, for example, their performative acts in society. The study of masculinities can be reflected through theories namely; (1) the essentialist theory which argues that masculinities are biologically determined, (2) the sex role theory which deals with assumed gender roles and norms and customs that outline acceptable behaviour (roles) of members of society based on gender - how society expects men to behave is different from how women are expected to behave (3) and social constructionist theory which argues that masculinities are socially constructed. All these roles differ from context to context and culture to culture.

In order to engage in masculinity in Africa we need to take into account the socio-economic, religio-cultural, colonial and political context and how it plays a role in men's psychological and spiritual minds. This is because in most societies, these are the main influencing factors to men's masculinity. Most African forms of masculinity are associated with the social responsibility of men. As a result, societal expectations on African men are very high. In some cases, such expectations result in aggression in men because they fear being seen as a failure in society's eyes while others become more timid or subversive. In Zambia, like in many other African countries, both in families and in the society generally, masculine identities associated with men's responsibilities seem to be acceptable and nurtured as an acceptable norm. This is often associated with the biblical principle of a good husband according to a specific (mis-)understanding of

Pauline theology.[8] These masculine identities are characterized by power, superiority, and authority, notions of headship, strength, decisiveness and courage. They are also culturally and religiously determined. In as much as these masculinities are relevant for a particular purpose, they can also be destructive, especially when used for the benefit of the person upholding these masculinities.

As men emerge as heroes, their performative masculinities also contribute to abuse of women and the girl child. Rhoda Semple argues that if manliness is primarily about policing a core set of values by men and for the benefit of men, then empire and its institutions offer valuable material for the historian inserted in the performance of masculinity.[9] Within Zambia, there are different masculinities that can be aligned to heroine and empire spirits in their operations. Like any other African society struggling with religio-cultural, missional and postcolonial empirical ideologies of their historical past, Zambian society has produced a heroic masculine identity of men as emperors in their own homes, churches and workplaces. In this chapter, I have decided to pick up three types of masculinities as discussed by Rhoda Semple.[10] In discussing these three forms I do not actually claim that these are the only masculinities present in this context, but rather that they are the most prominent types, especially when it comes to the oppression of women. These three forms also share a hegemonic kind of masculinity. Before I look at the three types of heroic masculinity, let me provide a brief understanding of hegemonic masculinity.

---

[8] Promoters of this ideology overlook Paul's injunction "that the husband should give himself up for the wife as Jesus did for the church" (Eph 5:25).

[9] Rhoda Semple, "Missionary Manhood: Professionalism, Belief and Masculinity in the Nineteenth-Century British Imperial Field," *The Journal of Imperial and Commonwealth History*, 36:3, 397-415 [1.4.2020].

[10] Ibid.

Hegemonic Masculinity

Robert Morrel argues that hegemonic masculinity is a key element of patriarchy. These kinds of masculinities are both developed and maintained in particular locations.[11] According to John Beynon, 'hegemonic masculinity' defines successful ways of 'being a man' in particular places at a specific time … In the process other masculine styles are rendered inadequate and inferior, what is termed as subordinate variants.[12] When masculinities are said to be subordinated it's not because they lack a particular historical factor or that they are inferior to others, but it is because they do not hold the same values as those seen to be the norm. Beynon further argues that:

> Hegemonic masculinity is established either through consensual negotiation or through power and achievement. At its most brutal, it is predicated upon raw coercion. The tension between hegemonic and subordinate masculinities is readily observable in many workplaces and organizations. Many are saturated by hegemonic masculine values which are embedded in their structures and practices. Power (which, of course, can be variously defined and displayed) is the crucial factor in hegemonic masculinity and resistance ensures that many sites are ones of ideological struggle for contested senses of masculinity[13]

Drawing from the above discussions, it is clear that hegemonic masculinities are power hungry, toxic and fluid. They are sometimes celebrated as a society's dominant way of doing things. They are not static, but are constantly produced and reproduced. This means that one can learn hegemonic masculinities from home or peers and later reproduce a different form of masculinity which is positive and life giving. Therefore, in order to address ways in which countries such

---

[11] Robert Morrel, *Journal of Southern African Studies*, vol. 24, no. 4, December 1998, 608, www.tandfonline.com/loi/cjss20.[22.6.2020]

[12] John Beynon, *Masculinities and Culture*, Celtic Court: Open University Press, 2002, 27; www.openup.co.uk.[20.6.2020].

[13] Ibid, 27.

as Zambia can produce positive masculinities, there is need to interrogate some of the negative masculinities that pose a danger to women and children.

Masculinity in Religion and Public Life

When dealing with masculinity in religion and public life, we do well to take cognizance of the fact that religion has the power to influence and affect the social fabric of any society. As a result, in most cases we as human beings are caught up in social systems that are engrossed in religion and we are denied of the opportunity to experience the fullness of God in our lives. Hence, in our discussion of the effects of masculinity on women, we cannot do so without looking at the role that religion and culture play in the lives of women. In the work of African Women Theologians, the church has been viewed as a home for different forms of masculine trends that are either oppressive or life giving. In his work on masculinities, Ezra Chitando focuses on how Christianity and African traditional religions have influenced the development of dangerous masculinities.[14] This is displayed in his studies of Pentecostal churches in Zimbabwe and their use of masculinity. His assessment of the need for Pentecostal churches to produce new masculinities provides a clear picture of the relationship between masculinity and religion. Chitando argues that:

> The theme of masculinities must find a place in the study of religion in Africa in the face of the HIV pandemic. If the discipline is to be contextually sensitive and relevant to the lived experience of Africans, it must grapple with the theme of masculinities.[15]

---

[14] Ezra Chitando, "Religion and Masculinities in Africa: An Opportunity for Africanisation," in Afe Adegame, Bolaiji Bayete & Ezra Chitando (eds), *African Traditions in The Study of Religion, Diaspora and Gendered Societies*, Farnham: Ashgate Publishing, 2013, 141.

[15] Ibid, 145.

Another scholar working in the field of masculinity and theology is Gerald West. Using the story of Tamar in 2Samuel 13, West has conducted numerous contextual bible studies on how different forms of masculinities played out in the rape of Tamar. In what he calls a coordinated rape case, West has also shown that each male character displayed a different kind of masculinity at a different time in the rape of Tamar, confirming that stories of the Bible also possess some form of masculinities that are violent, especially to women. The use of the Bible to promote dangerous masculinities is also alluded to by Madipoane Masenya who is writing from a feminist Biblical perspective addresses masculinity through themes such as male headship. In her article _The Sword that Heals: The Bible and African Women in African - South African Pentecostal Churches_ demonstrates how male headship is viewed as God ordained and this biblical interpretation is used in these churches to assign power and authority to men.[16] Masenya reflects on marriage as a patriarchal space that has contributed to HIV infections. She concerns herself with the way in which biblical metaphors are used to elevate men furthering the hegemonic masculine agenda in the church and in the home.[17]

Three Types of Masculinities Prominent in Zambia

Although African culture is said to be the thread through which Africans define being, there are so many things that African women do not understand about culture. In many ways, African women remain trapped in their own culture both as custodians and as

---

[16] Madipoane Masenya, "Trapped between Two 'Canons': African-South African Christian Women in the HIV/AIDS Era," in Isabel Phiri, Beverly Haddad & Madipoane Masenya (eds), _African Women, HIV/AIDS and Faith Communities_, Pietermaritzburg: Cluster, 2003, 113-127.

[17] Ibid.

enemies of their own culture.[18] In this dilemma cultural masculinities manifest themselves. Men who are the gatekeepers of their culture use them to their advantage. In most of the Circles of Zambian culture, one is always confronted by statements such as this even when the act itself is not culturally-oriented and is life denying to humanity. Hence, in the name of respecting culture, women have succumbed to dangerous masculinities. Rhoda Semple outlines three types of masculinities that can be associated with hegemonic masculinity.[19]

Traditional Manliness

The first type of masculinity is the one which depicts the traditional manliness elites. According to Rhoda Semple, these kinds of masculinities teach how a "man" is defined within a particular cultural domain of a particular ethnic group. Within Zambian society, different ethnic groups have different ways of defining a man's rights such as the hierarchical respect accorded to a man. In this context, a man is a superior being that needs to be respected, especially by women, and he is expected to provide leadership and security to the family. In most cases proverbs, praises and idioms associated with this phenomenon are poured over a man. Sayings such as *mulombwana munyati* for the Tonga, literally meaning "the man is a Buffalo," and *umwaume ni nkalamu* for the Bemba, meaning "the man is a lion" are some of the masculine sayings that are promoted in these cultures. Positive as these sayings may seem to be, they have serious negative repercussions on the ways in which women are perceived. The buffalo and the lion metaphor both have masculine connotations

[18] Musimbi Kanyoro, '*Introducing Feminist Cultural Hermeneutics – An African Perspective, Introductions in Feminist Theology,*' Cleveland: Pilgrim Press, 2002.

[19] Rhoda Semple, "Missionary Manhood: Professionalism, Belief and Masculinity in the Nineteenth-Century British Imperial Field," *The Journal of Imperial and Commonwealth History*, 36:3, 397-415 [1.4.2020].

associated with power and dominion. Another common saying that is associated with traditional manliness is one which says _buchende bwa mwaume tabupwisha echupo_ (man's infidelity does not end marriage). This saying is often used when a couple is going through marital problems. The proverb and the attitudes it expresses have 'serious implications" for the abuse of women, as the man is given leverage to have as many sexual partners as he likes at the expense of his marriage. In most Zambian cultures, traditional teaching goes that when a man comes back home late in the night, you do not ask him where he has been neither do you pick a quarrel with him.[20] In one of my postgraduate classes which I taught on masculinity, one student from Kenya informed us that his mother used to shout at him if he came back too early in the night from wherever he had gone. Meaning a man should not wait for dinner at home. Such gender constructs that are damaging relationships are what Rhoda Semple is trying to discourage. Rosemary Radford Ruether argues that the naming of males as norms of authentic humanity has caused women to be

---

[20] Rachel NyaGondwe Fiedler records this initiation song from South Eastern Malawi with the same message:

Tsegulire, tsegulire!	Open for me, open for me!
Ndakana, ndakana.	I have refused, I have refused.
Apanja, apanja	Those outside, those outside
Mulibe mwambo.	Have no behaviour.
Anyumba, anyumba	Those in the house, those in the house,
Mulibe mwambo.	You do not have behaviour.

Then, one _mlangizi_ sang _kunkhani, kunkhani_, and said: if a man sleeps outside and comes very late, you should not refuse him entry into the house, do not leave him outside because an animal can kill and eat him. If this happens you will be sorry. So do not be jealous with your husband. (Rachel NyaGondwe Fiedler, _Coming of Age. A Christianized Initiation among Women in Southern Malawi_, Zomba: Kachere, 2005, 91).

scapegoated for sin and marginalized.[21] Speaking on women's sexual and reproductive health struggles in marriage in Malawi, Fulata Moyo narrates her own story of how she was subjected to the words of "forgive and let go" when she found out that her husband was unfaithful. She further argues that sexual autonomy practiced by men in marriage influences women's failure to negotiate for safe sex and socializes men to think that they are more entitled to sex.[22] A study by Isabel Phiri on violence against Christian women in their marriages revealed how their husbands, who were mostly pastors, used scripture to oppress women.[23] This kind of violence is very common in Christian homes and it is sad that the silence that goes with the abuse elevates masculinities where these husbands demand religious titles that sacralize them and make them untouchable.[24] Hence, both African and Christian traditions embody the traditional manliness elite masculine identity which benefits men. Rosemary Radford Ruether contends that a religious tradition remains vital as long as its revelatory pattern can be reproduced generation after generation, continues to speak to the individuals in the community and provides for them redemptive meaning of individual and collective

---

[21]   Rosemary Radford Ruether, _Sexism and God Talk: Towards a Feminist Theology_, Boston: Beacon Press, 1983.

[22]   Fulata L. Moyo, "Sex Gender, Power and HIV/AIDS in Malawi: Threats and Challenges to Women Being Church," in Isabel Phiri & Sarojini Nadar (eds), _On Being Church: African Women's' Visions_, Geneva: WCC, 2005, 127-146.

[23]   Isabel Apawo Phiri, "Why does God Allow our Husbands to Hurt us? Overcoming Violence against Women," _Journal of Theology for Southern Africa_, 114, Nov 2002, 19-30.

[24]   For a detailed story of a pastor's infidelity, which the wife endured for 13 years before finally leaving him, see Molly Longwe, _African Feminist Theology and Baptist Pastors' Wives_, Mzuzu: Luviri Press, 2019, 216-223. Also see Isabel A. Phiri, "Why does God Allow our Husbands to Hurt us? Overcoming Violence against Women," _Journal of Theology for Southern Africa_, 114, Nov 2002, 19-30.

experience.[25] A good example of this is the practice of child marriage which is both culturally and religiously embedded.

As child marriage is prevalent in Zambia, I conducted a study on child marriage and found that although the practice is viewed as a cultural norm, its patriarchal roots perpetuate the oppression of the girl child. Through the interviews with girls involved in child marriages it became very clear that the practice has been normalized by those involved in it despite the fight put up by the government and international bodies to end the practice.[26] Hence, in discussing cultural masculinity, my argument is that, until men are involved in the fight against child marriage and violence against women, these practices will continue. This is because this is a safe space for men who exercise their sexuality masculinities. This was proved in another study I conducted on the same topic among men in the United Church of Zambia. The study revealed the power of masculinities in the practice of child marriage.[27] Using the story of Abigail and King David in 1Kings 1:1-4, I conducted a Contextual Bible Study with male church leaders of all ages in three different regions.[28]Some of the elderly male

---

[25] Rosemary Radford-Ruether, _Women-Church. Theology and Practice of Feminist Liturgical Communities,_ Eugene: Wipf & Stock, 1985, 43.

[26] Lilian Cheelo Siwila, "Problematizing a Norm: A Religio-cultural Gender Analysis of Child Marriage in the Context of HIV and AIDS," _Journal of Gender & Religion in Africa,_ (17)1, 2011, 27-49.

[27] Lilian Cheelo Siwila, "Gender, Culture and HIV and AIDS: United Church of Zambia's Response to Traditional Marriage Practice," PhD, University of KwaZulu Natal, 2011.

[28] According to the Bible narrative, this is the story of King David during his last years of life. The story narrates that when the King was very old, he could not keep warm even if they put many warm blankets over him. So, the servants said let us look for a young virgin girl who will lie in his arms to keep him warm. The girl made every effort to warm the King as she lies in his bosom but the king had no sexual intercourse with her.

participants argued that the idea of bringing the young girl, Abigail, to King David in his dying bed was an acceptable practice which is also commonly practiced in some parts of Zambia. 'To warm the king' as it is stated in the Bible is in some cases interpreted as keeping the king sexually active. According to one participant, this was a held belief that a man needs to remain sexually competent no matter how old he was, it was part of a man's way of improving his manhood. Therefore, as men grow old and begin to struggle with low sexual libido, they may choose to reduce their intimacy with their wives. Their male egos tend to influence them to find alternative ways of improving their sexual competence. Some end up marrying young girls who are sexually active to provide them with a sexual boost. Hence, in the context of child marriage, the main problem is not the marriage per se but sexual masculinity. Practices such as _impokeshi_[29] are associated with aspects of masculinity related to sexual competence.

Another thing to consider is that in child marriage, the girl child's reproductive health rights are domesticated by both economic and cultural ideologies, because at the centre of all these practices is a male figure who controls the girl child's reproductive health rights through religio-cultural, social and economic factors. From a cultural perspective, in most African communities, a girl child's reproductive health rights belong to the father or uncle who controls the _lobola_. A study by Thandi Ntuli on _Ubuntombi_ among the Zulu people reveals the value put on the virginity of a girl child in the Zulu culture, stating that when the girl is of marriageable age the father would host a

---

[29] This is a practice where, when a couple is old and the wife is beyond menopause, the wife will look for a sister to the wife or a related young girl to get married to her husband. The practice was very common among the Namwanga and Tumbuka in Zambia.

ceremony called *umemulo* to thank the girl for keeping her virginity.[30] The author states that within this culture in the past, a grandmother would inspect her granddaughter every day to make sure that she has not lost her virginity. Each time she comes back from playing outside, the grandmother would ask her to open her legs so that she could check *isibaya sikababa* (the father's kraal), literally associating her virginity with lobola which was given[31] in the form of cows when the girl gets married.[32] Other scholars who have investigated the same issue include Patricia Bruce, whose work focuses on how in the Old Testament, virginity was associated with male power.[33] Gyaviira Kisitu and Lilian Siwila's work focuses on how women's bodies are talked about and governed by male power.[34] All these scholars focus on one thing, on women's experiences of hegemonic masculinities. Rosemary Radford Ruether argues that the uniqueness of feminist theology lies not just in its use of experience, but in its use of women's

---

[30] Thandi Ntuli, "Ubuntombi – A Zulu Religio-cultural Heritage and Identity: A Path to Adulthood and Sex Education Practices," PhD, University of KwaZulu-Natal, 2018.

[31] This is an everyday routine and it's done for the purpose of preserving the virginity of the girl for the purpose of the *lobola* to be paid upon her marriage.

[32] Thandi Ntuli, "Ubuntombi – A Zulu Religio-cultural Heritage and Identity," 2018.

[33] P.F. Bruce, "The Mother's Cow: A Study of the Old Testament References to Virginity in the Context of HIV/AIDS," in Isabel Phiri, Beverly Haddad & Madipoane Masenya (eds), *African Women, HIV/AIDS and Faith Communities*, 2003, 44-70.

[34] Gyaviira Kisitu and Lilian Cheelo Siwila, "Whose Body Whose Language? A Feminist Critique of the Construction of Discourses on a Woman's Body in African Religious Spaces and its Effect on Well-being," in *Alternation* 23(2), 2016, 185–200.

experiences which were almost shut out of theological reflection in the past.[35]

White Collar Masculinity

The second form of masculinity is white collar masculinity with some historical colonial mentality which lies in being able to hold a good job and provide financial support to the family. Rhoda Semple states that employability masculinity demands 'a real man' be someone who has a job. Hence, the myth of independence and a respectable man becomes the measuring stick of acceptable manliness in society. In Zambia, the common phrase *ee baume balya* – ('those are the real men') is usually heard when a man is progressing well economically. What is very sad about such kind of perception is that the phrase is sometimes also used on women. If a woman is progressing well economically or gaining some kind social status, she will be called *uli mwaume* – (you are a man). This kind of perception that associates economic and social status with manliness simply shows that society has failed to accept the fact that employability and white-collar job masculinity has no gender. While this kind of 'being a real man' becomes the norm, in the African traditional worldview the concept of white-collar job masculinity is a new phenomenon. Our fore-fathers and mothers had shared equal labour gender roles. Pro-fessionalism which demands a white-collar job in order for a man to be recognized in society has a colonial mindset and remains a challenge in most African countries such as Zambia, where the economic standing of the country does not afford most of the men a chance to attain what is an acceptable standard of education for a 'real' man. This kind of masculinity undermines other men who are not able to acquire a white-collar job. It also sometimes misrepresents the concept of work by taking on the Victorian model of work that

---

[35] Rosemary Radford Ruether, *Sexism and God Talk: Towards a Feminist Theology*, Boston: Beacon Press, 1983, 13.

placed women in the kitchen as housewives, and removed an African man from his traditional understanding of work that was done in the fields and placed him in a professional paid labour.

Clerical Hero Masculinity

The third type of masculinity I wish to discuss is the missionary kind of masculinity which Rhoda Semple calls the 'Clerical hero masculinity.'[36] This kind of masculinity sees ordination as an elite form of power, authority and subordination of others, especially women. Many of the mission churches introduced ordination of women after much deliberation as to why women should enter a traditionally male space.[37] African Women Theologians have written vastly on the issue of ordination of women focusing mainly on how ordination has been used as a hindrance for women to attain their full humanity and their call to ministry. In the book _Her-Stories: Hidden Stories of Women of Faith in Africa_ contributors review stories of women and their struggles in the church under male leadership.[38] In the same volume, Isabel Phiri relates the story of a woman who was called to ministry at 23 and was only ordained at 73.[39] The reason for this delay reflects how women are viewed by men in ministry. These kinds of stories show how

[36] Rhoda Semple, "Missionary Manhood: Professionalism, Belief and Masculinity in the Nineteenth-Century British Imperial Field," _The Journal of Imperial and Commonwealth History_, 36:3, 397-415.[1.4.2020].

[37] For one example of this process in Zambia see Lazarus Chilenje, _Paul's Gender Theology and the Ordained Women's Ministry in the CCAP in Zambia_, Mzuzu: Mzuni Press, 2021, 13-50.

[38] Isabel Apawo Phiri et al, _Her-Stories Hidden Stories of Women of Faith in Africa_, Pietermaritzburg: Cluster, 2002.

[39] Isabel Apawo Phiri, "Called at Twenty-Seven and Ordained at Seventy-Three! The Story of Rev. Victory Nomvete Mbanjwa in the United Congregational Church in Southern Africa," in Isabel Phiri et al (eds), _Her Stories. Hidden Stories of Women of Faith in Africa_, Pietermaritzburg: Cluster, 2002, 119-138.

patriarchy has stopped women from being behind the pulpit. Speaking from a gender perspective, Rhoda Semple believes that clerical hero masculinity has contributed to the delay of women's ordination in most mainline churches, and where it has taken place, women still struggle to find space in these contested male spaces that seem to be occupied by power as reflected in some of the stories in this volume.[40] 'Clerical hero' as a masculinity is still very active and strong even today both in mainline and Pentecostal/Charismatic churches. Most of the church leaders are no longer striving for servanthood leadership, instead they are immersed in patriarchal leadership where they hold titles of fatherhood, papa, Abba, apostle and prophet in the name of power and dominion.[41] In this book volume there are a number of articles focused on 'clerical hero' as a dangerous masculinity towards women where stories of ordained women have experienced the oppression of men who identify with clerical hero masculinity. While most churches in Africa are filled with women and children, the clerical hero masculinity still encompasses the concept of "men on the pulpit and women in the pew" narrative.[42] 'Clerical hero' masculinity has also subjected women to sexual abuse as demonstrated by Nelly Mwale in this volume. In some churches, male leaders abuse their positions, take advantage of the reverence given to them by women and use their clerical power to sexually abuse them. Therefore, when talking about a masculine empire from within, it is important to note the three types of

---

[40] Rhoda Semple, "Missionary Manhood: Professionalism, Belief and Masculinity in the Nineteenth-Century British Imperial Field," *The Journal of Imperial and Commonwealth History*, 36:3, 397-415. [1.4.2020].

[41] This is what is currently happening in most of the Pentecostal/Charismatic churches where the leaders of these churches have taken on new titles that accord them power over their members.

[42] Brigalia Bam, "Women and the Church in (South) Africa: Women are the Church in (South) Africa," in Isabel Phiri & Sarojini Nadar (eds), *On Being Church: African Women's Voices and Visions*, Geneva: WCC, 2005, 8-16.

masculinities addressed by Rhoda Semple and how they are masked as empire. Violence against women that emerges from any of these three forms of masculinity is often condoned and seen as normal. For example, a woman who is not able to provide for herself could be subjected to abuse by the breadwinner husband and be advised to stay on and pray about the abuse because he is the main provider financially. While some women may try to fight these kinds of masculinities, others have succumbed to them. Hence, the need to promote positive masculinities that are life giving. To sum up this section, I agree with Ezra Chitando and Sophie Chirongoma who argue that most of the scholarship on masculinity seems to be trapped in negative ideas of what it means to be a man.[43] This kind of approach has put a lot of pressure on men who, in many ways, have to negotiate with societal norms that have seen men as irredeemable beings when it comes to the oppression of women.

Towards a Transformative Masculinity

The need to revisit masculinities and gender inequality cannot be over-emphasized in a country such as Zambia where issues of violence against women are still an issue of debate. Practices such as incest, silenced rape and child marriage are still rampant. In this chapter, I call for a need for a redemptive form of masculinity that is life giving, because both in religion and public life, dangerous masculinities have been condoned and nurtured at the expense of women's lives. So, there is need to promote and uphold the kind of masculinities that promote the health and wellbeing of women. Transformative masculinity emerges as a way in which men begin to revisit the ways in which they express their masculinity. Transformative masculinity helps men to seek transformation from within. This

---

[43] Ezra Chitando & Sophie Chirongoma (eds), *Redemptive Masculinities: Men, HIV and Religion*, Geneva: WCC, 2012.

is the kind of transformation that Paul talks about in Romans 12:1-2 as the renewal of the mind.

Statements such as all men are trash have not made it any easier for a call for men to join the fight against negative forms of masculinity. Most African churches have been accepting the patriarchy inherited from both western missionaries and African cultures. The ideology of patriarchy has been internalized in such a way that even when dealing with issues of oppression and exclusion, African theologians have not been able to make the connection. Therefore, ideologically and spiritually, African theology has remained largely beholden to supremacist ideas related to gender issues. Transformative masculinity should not only transform men's behaviours from being the bad man to the 'real man,' but rather help men to realize their privileged positions and work towards change. Transformation is a process that needs to be addressed by both men and women. There is further a need for a gender sensitive transformative approach to addressing toxic masculinities. This is a kind of transformative masculinity which calls for a will to change and embrace new ways of being men. Rosemary Radford Ruether argues that

> The critical principle for feminist theology is the promotion of the full humanity of women. Whatever denies, diminishes or distorts the full humanity of women is, therefore, appraised as not redemptive. Theologically speaking, whatever diminishes or denies the full humanity of women must be presumed not to reflect the divine or as authentic relation to the divine[44]

Feminist ethics demands that we re-evaluate and rethink what has been seen as the norm in our societies. There has been so much wounding and scarring in the name of 'keeping our traditions' at the expense of women's lives. The history found in our theology and cultures has in many ways, informed the way in which we respond to issues of gender and masculinities. The understanding of the image

---

[44] Rosemary Radford Ruether, *Sexism and God Talk*, 1985, 9.

of God should be viewed both from a historical and current context. In our discussion of gender and women there is a need to revisit the way in which our theology is influenced by our history and how this has perpetuated the subordination of women in the church today. Women's bodies are still seen as a centre of political contestation. The tripartite alliance of culture, religion and societal construction of women needs to be addressed by using a gender lens.

Dealing with the Empire from within

In this chapter, I have related masculinity as a form of empire. In most of the scholarship on empire, it is understood as an external force that operates through oppression of those who are on the margins of society and economically less privileged. Most scholars' writing on empire from a third world perspective tend to hold a general assumption that empire is about the west with all its empirical ideologies while third world countries are seen to be an empire free zone that is subjected to imperial oppression. While this may be true to a certain extent, this chapter argues that hegemonic masculinity is one form of empire which the church has struggled to overcome. The main reason why trends such as hegemonic masculinity are often not associated with empire is because whenever we think of empire, our minds think of the grand-narrative in which empires in our own contexts do not exist. Unless we re-define and identify the locations of these empires with a small narrative within our contexts that in most cases are condoned in the name of culture and ecclesial traditions, women's lives will continue to be subjected to these hege-monic masculinities.

In this context, the real question would be how to resist these life denying masculinities that are perpetuated in the name of religion and culture. This question is not only about checking the abuses of power by others, but also about checking our own abuse of power even as women oppressing women, bearing in mind that although masculinity is more about manliness, there are women who carry masculine behaviours that are oppressive towards their fellow women. In many cases these masculinities are also nurtured by women in the name of religion and culture.

Conclusion

In conclusion, I would like to state that issues of masculinities in Zambia, especially in the church, have been treated as silent waters. When the water is still, it's difficult to assess the level of contamination. Until the water is tested chemically, only then will we know the depth of contamination. Masculinity, as it is presented in the Zambian context, will require testing to assess the extent to which it has influenced gender-based violence, especially on women. In the name of religion and culture, a number of negative masculine trends have been accepted as norms and used against women and children. Like African Women Theologians and some male theologians, the Circle in Zambia needs to stand against hegemonic masculinities that are condoned in the name of religion and culture. Hence, in this context, both empire and patriarchy have been treated as still water, which looks clean on the surface but is dirty at the bottom. Masculinities are a complex concept that needs careful analysis in order to understand how it operates. Hegemonic masculinity is not only about the oppression of women. Men have also made huge sacrifices in order to meet society's demands related to hegemonic masculinity.

The aim of this chapter was to show the different forms of masculinities that are found in the Zambian context as outlined in the chapter and how they affect the lives of women. I deliberately focused on this aspect so as not to lose the focus of this volume which is about women's experience of patriarchy and empire.

Chapter Two

Prophecy for Prayer and Profit: Women's Experiences and their Contestation of the Empire in the Media in Zambia

Nelly Mwale

Introduction

The current scenario of prophetic ministry has proved that media can be a powerful space for women's contestation of the prophetic empire. Therefore, there is need for a women's generation empowered through religious literacy that can deconstruct and reconstruct women's approaches to prophecy and prayer in a context awash with self-acclaimed 'prophets' or 'men of God' (the empire traits) and the consequent rising vulnerability of women. Using a religion and media approach in which religion is mediatized by way of conveying ideas and experiences relating to prophecy, the chapter draws on narratives of women's experiences of the prophetic empire and the ensuing discourses of rescuing women from the prophetic empire.

The chapter seeks to make a modest contribution to religion, gender and media scholarship in Zambia by reflecting on how religion can be engaged in empowering practices as opposed to destructive practices that promote the prophets' prosperity and power at the expense of women's prosperity in prayer and prophecy.

Context of the Study

Zambia is a multi-faith society. However, over 20 years since it's declaration as a "Christian nation,"[1] the religious landscape in the country has completely changed. First, a Religious Desk was established at State House, and in 2016 it was replaced with the Ministry of National Guidance and Religious Affairs with the mandate of actualizing the declaration of Zambia as a Christian nation. The "Declaration of Zambia as a Christian" nation has widely been studied by different scholars.[2]

Apart from these developments, the religious landscape was characterized by the growth of Pentecostalism[3] seen in the 'mushrooming of new churches and a new wave of prophetic discourses.[4] As a result, the media was not short of reporting on miracles performed by self-proclaimed prophets (sometimes other

---

[1] On the process see: Austin Cheyeka, *Church, State and Political Ethics in a Post-colonial State. The Case of Zambia,* Zomba: Kachere, 2005, 83-123.

[2] Austin Cheyeka, *The Politics and Christianity of Chilubaism, 1991-2011*, Ndola: Mission Press, 2014; Isabel Apawo Phiri, "President Frederick JT Chiluba of Zambia: The Christian Nation and Democracy." *Journal of Religion in Africa*, 33(4), 2003, 401-428; Chammah J. Kaunda, 'Christianising Edgar Chagwa Lungu: The Christian Nation, Social Media Presidential Photography and 2016 Election Campaign.' *Stellenbosch Theological Journal* 4 (1), 2018, 215-245.

[3] I employ the commonly used term "Pentecostal." This includes the Charismatic Churches (as described by Austin Cheyeka) and those Pentecostal Churches which have in many ways conformed to Charismatic patterns and theology (like the Assemblies of God Africa, AGOA).

[4] Austin Cheyeka, "Toward a History of the Charismatic Churches in Post-colonial Zambia," in J. Gewald et al (eds), *One Zambia, Many Histories: Towards a History of Post-colonial Zambia,* Leiden: Brill, 2008; N. Haynes, "Why can't a Pastor be President of a Christian Nation? Mapping the Diverse Political Theologies of Zambia's Pentecostals," 2016, (unpublished); Bernhard Udelhoven, *The Changing Face of Christianity in Zambia,* Fenza documents. https://fenza. org/docs/ben/ changing_face.pdf.

terms were used for self-identification). These miracles included turning water into wine, petrol, and paraffin, unblocking urinary tracts, healing any kind of sickness such as cancer, HIV and AIDS (even raising the dead) and making predictions of events that would happen in the near and distant future, including deaths, and soccer and election results.[5]

Pentecostalism and prophecy have received considerable attention in Zambian scholarship. Numerous scholars such as Austin Cheyeka have traced the growth of Pentecostalism,[6] and there has been a general acknowledgement on the Pentecostal contribution to chang-ing the religious landscape of Zambia and the course of its church history.[7] Some studies have focused on the prosperity gospel,[8] while others have linked Pentecostalism to political discourses.[9] The emerging gendered perspectives in Pentecostal studies in Zambia have only been used to analyze how African Pentecostal women politicians have utilized the religious discourse of wifely submission in exercising religio-political powers.[10] Zambian prophecy as a whole

---

[5] Austin Cheyeka, "Toward a History of the Charismatic Churches," 2008.

[6] Ibid.

[7] Bernhard Udelhoven, *The Changing Face of Christianity in Zambia*, Fenza documents. https://fenza. org/docs/ben/changing_face.pdf.

[8] Hermen Kroesbergen, "The Prosperity Gospel: A Way to Reclaim Dignity?" *Word and Context Journal*, 2003, 78-88; E. Zulu, "'Fipelwa na ba Yahweh': A Critical Examination of Prosperity Theology in the Old Testament from a Zambian Perspective," *Word and Context Journal*, 2013, 27-35.

[9] Naomi Haynes, "Why Can't a Pastor Be President of a 'Christian Nation?'" 2016; Chammah J. Kaunda, "From Fools for Christ to Fools for Politicians: A Critique of Zambian Pentecostal Theopolitical Imagination," *International Bulletin of Mission Research*, 41(4), 2017, 296-311.

[10] M.M. Kaunda & C.J. Kaunda, "Pentecostalism, Female Spirit-Filled Politicians and Populism in Zambia," *International Review of Mission*, 107(1), 2018, 23-32.

is a gendered discourse as most prophets are male while mostly women receive prophecies and are the victims of reported abuse (theft, sexual abuse) by these same prophets.[11] Studies so far neglected to investigate the exploitation of women by the prophetic empire at the intersection of prayer, profit and prophecy. Hence, this chapter seeks to understand the experiences of women with the prophetic empire through the use of narratives of prayer and profit in order to demonstrate how the media was used as a space for women's assertiveness and their contestation of the empire in a broader religion and the media framework.

Situating Prophecy and the 'Prophets' in Discourses of the Empire in Contemporary Zambia

The Concept of Empire

The discourse of empire is used with reference to the self-proclaimed prophets who have become the new icons of prophecy that are not detached from personal gain in the media. As observed by George Steinmetz, the concept of empire encompassed colonialism and imperialism and was associated with political organizations that were expansive, militarized, and multinational and that placed limits on the sovereignty of populations in their periphery.[12] In colonialism, conquered populations were not just ruled by the conquerors but were seen as inferiors to their rulers in legal, administrative, social and cultural terms. Imperialism involved political control over foreign lands without necessarily the annexation of territory. Empire is a relationship, formal or informal, in which one state controls the

---

[11] Nelly Mwale & Joseph Chita, "Pentecostalising the Voice in Zambian Charismatic Church History: Men of God's Expression of Spiritual Identities, 1990 to Present," *Studia Historiae Ecclesiasticae*, 44(3), 2018, 1-13.

[12] George Steinmetz, "The Sociology of Empires, Colonies and Post-colonialism," *Annual Review of Sociology*, 40, 2014, 77-103.

effective political sovereignty of another society, a system of interaction between two entities, where the dominant metropole exerts control over the subordinate periphery.[13] What underlies the general notion of "empire," is any form of hegemonic domination or influence.[14] This hegemonic domination is present in different spheres, including religion.

The chapter therefore relates the notion of empire to the activities of the self-proclaimed prophets as portrayed in the media, because in the Zambian context, the growth of neo-Pentecostalism and the consequent popularity of the 'prophets' awakened the notion of empire in religious circles, as an increasing number of self-proclaimed pastors chose 'prophet' as their title because of the reverence and even idolization attached to it.[15] The concept of empire has been linked to prophecy in this chapter because many of the activities of the so-called prophets in the public sphere point to domination, exploitation, and the protection of the prophets' own interests at the expense of those who seek help.

The self-proclaimed prophets are associated with the exploitation of women who are in search of prophecy and healing as the prophets are only interested in profiting from the members at the expense of human dignity and service to humanity. All this resonates with the traits of the empire. Most importantly, religion is used to colonize the minds of the followers through an imperial logic, a scenario that easily points to the possible replacement of the God of the oppressed by ungodly ideologies of power and prosperity. This resonates with the

---

13 Michael Doyle, _Empires_, New York: Cornell University Press, 1986, 12, 14.

14 John Darwin, _After Tamerlane: The Global History of Empire since 1405_, London: Bloomsbury, 2008.

15 Chima Agazue, _The Role of a Culture of Superstition in the Proliferation of Religio-Commercial Pastors in Nigeria_, Bloomington: AuthorHouse, 2015.

numerous historical situations in which the dominant hegemony has used religion, religious institutions and rituals to create and legitimize new idols which guaranteed them prosperity and power, all at the altar of patriarchy.

Mediatization as an Analytical Framework

Apart from the concept of empire, the chapter is also situated in the wider discourse of religion and the media through mediatization as a framework. This framework has aided in understanding how the media have worked as agents of religious change because religion has become increasingly subsumed through the process of mediatization.[16] For example, the media has been a conduit for religious ideologies that have shaped religious imagination in popular culture while providing both moral and spiritual guidance, and a sense of community. The mediatization framework was therefore used to understand how the media conveys religious experiences that mainly affect women.

Brief Perspectives on Religion and the Media in Zambia

"Religion and media" has not attracted as much scholarly attention in the Zambian context as in other Sub-Saharan countries.[17] The development of religion in the media can be traced to Christian missionaries in Zambia. For example, when television was introduced in the country in 1961, some of the churches used this medium to

---

[16] Stig Hjarvard, "The Mediatisation of Religion: A Theory of the Media as Agents of Religious Change," *Northern Lights: Film and Media Studies Yearbook*, 6(1), 2008, 9-26.

[17] Muhammed Haron, "Religion and the Media: Reflections on their Position and Relationship in Southern Africa," *Global Media Journal*, 4, no. 1, 2010, 28-50; Lee-Shae Salma Scharnick-Udemans, "A Historical and Critical Overview of Religion and Public Broadcasting in South Africa," *Journal for the Study of Religion*, 30(2), 2017, 257-280.

promote their activities. The Catholics, in particular, were renowned for religious programmes on the then Zambia Broadcasting Services, but it was only later in the 1990s that religion and the media were popularized with the growth of tele-evangelism and other forms of religious media. The liberalization policies of Zambia in the 1990s further contributed to the mediatization of religion. So, the interest in this chapter is to understand how the media was religionized through women's experiences of prophecy and how they contested the prophetic empire in contemporary times.

Methodology Used for the Study

Guided by the concept that narrative research is the study of any text or discourse with a specific focus on stories told by individuals,[18] this chapter uses a narrative research design that is informed by content analysis of media's portrayal of women, prayer and prophets in Zambia. Given that religion and the media are often linked in the new media technologies, the chapter analyzes through re-storying[19] different forms of media such as television, newspapers, and social media because these are widely used in Zambia.[20]

---

[18] Donald E. Polkinghorne, "Narrative Configuration in Qualitative Analysis," *Qualitative Studies in Education*, 8, 1995, 5-23. See also J.W. Creswell, *Qualitative Inquiry and Research Design*, London: Sage, 2007.

[19] J.W. Creswell, *Qualitative Inquiry and Research Design*, London: Sage, 2007.

[20] As Hackett et al observed, social media is an area for research just as religious websites are dynamic archives of religious worlds (R. Hackett, A. Melice, S.V. Wolputte & K. Pype, "Interview: Rosalind Hackett Reflects on Religious Media in Africa," *Social Compass*, 61(1), 2014, 67-72.

Media as a Space for Conveying Women's Experiences of the Prophetic Empire

Religion was mediatized by women being depicted as vulnerable in their quest for prophecy and prayer at the hands of the 'new prophets'. This vulnerability includes narratives of sexual abuse. For example, a 26-year-old female recounted how she was abused emotionally and sexually by prophets whom she would not name.

> In 2014, one prophet told me that I was going to be diagnosed with HIV and eventually die in 2015. That prophecy depressed me. I started drinking and clubbing just to cheer myself up. Seeking help, I started visiting another prophet who offered to pray against the spirit of death. This prophet would invite me for prayers and he started saying that God had told him that I was his wife and eventually convinced me to be having sex with him … I later discovered that he was actually having sex with a lot more other girls in the church; that is how I left his church.[21]

Sexual abuses in the name of prophecy were also through some prophets "ministering healing" to female congregants through rape and other sexual assaults.

> I went for prayers for the first time after my friend advised me to try and get help. I went there several times and began to trust the prophet. He seemed to understand my problems. He spoke in tongues and would give me holy water. One day when I was absorbed in prayer, he pushed me to the floor and raped me. I struggled to free myself, but he overpowered me.[22]

In addition, some prophets "minister" in ways that violate the principles of human dignity and integrity. For example, one self-proclaimed prophet kicked the abdomen of a pregnant woman as a way of "transmitting a miracle," while another jumped and sprang on

---

21 Prudence Phiri, "Zambia Begins Crackdown on Self-Proclaimed Prophets," *Global Press Journal,* 21 June, 2017.

22 "Women Stop being Naive, Prophets & Pastors won't Solve your Problems," *Lusaka Voice Newspaper,* 1 May 2015.

the back and buttocks of a woman lying on the floor to demonstrate that all things were possible.[23]

Some women's experiences with the prophets are related to financial fraud. For example, a widow from Lusaka was swindled out of K260,000 by her pastor.[24] In 2016, the widow had given the pastor K170,000 with a view that he would buy her a house. In 2017, he asked for an additional K90,000 for starting a business, money which he never returned; neither did he buy her the house.[25] Another woman was swindled out of K10,000 by a 'prophet' on the pretext that he would raise her husband from the dead.[26]

These stories not only point to how the prophets objectify women, but also how they cause suffering to them through their traits of domination, empire and exploitation in the name of prayer. While some offences were reported to the law enforcement agencies, it is probable that numerous other cases of abuse remained unreported. Many pastors' victims still live in fear of further victimization and therefore will never disclose their ordeal and die in silence.[27] These narratives of vulnerability also signify the broader patriarchal nature of society. Chima Agazue argues that the women's biological clock,

---

[23] Munshya wa Munshya, "In the Name of God: Miracles in Zambia's Pentecostal Movement" *Daily Nation*, 26 June, 2015.

24 In 2016 a $US was worth about 10 Zambian Kwacha, (Bank of Zambia, Summary Exchange Rate Data Bank of Zambia Mid-Rates, accessed from https://boz.zm/StatisticsFortnightly2017Vol25No3.pdf).

[25] As reported by Phiri, *Zambia Reports*, on 15 September, 2018:25.

[26] "Prophet Sued for Swindling Widow on Pretext that he would Raise her Husband from the Dead," *Muvi TV News*, 15 July 2017.

[27] Chima Agazue, "'He Told me that my Waist and Private Parts have been Ravaged by Demons': Sexual Exploitation of Female Church Members by 'Prophets' in Nigeria." *Dignity: A Journal on Sexual Exploitation and Violence*, 1(1), 2016, 9-10.

the culture that prohibits child bearing outside marriage and that does not allow women to make the first move to approach a man for marriage account for many unmarried women who are financially and sexually exploited by their prophets.[28] In as much Chima Agazue links cultural reasons with exploitation, it is also true that other factors have made women vulnerable in Zambia. In any case, in the quest for some women to meet societal expectations, the prophets find a fertile ground for the exploitation of women.[29]

In addition, women's narratives of prophecy in the media revealed that the prophets had commodified numerous items for sale that targeted women. Some women revealed how they bought anointed underwear, brooms, oil, water and light bulbs among other items from some prophets. For example, some 'prophets' in Lusaka were selling underwear to unsuspecting and desperate female congregants, which they claimed were anointed for marriage protection and preservation.

> A prophet visited me to offer some prophetic solutions after clandestinely learning about my marital disputes with my husband. The prophet told me that I was possessed with a spiritual husband and all I needed to do was to buy new anointed underwear from him at a cost of K100 to repel the provocative spiritual husband. I looked for K100 [US$10 at the time] because I wanted my problems to end and bought the underwear, but despite wearing the underwear, there was no improvement at all.[30]

While a lot of women reported to have bought anointed underwear, other women were buying anointed brooms, which were being sold by another prophet with instructions to sweep every area of the house that was a source of problems. Other women bought anointed water, oil and light bulbs. What was remarkable was that these items were

---

[28] Chima Agazue, *The Role of a Culture of Superstition in the Proliferation of Religio-Commercial Pastors in Nigeria*, Bloomington: AuthorHouse, 2015.

[29] Lucas Soko, "Zambia Dziko la Chonde," *Word and Context Journal*, 2013, 90-99.

[30] Sam Phiri, "Anointed Pants on SALE!" *Times of Zambia Newspaper*, 3.10.2015.

sold at exorbitant prices. This exorbitant pricing could be understood in relation to the fact these items fetched well below K100 on the market. Financial exploitation has become a major practice of these so-called prophets.[31]

These narratives are associated with densely populated areas in Lusaka. This confirms the conclusions that have been drawn in existing literature. For example, for Nigeria Asonzeh Ukah and Magbadelo concluded that religious participation and activities tended to be more prevalent in societies experiencing economic hardship and political tension, while Chima Agazue adds that social ills such as insecurity and violence cause many to seek the divine protection that the prophets seem to guarantee.[32] I argue that the African religious worldview which sees a connection between any misfortune and the spiritual world also fueled this vulnerability and was exploited by the prophets.

Ultimately, these narratives point to the empire's grip on the women who are exploited in their quest for healing, prayer and general wellness. Poverty and desperation make people vulnerable to prophets, 'there is so much poverty, so much hopelessness that when people promise miracles, everyone rushes hoping for a better life.'[33] The factors that increase women's vulnerability are therefore closely related to the discourses and traits of the empire in the hope of prayer and prophecy because the 'prophets' are the ones who profit from

---

[31] Anthonia Essien, "Proliferation of Churches: A Leeway to Commercialisation of Religion," _European Journal of Scientific Research_, 45, 2010, 649-657; for Nigeria see: Asonzeh Ukah, "Banishing Miracles: Politics and Policies of Religious Broadcasting in Nigeria," _African Sociological Review_, 5, 2011, 39-60.

[32] Chima Agazue, _The Role of a Culture of Superstition_, 2015.

[33] Prudence Phiri, "Zambia Begins Crackdown on Self-Proclaimed Prophets," _Global Press Journal_, 21 June, 2017.

the women, as it is a common sight to see well-dressed charismatic preachers and prophets leaving their big mansions as they drive their super expensive cars to the bank to deposit money contributed by mostly poor church members.[34]

Media as a Space for Contesting the Prophetic Empire

Apart from mediatizing religion by using the media for women to recount their traumatic experiences with the prophets, it was also a space for contesting the prophetic empire. This contestation called women to stop being naïve and to be wary of fake prophets. For example, a woman who identified herself as "Aunt Molly" hinted that

> the women are threatened with all manner of afflictions if they squeal; you will go mad, you will lose your child, I will unleash evil spirits upon you, you will suffer a nervous breakdown and the list is endless … it's time for women to stop being naïve and trusting people who hide behind the word of God.[35]

Another woman, Juliet Kawanda (the Executive Director of Women's House for Africa) noted that it was disappointing that false prophets and prophetesses extorted money from women who were desperate to get married and swindled them out of their money or sexually assaulted them. As such, women were urged to position themselves as women of substance and watch out for fake clergymen and women.[36]

Such remarks point to the need for women to be assertive, as the prophets will not solve their problems. Another woman remarked:

> Most of these prophets are fake, they are asking people to go to their churches for healing prayers and in the process demand for money to be

---

[34] Mwansa Besa, "The Curious Case of the Prophets," *Lusaka Voice*, 22.5.2017.

[35] Lusaka Voice Opinion, "Women Stop Being Naïve, Prophets and Pastors won't Solve your Problems," *Lusaka Voice*, 1 May, 2015.

[36] Chambo Ng'uni, "Be Wary of False Prophets who Promise Marriage," *Daily Mail*, 10 January 2018.

blessed … on many occasions, the prophets swindle residents out of their money through false prayers.[37]

The foregoing remarks point to a call for women's emancipation, because many women have been exploited while seeking help for various problems like barrenness, joblessness, and marital troubles. This call for women's assertiveness is significant in a context where the prophetic enterprise is partly driven by the women in need. As such, the media become a conduit for conveying liberative messages for women oppressed and exploited by the prophetic empire.

Apart from addressing the women, the so-called prophets were also challenged in the media to desist from prophesying miracles that violated human dignity and integrity.

The idea that some prophets are using the anointing in ways that violate human dignity is repugnant to the Bible and gives the good movement of Pentecostalism a very depraved image. "Kicking a pregnant woman is a violation of human dignity and integrity … The jumping on the bodies of people lying on the floor and springing on the back and buttocks of a woman does not add to the biblical causes."[38]

Thus, as women are not receiving benefits from prayer and prophecy, the media present the prophets as the profiteers, hence the prophets are asked to revisit their theologies. In this way, the media was used to condemn traits of the empire such as exploitation and convey the need for liberating theologies.

---

[37] Daily Nation Staff, "False Prophets Stealing from Worshippers in the Name of God," *Daily Nation*, 20 January 2016.

[38] Munshya wa Munshya. "In the Name of God: Miracles in Zambia's Pentecostal Movement," *Daily Nation*, 26 June, 2015.

Fleeing from the Prophetic Empire

The intersection of religion and the media in the context of the prophetic empire points to education as the escape route to women's liberation:

> In addition to the anointing, we need common sense and some exposure to education ... Education helps to preserve a revival.[39]

While this points to the need for the so-called prophets to embrace theological education, this chapter also advocates mass religious education for women, with the starting point in the media. 'Prophets' are thriving on ignorance.[40] As a communication channel, the media would be used to transmit religious ideas that are critical of destructive religious discourses. This chapter wants to motivate the media to be the starting point because it has the potential to foster religious literacy.

Apart from advocating for critical religious education in the media, the chapter calls for an intentional focus on women because the abuse is largely driven by their quest for well-being, which the prophets exploit. This vulnerability is entrenched in the socio-economic, religio-political and cultural context that provides a fertile ground for the empire to exploit women in the name of prayer and prophecy. Therefore, critical religious education needs to be integrated into existing women's programmes. As Sophie Chirongoma has argued, 'women, especially mothers, are the best teachers' and would contribute to freeing the present and next generation from exploitation by the prophetic empire.[41] Similarly, the education

---

[39] Ibid.

[40] Emelda Musonda, "False Prophets Thriving on Ignorance," *Daily Mail*, 25.8.2017.

[41] Sophie Chirongoma, "Karanga-Shona Rural Women's Agency in Dressing Mother Earth: A Contribution towards an Indigenous Ecofeminist Theology," *Journal of Theology for Southern Africa*, 142, 2012, 120.

system should incorporate a religious curriculum that is anchored in discernment so that both the young and old could be made aware of destructive tendencies of religion. This would also deconstruct the patriarchal (mis)behaviour perpetuated through religious discourses and consequently contribute towards a generation that would be free from abuse in the name of prophecy.

Conclusion

The chapter interrogated the traits of empire in the narratives of women's experiences of the prophets in the media in order to understand how the media is used to contest the prophetic empire. While women sought divine intervention they are exploited; instead of reaping the benefits of prophecy and prayer, the prophets as part of empire benefit from the women in ways that perpetuate their oppression. The chapter has argued for mass religious education integrated into existing women's programmes and the education system to empower a generation that is free from exploitation disguised as religion and independent from enslaving prophecies and prayers associated with the traits of the empire of the so-called prophets.

Chapter Three

Kenosis as a Theological Response to the Culture of Sexual Abuse in the Catholic Church

Sr Petronella Bweupe Bwalya

Introduction

This chapter discusses the clerical sexual abuse scandals of recent decades, revealed within the Catholic Church, in the light of the Christological hymn of Philippians 2:5-7. Insights from research findings from the United States of America (USA), the Netherlands and Australia inform the thematic analysis in this chapter. It concludes by examining the relationship between the self-emptying of Christ and the Catholic Church's response to the clerical sexual scandals.

Analysis of Philippians 2:5-11 as a Christological Hymn

The Christological hymn in its immediate historical context proceeds from the opening chapter of the epistle (1:27-30).[1] What prompted Paul's Christological hymn of Philippians 2:5-7 were the divisions that prevailed in the church at Philippi and the persecutions that the faithful experienced from the surrounding pagan communities. Thus, the hymn comes as an exhortation to the Christian community in Philippi to put aside their internal conflicts and take an attitude of humility and respect (2:1-16). Paul encourages the Philippians to be selfless and mindful of the other, to put others before themselves. "Do nothing out of selfish ambitions and vain deceit, but rather in

---

[1] "Whatever happens, conduct yourselves in a manner worthy of the gospel of Christ" (Phil. 1:27).

humility, put concern for others before yourselves."[2] Paul is quick to urge the believers to have the mind of Christ. To emphasize his exhortation, he cites the Christological Hymn of Philippians 2:5-11.

> Have among yourselves the same attitude that is yours in Christ Jesus, who, though he was in the form of God, did not regard equality with God something to be grasped. Rather, he emptied himself, taking the form of a slave, coming in human likeness; and found human in appearance, he humbled himself, becoming obedient to death, even death on a cross. Because of this, God greatly exalted him and bestored on him the name that is above every name, that at the name of Jesus every knee should bend, of those in heaven and on earth and under the earth, and every tongue confess that Jesus Christ is lord, to the glory of the God the father (The African Bible).

He gives what theologians and scholars perceive as kenosis: "Although Jesus was equal with God, he made himself nothing, he demonstrated God-like against self-ambition,"[3] by depriving himself, taking the form of a slave, being made in human likeness and by the obedience of his death on the cross.[4] In the Christ hymn Paul brings out what prompted Jesus to become human, and how he led a humble and self-sacrificing life while on earth.[5]

The significance of the Christ hymn is the notion of kenosis; the self-emptying, the self-limitation, the radical moral initiative taken by Christ to show solidarity with humankind. Paul looks at kenosis as a very significant virtue that Christ took of giving up the glory he shared with the Father. Kenosis brings out a pastoral and moral role among the Christians at Philippi because it challenges self-

---

[2] Gordon Fee, "The New Testament and Kenosis Christology," in C.E. Evans (ed), *Exploring Kenotic Christology – The Self-Emptying of God*, New York: Oxford University Press, 2006, 25-44 [30].

[3] Ibid.

[4] Ibid.

[5] Ibid.

centeredness and attitudes of power and self-ambition. The kenosis of Christ provides us with an example of self-humbling and self-sacrificing for the other, and humiliation and self–sacrifice are the very nature of God.[6]

The Christ hymn is important to Catholic theology. J.B. Lounibos observes that for the Catholic community, Vatican II documents give a complete exposition of the Christ hymn of Philippians 2 as an invitation to all her members to perfection.[7] Lounibos asserts that Chapter Five of *Lumen Gentium,* the "Constitution on the Church" and the "Degree on Ecumenism #4", exhort the Church to a self-transformation so that she may reflect the life of Christ to the world.[8]

If kenosis, as portrayed in the Christ hymn of Philippians, is so important for the church, one would ask, how this kenosis of Christ links to the self-understanding of the Church at this moment in time when faced with clerical sexual scandals. John Paul II's approach to the past scandals of the Catholic Church effects the link. Jeanmarie Gribaudo observed that in order to have meaningful millennium celebrations, the pope sought pardon for the faults committed by the clergy in the Catholic Church.[9] The other humbling statement came from Pope Benedict XVI who, during the interview on his flight to Australia on 12th July 2008, conceded that the clerical sexual scandals have brought shame to the Church and were a call for the Church to strictly evaluate the manner in which she prepares the candidates who

---

[6] Bruce N. Fisk, "The Odyssey of Christ: A Novel Context for Philippians 2: 6-11," in C.E. Evans (ed), *Exploring Kenotic Christology - The Self-Emptying of God,* New York: Oxford University Press, 2006, 45-73.

[7] J.B. Lounibos, *Self-Emptying of Christ and the Christian: Three Essays on Kenosis,* Eugene: Wipf & Stock, 2011, 42.

[8] Ibid.

[9] Jeanmarie Gribaudo, *A Holy Yet Sinful Church: Three Twentieth-Century Moments in a Developing Theology.* Collegeville: Liturgical Press, 2015, 148.

aspire to priesthood. But he also called for an apology to the affected individuals and communities.[10]

The Clerical Sexual Abuse Scandals in the Catholic Church

In his research on childhood sexual abuse in the Netherlands, Wim Deetman asserts that for the period under review (1945-2010) "one in ten" of the Dutch population experienced sexual violence from strangers[11] and that higher incidences of such cases were recorded for those brought up within the Catholic Church.[12] This shows that the phenomenon of childhood sexual abuse is a serious problem in the Catholic Church.[13] He adds that in the Netherlands among the Catholic populations, "between one in a hundred (0.9%) and one in three hundred (0.3%) citizens aged forty and above were sexually violated before they reached the age of eighteen."[14]

A report from Sandra Fernau indicates that in the United States of America (USA), childhood sexual abuse by priests started when the victims were between the ages of four and fourteen.[15] She shows that

---

[10] Christopher Bailey, *The Priest. A Bridge to God,* Huntington: Our Sunday Visitor Publishing Press, 2012, 110.

[11] This is 9.7% of his study population of 34,234 (Wim Deetman, "Sexual Abuse of Minors in the Roman Catholic Church," 2010, 51, www.onderzoe krk.nl/fileadmin/commissiedeetman/data/downloads/eindrapport/20111216/Sa men vatting_eindrapport_Engelstalig.pdf [29.3.2019]).

[12] Wim Deetman indicates that figures of the people abused within Catholic settings outweigh those from other traditions by 12.4% to 8.4% respectively (Wim Deetman, "Sexual Abuse of Minors in the Roman Catholic Church," 2010, 51).

[13] Ibid, 55.

[14] Ibid, 55, 361.

[15] Sandra Fernau, "Sexual Abuse by Catholic Clergy: Patterns of Interpretation and Coping Strategies of Victims, in the Light of a Religious Socialization," 2016, 8, www.jostor.org/stable/j.ctvsz3.12 [13.5.2019].

most of the highly affected were male children whose abuse would last as long as nine years. She observes that the abusers took sexual acts as an absolution for sins after confession and as a blessing being bestowed on the victim. The worst scenario was when sexual violence was used as an exorcism which was reported by the one victim whose abuse started when she was four years old.[16] Given that both sex and religious rituals are believed to be sacred spaces in the Catholic Church, these acts were an exploitation of the sacredness of religious beliefs *and* of innocent children who are made in the image of God. In secular discourses, these acts are not only immoral but also criminal, as innocent children are exploited in order to fulfil selfish desires.

Wim Deetman confirms that sexual abuse of children took the nature of "very mild to extremely sexual acts" and this included continuous sexual intercourse, coercion and sexual violence.[17] For instance, one victim narrates a serious incident in his life:

> When I reached the age of first communion, it was the parish priest that was in charge of the proceedings. The parish priest thought that I could benefit from private lessons in the catechism, which took place once a week. Only, I didn't learn much about the catechism, since within half an hour his hands were down my trousers. I was forced to perform oral sex and on several occasions, he would then penetrate me anally. This continued for several months until I took my first communion. I never talked about it to anyone because the parish priest was someone to be respected – unlike me apparently.[18]

---

[16] Sandra Fernau, "Sexual Abuse by Catholic Clergy: Patterns of Interpretation and Coping Strategies of Victims," 2016, 15.

[17] Wim Deetman, "Sexual Abuse of Minors in the Roman Catholic Church," 2010, 51, www.onderzoekrk.nl/fileadmin/commissiedeetman/data/downloads/eindrapport/20111216/Samenvatting_eindrapport_Engelstalig.pdf [29.3.2019].

[18] Ibid, 40.

Wim Deetman presents us with a very serious moral issue in the life of a priest. According to Deetman, of the 720 victims in the study, 70 victims experienced penetrative sexual intercourse, 437 had prolonged relationships with their abusers, while 200 victims experienced abusive acts for more than a year. He observes that while childhood sexual abuse reached its peak in the 1950s and 1960s, a decline was observed from 1970 to 1980 and thereafter.[19] According to the John Jay report for the USA, a total number of 4392 clerics were accused of childhood sexual abuse, translating to 4% of the priests who were in ministry at that time.[20] The authors observe that among them 1.5% were falsely accused.[21] Cahill & Wilkinson argue that it is worth noting that the Church leadership had received allegations of childhood sexual abuse long before the peak of the revelations of 2000 to 2003. The researchers report that in the USA, clerical sexual abuse of minors increased in the 1960s to the 1980s and saw a decline from the 1980s to 2000.[22] For them, the decline can be attributed to many factors, including the vigilance of the victims and their families, the media and the aggressiveness of the bishops who made sexual abuse talks top of their agenda.[23]

Elizabeth Cullingford reports that 81% of the abused children were male. Responding to the media allegations that the abusers were homosexual by nature,[24] she argues that the fact that the majority of

---

[19]   Ibid, 40-56

[20]   2004_02_27_John_Jay_Main_Report_Optimized.pdf.

[21]   Desmond Cahill & Peter Wilkinson, *Child Sexual Abuse in the Catholic Church: An Interpretive Review of the Literature and Public Inquiry Reports*, Melbourne: RMIT University, 2017, 73, 173.

[22]   Ibid. This agrees with Wim Deetman's findings for the Netherlands.

[23]   Ibid, 75.

[24]   Elizabeth Cullingford, "Evil, Sin or Doubt? The Dramas of Clerical Child Abuse," 2010, 4-6, www.jostor.org/stable/40660605 [13.3.2019].

the victims were male children does not mean that those who committed the acts were homosexuals. She asserts that paedophilia is associated with age and not gender, thus individuals can commit acts that are homosexual by nature while they are not homosexuals.[25]

Causes of Clerical Sexual Scandals in the Catholic Church

Cahill &Wilkinson observe that priest offenders were deprived of the community support systems that they usually depend on. They assert that the offending priests suffered from the psychological effects of loneliness, sadness and isolation, thus they were rendered sexually and emotionally weak to resist temptation,[26] and that the availability of the children in their care provided easy access to them.[27] The researchers observe that, although the figures show the number of serial offending priests ranging from one to five in a study, hundreds of children suffered at their hands for many years. Here serial offenders according to the authors are those priests who have repeatedly abused about ten children.

According to Cahill & Wilkinson, the shortage of priests against the demanding missionary activities in the church resulted in the ordination of priests with psychological problems against the will of the training staff in the seminaries. They observe that priests, brothers and seminarians were 'recycled.'[28] Here seminarians were moved from one seminary to another and religious brothers who felt called to a priestly life were allowed to change their vocations to priesthood, while Priests who committed crimes were transferred from one diocese to another and from one country to another, even though the

---

[25] Ibid.

[26] Desmond Cahill & Peter Wilkinson, *Child Sexual Abuse in the Catholic Church*, 207.

[27] Ibid.

[28] Ibid, 190.

church as early as Trent and the Code of Canon Law (1363 #3) of 1917 forbade the practice of transferring offenders from one place to another.[29]

Cahill & Wilkinson observed that in as much as the reports on sexual abuse indicate a low incidence of childhood sexual abuse among female religious congregations, there is clear evidence of many cases of severe physical and psychological abuse of children in female religious institutions, as the religious sisters' insensitivity and naivety related to sexual issues allowed male strangers easy access to children's homes.[30]

Other factors driving sexual scandals were linked to institutions such as orphanages, seminaries and boarding schools which recorded the highest incidences of childhood clerical sexual abuse. For example, Deetman observes that the lack of supervision from the people running these institutions and the lack of action from authorities fuelled the abuse.[31] Cahill & Wilkinson add that childhood sexual scandals were witnessed in migrant homes and in schools for physically and mentally challenged children.[32] They assert that the offending priests used the comfort of their cars to molest children. They added that some priests took advantage of the generosity of family friends who welcomed them into their homes so they could commit the crimes. For instance, two priests sexually abused two siblings in their own bedrooms. On several occasions, children were

---

[29]   Ibid, 190-191.

[30]   Ibid, 190-192, 307.

[31]   Wim Deetman, "Sexual Abuse of Minors in the Roman Catholic Church," 2010, 52-56.

[32]   Desmond Cahill & Peter Wilkinson, *Child Sexual Abuse in the Catholic Church: An Interpretive Review of the Literature*, Melbourne: RMIT University, 2017, 152.

abused during spiritual programmes such as youth camps organized by their priests.[33]

According to Cahill &Wilkinson, Vatican II and the sexual revolution were major contributing factors to the clerical sexual scandals.[34] They affirm that the sexual revolution brought enormous changes in the manner in which seminarians and priests managed their sexuality. They assert that clerical life suffered from moral corruption causing priests to express their sexual desires on innocent children.[35] Supporting the argument, Doyle & Benkert concede that after Vatican II the Catholic Church witnessed an enormous 'exodus' among priests and religious brothers.[36] According to him the church faced a difficult time as the life of celibacy was questioned by the secular world, thus hundreds of intelligent priests and seminarians abandoned their vocations.

Hamilton observes that the current practice that allows religious institutions to handle cases internally must be viewed with a suspicious eye, since it is a major contributor to childhood clerical sexual abuse. He argues that the system is only interested in protecting the dignity of the offenders while constantly putting the victims at risk. The law regulating the 'statute of limitation' is another hindrance in addressing sexual scandals by the clergy since it deprives the victims of the chance of reporting their abusers, once a specific time period has passed. He further observes that the "church autonomy clause" in the law creates another dangerous gap in legal matters because it prevents religious and priests from being

---

[33] Ibid, 306.

[34] Ibid.

[35] Ibid, 193.

[36] Thomas P. Doyle & Marianne Benkert, *Clericalism, Religious Duress and its Psychological Impact on Victims of Clergy Sexual Abuse*, New York: Spring Science + Business Media, 2009, 7.

prosecuted.[37] Furthermore, the offenders must not only be held accountable for their criminal behaviours, but they must also *not* be excluded from the 'legal obligations' imposed on other people.[38]

A culture of silence was (and often still is) dominant in the Catholic Church, and it is manifested in different ways. For instance, Marci Hamilton observes that to cover up the abuse, the Church authorities did not only transfer the offenders but concealed the fact that they knew anything about the challenges the offending priest had and they made private payments to silence victims.[39] Adding to the debate, Cahill & Wilkinson affirm that at the centre of the Catholic Church structures is a culture of 'secrecy, secretiveness and denial'.[40] According to them, the practice of silence does not end in the confessional box, but rather extends to the protection of information and offenders. The researchers assert that this culture of silence is not only applied to institutional cover-ups of clerical sexual scandals but it also denies legal agencies from accessing relevant information that could help in prosecuting priests and religious offenders. Cahill & Wilkinson argue that the Church emphasizes secrecy to protect the Catholic community from knowing the weaknesses of their priests.[41]

---

[37] This is the Church Autonomy Clause in the *Tort and Criminal Law* which allows the church hierarchy to internally solve the problems of the clergy. The law provides immunity to the clergy from facing 'judicial examination' (Marci Hamilton "The Waterloo for the So-Called Church Autonomy Theory: Widespread Clergy Abuse and Institutional Cover-Up," www.researchgate. net/publication/2281 60852, 2007, 12-13).

[38] Ibid, 10.

[39] Ibid, 3-4.

[40] Desmond Cahill & Peter Wilkinson, *Child Sexual Abuse in the Catholic Church: An Interpretive Review of the Literature*, Melbourne: RMIT University, 2017, 273.

[41] Ibid, 273.

Cahill & Wilkinson conclude that while the well-intended work of providing support and a decent life to vulnerable children is appreciated, it is evident that institutional care provided a fertile ground for sexual abuse, physical torture and psychological damage to the children.[42] One would conclude that good will in providing care to the children is supported by relevant professional skills and self-sacrifice. This section of the study explored the clerical sexual scandals that were highly reviewed in 2002 conducted by some members of the clergy in the Catholic church.

As the author I am not trying to point a finger on anyone in the Catholic Church, but to reflect on the kenosis of Christ as a critical tool to respond to the matter. Certainly, the church today has taken a prophetic stand to address the issue. The encouragement coming from Pope John Paul II is of great importance. During the World Youth Day celebrations in July 2012, the pope encouraged the youth that they should not be discouraged by the faults and weaknesses of a minority of the individuals in the church, as the majority of Catholic clergy and religious are living saintly lives and witnessing to the gospel in the various charitable works they are doing across the world.

Effects of Childhood Clerical Sexual Abuse on Victims

The sexual wrongdoings of clerics in the Catholic Church have a long-lasting impact on the victims. These psychological effects are vast and vary in their presentations. For instance, in her observations, Diane Shea states that victims of childhood clerical abuse suffer from despair as they are powerless to defend themselves and thus are rendered hopeless, and consequently, they suffer from depression.[43]

---

[42] Ibid, 162.

[43] Diane J. Shea, "Effects of Sexual Abuse by Catholic Priests on Adults Victimized as Children: Sexual Addictions and Compulsivity," *Research Gate* 15 (3), 2008, 250-268, www.researchgate.net/publication/232959291 [13.3.2019].

For her, the victims lose their value in religious beliefs and the tradition that had guided their moral and spiritual lives. The author observes that since the perpetrators of childhood sexual abuse are men, male victims live with the fear that they will become homosexuals. She says that male victims suffer from self-stigma and thus fail to talk to anyone about the abuse. Moreover, the social construct that males are defenders of themselves is a major challenge for male children to disclose their abusive experiences as this will make them look weak.[44] She asserts that the 'statute of limitation,' which makes legal proceedings impossible after a number of years, leaves victims in a helpless state as no one fights for their justice, hence, victims develop suicidal tendencies.[45]

Similarly, Sandra Fernau observes that victims of childhood clerical sexual scandals do not want to disclose their abuse because by sharing, they are forced to re-live their traumatic experiences.[46] For her, the trauma instilled in the victims is related to the "fear of stigmatization and loss of affiliation with the church community."[47] Here, the survivors fear being blamed for the abuse and the people around them to whom they look for spiritual support, such as family members and faith communities, might reject them. Since victims of abuse are often active members of their parishes, they fear that by disclosing their sexual abuse, they will lose their connection to their parish life. Sandra Fernau asserts that since priests have an influential role in society, abused children do not report their abuse because they

---

[44] Ibid, 13.

[45] Ibid, 14.

[46] Sandra Fernau, "Sexual Abuse by Catholic Clergy: Patterns of Interpretation and Coping Strategies of Victims in the Light of a Religious Socialization," 2016, 10, www.jstor.org/stable/j.ctvsz3.12.[13.5.2019].

[47] Ibid, 10.

fear that their community and family will not 'forgive' them for tempting the man of God to commit sexual acts.[48] It is worth noting that since victims have relied on their religious, social and family ties in which they find security, they fear being blamed by this very system as they would lose their support network and 'affiliation.'[49] She argues that male victims live in denial of the trauma they have experienced by trivializing the abuse when it happens and afterwards.[50]

According to Michael Doyle[51] the priests use their powerful positions to intimidate their victims and to sustain their "trauma bonding" relationships with their victims. Offenders exercise their spiritual powers over the victims who see them as representatives of God. This leaves the victims with severe psychological, spiritual and emotional wounds. Here victims are vulnerable as they do not have the capacity to defend themselves against the powerful influence of their perpetrators, who are, at the same time, their spiritual fathers. This leaves victims traumatized. During the whole period of such relationships, victims are not able to distinguish between genuine love and an abusive relationship.[52] Doyle and Bankert assert that the Catholic Church teaches that sexual sin, including homosexuality, sex outside marriage, sexual thoughts and acts, whose remission is the prerogative of a priest, leave the victims of clerical sexual abuse confused and in a dilemma as their spiritual system crumbles. Here, victims fail to internalize the double standards of their priests, suffer from anxiety and become nauseous at not only the sight of their

---

[48]   Ibid, 11.

[49]   Ibid, 12.

[50]   Ibid, 14.

[51]   Thomas Doyle, "Roman Catholic Clericalism, Religious Duress and Clergy Sexual Abuse," 2003, 223, www.researchgate.net/publications/251344, 247, [18.3.2019].

[52]   Ibid, 223-226.

abusers but the church. The victims' horrific experiences cause them to lose faith in church teachings, religious systems and the clergy because the priest is not only the source of spiritual support but also the source of the abuse.[53]

The implication of the foregoing is that clericalism has a culture of authoritarianism which defines holiness and grace of the church with the clerics. This clerical nature empowers priests with both prestige and status and becomes the root cause of "religious duress"[54] whereby victims and their family members are intimidated with fear when they are taught the truth about sexual sin by the very same clerics. Therefore, this leaves them feeling betrayed.[55] It is fitting to say that the scandals call for the Church to face the reality of the problem. It is with this deep sorrow that Pope Francis acknowledges the damage the priests have inflicted not only on the victims but also on their families and communities who have witnessed and suffered from the phenomenon.[56]

The Catholic Church's Response to the Clerical Sexual Abuse Scandals

The response of the Church to childhood clerical sexual scandals illustrates the sense of responsibility that the Church feels for the

---

[53] Thomas P. Doyle and Marianne Benkert, *Clericalism, Religious Duress and its Psychological Impact on Victims of Clergy Sexual Abuse*, New York: Spring Science + Business Media, 2009.

[54] Ibid, p. 234.

[55] Ibid, 232-237.

[56] Pope Francis, "Letter to the People of God," 2018, 1, http:// w2.vatican.va/ content/francesco/en/letters/2018/documents/papa-frances co_20180820_lettera-popolo-didio.html.[14.4.2019]; http://w2.vatican.va/co ntent/francesco/en/speeches/2019/february/documents/ papa francesco_20 190224_incontro-protezi oneminori-chiusura.html.[14.4.2019].

wrongdoings of the offending priests. Here, one would agree that the notion of self-emptying has been demonstrated by Pope Francis who has embraced a kenotic way of dealing with the clerical sexual scandals. For instance, in his letter to the people of God dated 20th August 2018, Pope Francis observed that the Church was not attentive enough to childhood clerical sexual scandals. He acknowledged that the Church, through its silence surrounding sexual abuse by its priests, perpetuated the crimes. He asserts that the Church neglected its prophetic role by not addressing the clerical sexual scandals.[57] With deep sorrow he wrote :

> With shame and repentance, we acknowledge as an ecclesial community that we were not where we should have been, that we did not act in a timely manner, we showed no care to the little ones.[58]

The Pope further calls upon the ecclesial body to collectively show sympathy and concern for and be in solidarity with the victims. He rejects the clerical culture, the egoistic notions of pride, self-satisfaction and self-sufficiency, asserting that these kinds of attitudes are motivated by spiritual immorality and perpetuate the institutional cover up of abusive behaviours in the church. He further calls for self-less and self-sacrificing attitudes that motivate the fight against all sorts of immorality.[59]

Kenosis, the self-emptying of Christ, is about acknowledging the wrongs and looking for ways to amend them. The clerical sexual scandals are a revelation that there is sin in the Church, a fact that the Holy Father attests to. He affirms that sin in the Church does not exclude anyone; ordained and non-ordained are all sinners and he

---

[57] Pope Francis, "A Letter to the People of God," 2018, 2, http://w2.vatican.va/content/francesco/en/letters/2018/documents/papa-francesco_201808 20_lettera-popolo-didio.html.[14.4.2019].

[58] Ibid, 2.

[59] Ibid, 2-3.

calls the whole community of believers to prayer and fasting for this motivates a transformation that seeks a more Christ-like attitude towards the other.[60]

It is worth noting that in responding to the childhood clerical sexual scandals, Pope Francis has exhibited the virtue of humility, which theologians have claimed to be the very nature of the Church. For example, Mc Brien echoes Congar's claim of the moral failures within the Church.[61] He observes that Congar acknowledged that 'throughout history,' the Church has failed: her desire for human-comfort, pride, her thirst for riches and power and her 'vulnerability to the sins of the flesh'.[62] Here one would conclude that by the mention of the `sins of the flesh,' Congar was aware of the gravity of clerical sexual immorality in the church.[63] According to McBrien, despite these failures, Congar is confident that the Holy Spirit accompanies the church in its mission to spread the Good News and its ultimate union with God.[64] Certainly one would agree that this kind of confidence in divine grace leading the Church in its mission in challenging moments is the consolation of a humble soul.

Similarly, Flannery observes that in *Lumen Gentium,* the exposition of the nature of the Church is found.[65] Here, the synod fathers insisted that the Church, apart from being a mystery and sacrament, is also a

---

[60] Ibid, 3.

[61] Richard P. McBrien, "I Believe in the Holy Spirit: The Role of Pneumatology in Yves Congar's Theology," in G. Flynn (ed), *Yves Congar: Theologian of the Church*, Louvain: Peeters Press, 2005, 303-327.

[62] Ibid, 317.

[63] Ibid.

[64] Ibid.

[65] Austin Flannery (ed), *Vatican Council II: The Conciliar and Post-conciliar Documents.* Collegeville, MN: Liturgical Press, 2014, 369.

whole community of God. In this context the synod fathers suggested a theological image of the Church as a collective journey and denied the clerical nature of the Church. It follows that the Church as a pilgrim people on the way to the final reign of God, is imperfect and sinful, seeking renewal (*Lumen Gentium*: 48). Agreeing to the notion of the eschatological nature of the Church as "a pilgrim people" (*Lumen Gentium:* 78)[66] Sullivan emphasizes on the Church embodying a community of believers who fight against the 'temptations and the weakness of the flesh'.[67] One will conclude that it is in this humble state that the Church attempts to respond to the clerical sexual scandals affecting the Church today. The revelations of these scandals have negatively affected the prophetic mission of the Church. In this context, kenosis becomes significant in the life of the Church at this time of crisis. It comes as a pastoral tool in addressing the immorality that has damaged the image of the Church. For example, the Servant Church indicates that the sexual immorality within the Church has revealed the 'hypocrisy' of her members.[68] According to the Servant Church, in this context, a kenotic approach comes from Pope Francis who has renounced all forms of clericalism and privilege and encouraged the leadership of the Church to reclaim the theological image of the Church as the 'community of the people of God' as this promotes equality and servanthood.[69] One would agree that the kenotic message teaches to accept the wrong echoed by the Servant Church. Here the author acknowledges that 'immorality, inequality, pride and greed' have rendered the church imperfect.[70] In this context, kenosis calls for a transformation of attitudes,

---

[66] Ibid.

[67] Francis Sullivan, *The Church we Believe in*, New York: Pauline Press, 1988, 78.

[68] *Servant Church: The Programme for Adult Formation*, Hinckley: St Peters Community, 2013-2014, 9.

[69] *Ibid*, 9.

[70] Ibid, 77.

values and desires and renounces a culture of dominance, privileges and power as these prevent not only individual growth but equally the growth of the entire body of Christ. After all the drama that has surrounded sexual abuse of minors in the Church, renewal and reform in the Church is what is at the heart of Pope Francis as he claims:

> the best results and the most effective resolution that we can offer to the victims, to the people of Holy Mother Church and the entire world, are the commitment to personal and collective conversion, the humility of learning, listening, assisting and protecting the most vulnerable.[71]

Similarly, one would agree that the Pope looks at a kenotic Church, as one that accepts her failures and humbly seeks forgiveness. It is in this spirit that Pope Francis meets the survivors of clerical sexual abuse. Pope Francis in his position could have sent any of his cardinals or bishops to talk to the victims of clerical sexual abuse. However, he saw (and sees) the matter as a pastoral need to personally provide a listening ear to the wounded souls. For him, a personal encounter motivates reconciliation and a change of attitude as he narrates in the letter to the bishops of Chile:

> I wanted to personally meet with some of the victims of sexual abuse, the abuse of power and abuse of conscience, to listen to them and ask forgiveness for our sins and omission.[72]

The Pope confirms that the meeting created an awareness of the Church's lack of responsibility in the past which deterred her positive

---

[71] Pope Francis, "Address at the End of the Eucharistic Celebration," 2019, 9. http://w2.vatican.va/content/francesco/en/speeches/2019/february/doc ume nts/papafrancesco_20190224_incontro-protezioneminori-chiusura.html. [14.4.2019].

[72] Pope Francis, "Letter to the Bishops of Chile," 2018, www.vaticannews. va/en/pope/news/2018-05/letter-of-pope-francis-to-the-chileanbishops.html. [14.4.2019].

growth. The kenotic love of Pope Francis painfully demands a 'never again' culture of abuse and to all systems that cover up the abuse while seeking to create a culture of love that reflects God's compassion and care for life, which promotes authentic relationships.[73] Certainly, Pope Francis sees kenosis as a means of attaining a communal spirit among believers. Pope Francis is aware that if kenosis was to be a pastoral tool, there is need for a consolidated effort from all baptized members in the Church. In this regard, the Pope turns to all the people of God and reminds them of their prophetic zeal inculcated in them by the Holy Spirit which collectively challenges the culture of clerical sexual abuse and brings about transformation in the church, one that reflects and upholds the dignity of every person.[74] His exhortation to all people baptized is demonstrated in the Servant Church:

> All the baptized, whatever their position in the church … are agents of evangelization, and it would be insufficient to envisage a plan of evangelization to be carried out by professionals while the rest of the faithful would simply be passive recipients … the task of proclaiming the good news of Jesus Christ is for all of us. We are called to carry the Lord and be carried by the Lord.[75]

Here the Pope breaks the boundaries of hierarchy in the proclamation of the Gospel and sees the whole [Catholic] church as a pastoral agency for all the faithful to be involved in evangelization.[76] Hans Urs von Balthasar looks to the self-sacrifice of Christ in obedience to his Father as a perfect example for a sacrificial Church. He argues that a kenotic Church does not exclude anyone from fulfilling their pastoral responsibilities and the ordained and non-

---

[73] Ibid, 4.

[74] Ibid.

[75] *Servant Church: The Programme for Adult Formation*, Hinckley: St Peters Community, 2013-2014, 108.

[76] Ibid, 112.

ordained have the duty to restore the damaged image of the Church.[77] In this case, Christians are called to denounce the culture of abuse, condemn and fight all systems that perpetuate such crimes and proclaim the love of God to all. The Church of kenosis is the church of the 'poor,' one which meets the oppressed in their desperate conditions.[78] In the context of clerical sexual scandals, the poor are the victims who cannot even express their vulnerability for fear that they will be rejected and consequently lose their connectedness to their support networks in society as discussed earlier. According to the Servant Church a kenotic Church is a place of safety, one which accommodates and liberates the rich and poor alike, where all share space and find consolation.[79]

Conclusion

This chapter was a discussion of past clerical sexual abuse scandals within the Catholic Church. It concludes that the approach taken by Pope Francis in addressing the clerical sexual scandals shows the link with the self-emptying of Christ. The Christological hymn offers a demonstration of the self-restriction which is the radical, moral initiative that Jesus took to reconcile humanity. Here, kenosis encourages all believers to have a self-limiting attitude as Christ did and to foster Christian thinking and attitudes towards life and other people. It is not a secret that the clerical sexual scandals have not only shaken the Catholic Church but have also destroyed its image and robbed it of its prophetic role, making it difficult to challenge evil in the world. Pope Benedict acknowledged the sinfulness of priests in

---

[77] Hans Urs von Balthasar, *Who is a Christian?* San Francisco: Ignatius Press, 2014, 122.

[78] Ibid, 126.

[79] *Servant Church: The Programme for Adult Formation*, Hinckley: St Peter's Community, 2013-2014, 112-113.

the Church and the lack of responsibility by the church authorities over the matter.[80] This requires a kenotic response, not only from the Church authorities but from all baptized individuals and communities.

Reflecting on the self-emptying of Christ provides a clear indication that the kenosis theory can offer a theological response to clerical sexual scandals affecting the Church today. The Christological hymn of Philippians 2:5-7 gives an exposition of the self-emptying of Christ, where Paul exhorts the Christian community at Philippi to imitate the mind of Christ. This is a self-divesting notion that allows the accommodation of others. This informs a Christian way of life.[81] The researcher observes that in the context of clerical sexual scandals, the self-emptying approach has been exhibited by Pope Francis who, in his *Letter to the People of God* dated 20th August 2018 with humility, he has exhorted the Catholic Christian community to seriously reflect on the current happenings in the church and urged them to show compassion, love and care to the victims while challenging the scourge of clericalism, which is the major contributing factor to the crime.[82] Furthermore, the Pope in his *Letter to the Church in Chile* of 15th May 2018, cautioned the Church leadership to refrain from all forms of silence on abuse as this perpetuates the clerical sexual abuse of innocent children.[83] The researcher was inspired by the Church's attempt to re-claim her theological image as the people of God, as stated in *Lumen Gentium* #48 of Vatican II. Here, the Church sees

---

[80]   C. Bailey, *The Priest. A Bridge to God,* Huntington: Our Sunday Visitor Publishing Press, 2012, 108-110.

[81]   John B. Lounibos, *Self-Emptying of Christ and the Christian: Three Essays on Kenosis,* Eugene: Wipf & Stock, 2011, 42.

[82]   Pope Francis, "Letter to the People of God," 2018, 4.

[83]   Pope Francis, "Letter to the Bishops of Chile," 2018, 4-5, www.vatican news.va/en/pope/news/2018-05/letter-of-pope-francis-to-the-chileanbishops .html.[14.4.2019].

itself as a community of believers on an eschatological journey towards the heavenly Father. In this context, it is an imperfect community striving for holiness. This self-understanding of the Church as the People of God can be used as a prophetic instrument to collectively address the clerical sexual scandals with humility.

Chapter Four

A Feminist Critique of the Concept of *Ishilu* and its Effect on Women with Mental Disability in Zambia

Lilian Siwila & Charity Mulalami

Introduction

This chapter is derived from the Master's thesis that focused on the ecumenical bodies' silence on the sexual abuse of women with mental disabilities in Zambia. The study draws from the researchers' observation of the sexual violence of women with mental disability in the streets of the Copperbelt province of Zambia.[1] The findings of the study were that, although the ecumenical bodies[2] are involved in social justice/gender-based violence activism, in all their joint

---

[1] This chapter is drawn from Charity Mulalami: 'A Feminist Critique of Ecumenical Bodies' Silence to the Sexual Abuse of the Women with Mental Disability in Zambia', MA, University of KwaZulu Natal, 2020. Among the many issues addressed in the dissertation, this chapter focusses on the issue of *ishilu* which was drawn from our encounters of sexual violence against women with mental disability in the Copperbelt province. Each one of us had a separate experience of the same incident, and we found ourselves concerned to reflect on the issue academically. Although incidents of sexual violence against women with mental disability are not well documented in Zambia, the practice on the ground is prevalent. In the Copperbelt province there is a tendency of men raping women with mental disability, especially those who sleep in the streets. And when this happens, passers-by could not seem to be bothered, instead they just despise the woman as *ishilu*, a social construct associated with being mentally sick. In the Zambian context *ubushilu* is a very serious term that is commonly used, especially on women.

[2] The three ecumenical bodies are: The Council of Churches in Zambia, the Evangelical Fellowship of Zambia and the Zambia Council of Catholic Bishops.

statements, there is no mention of advocacy for women with mental disabilities who are also the victims of sexual abuse. The study also observed that there are robust religious and cultural beliefs and attitudes towards disability which have led to the dehumanization, devaluation, discrimination, rejection, stigmatization, and marginalization of persons with disabilities. The social construction of naming someone *ishilu*[3] in society removes the human dignity of a person – implying that they are no longer the image of God, since the image of God seems to be associated only with those viewed as normal in society. It is from this background that this chapter hopes to draw out a debate on the conceptualization of mental disability as *ishilu* in Zambia and its effect on the rape of women who are mentally challenged.

Disability in Zambia

Disability is both a public health and a human rights issue and as such, it has drawn the attention of key stakeholders globally, who are trying to determine how best they can render support to persons with disabilities worldwide.[4] Zambia as a developing country has many people with disabilities whose living conditions are poor, and most of whom are found in the street. James Mung'omba states that in Zambia there were in 2008 an estimated 256,000 people that had

---

[3] *Ishilu* is a Bemba word, the language of one of the major tribes from the northern part of Zambia. It is a very derogatory word that devalues, demeans, and takes away the dignity and humanness of someone, thereby rendering one useless. It is not only used to express mental disability or illness but it is also applied to those who don't have a mental illness.

[4] One of the major books from the region, using a theological approach, is: James Amanze & Fidelis Nkomazana (eds), *Disability is not Inability. A Quest for Inclusion and Participation of People with Disability in Society*, Mzuzu: Mzuni Press, 2020.

some form of disability, and out of these, about 13,800 lived with intellectual disabilities.[5]

In addition to this, the national policy on disability reveals that women with disabilities can be more vulnerable to sexual abuse than men.[6] Though statistics about disabilities have been increasing in the country, addressing disability as an issue has received very little attention in the planning and development strategy of the nation.[7] The assumption is that the government regards disability as a non-threatening life condition and so it is not amongst the public health priorities. And yet, both disability and gender-based violence [GBV] are public health issues.[8]

Gender Based Violence in Zambia

Cases of gender-based violence are escalating in Zambia, and this has attracted the attention of the government through the Ministry of Gender and Child Development [MGCD], of the Non-Governmental Gender Organisations Coordinating Council [NGOCC], the Young Women's Christian Association [YWCA], and the Women for Change Lobby Group [WCLG], to mention only a few, as well as the church through the three ecumenical bodies. Despite the high presence of GBV cases, there is also a high possibility that the numbers of women with mental disability who are also sexually abused are not represented in these statistics. This is because in

---

[5] James Mung'omba, "Comparative Policy Brief: Status of Intellectual Disabilities in the Republic of Zambia," *Journal of Policy and Practice in Intellectual Disabilities*, 5(2), 2008, 142-144.

[6] Central Statistical Office, *Zambia National Disability Survey*, 2015.

[7] Ibid.

[8] Isabel Allende, "Violence against Women: The Health Sector Responds," World Bank, http://web.worldbank.org/archive/website01213/web/images/ vaw_ heal. pdf. [30.11.2019].

Zambia, like in many other countries, there are a number of gender-based violence cases that are not reported. Women fail to report cases due to stigma and victimization that they encounter, especially from the police.

Although Zambia is believed to be a Christian nation, sexual and gender-based violence has become one of the key concerns in the country. The Non-Governmental Gender Organisation Coordinating Council [NGOCC] recently convened a national indaba on SGBV from the 11th to 12th September 2019, on the theme, *"Zambia Unite! End Sexual and Gender Based Violence."*[9] Elizabeth Phiri, the Minister of Gender officiating at the first-ever national indaba on sexual and gender-based violence, highlighted in her keynote speech that sexual and gender-based violence (SGBV) is not only evolving at a fast rate but has turned into a national crisis.[10]

Zambia passed one of the most comprehensive (inclusive) laws on gender-based violence in the SADC region, the "Anti Gender Based Violence Act no. 1 of 2011." Not only does the Act offer a comprehensive framework for the protection of victims, it also offers a means of survival in form of support systems for victims and survivors of gender-based violence, and prosecution of perpetrators.[11]

---

[9] NGOCC, http://ngocc.org.zm/2019/09/13/zambia-unite-end-sexual-gend er-based-violence.[14.9.2019].

[10] Elizabeth Phiri, "Minister Bemoans Rise in GBV Cases," *Lusaka Times*, September 11, 2019, www.lusakatimes.com/2019/09/11/gender-minister-bem oans-rise-in-gbv-cases [11.9.2019].

[11] Rumbidzai Elizabeth Chidoori, "Putting Women First – Zambia's Anti gender-based Violence Act of (2011)," https://au.int/sites/default/files/ documents/-31520-ocputting_women_first__zambias_anti_gender_based_vio lence_act_of_ 2011_by_chidoori_rumbidzai_elizabeth.pdf.[20.5.2019].

Society's Perception of Disability

African countries, including Zambia, have different experiences of disability due to religious and socio-cultural constructions, thereby producing either positive or negative societal attitudes. Most African societies associate disability with religious beliefs; this has been embraced for generations, and it is still a trend. According to Micheline Kamba Kasongo, in the Democratic Republic of Congo, there is a negative portrayal of persons with disabilities.[12] There is the belief that disability is a misfortune, and this socio-cultural concept of disability has been influenced by the biblical interpretation of it, making people with disabilities seem to be lesser human beings.[13] Louise Kretzschmar agrees with Micheline Kamba Kasongo and affirms that "when one has a disability, they are perceived as having a lower social status, sometimes dehumanized."[14]

According to Kasongo, the perception of disability as a misfortune has strongly influenced the mind-set of many people in the Democratic Republic of Congo [DRC].[15] She also asserts that, although the DRC is a Christian country and people have much faith in the Bible, there is a challenge to separate some cultural beliefs from biblical texts.[16] Retief and Letšosa maintain that "one of the primary forms of moral or religious models of disability regards disability as a

---

[12] Micheline Kamba Kasongo, "Developing a Holistic Educational Pro gramme through Contextual Bible Study with People with Disabilities in Kinshasa, Democratic Republic of Congo: Iman'enda as a Case Study," PhD, University of KwaZulu-Natal, Pietermaritzburg, 2013.

[13] Ibid.

[14] Louise Kretzschmar, *The Church and Disability*. Pietermaritzburg: Cluster, 2018, 24.

[15] Micheline Kamba Kasongo, "Mission to Persons with Disabilities: A Transforming Love for Justice in 1 Samuel 9: 1-11," *International Review of Mission*, 108(1), 2019, 18-24.

[16] Ibid.

punishment from God for sin(s) that may have been committed by the persons with disability."[17] Given this line of argument, Mwale and Chita, writing from the Zambian context, remark that "individual Pentecostal ministries depict disability as that which needs healing through the operation of the Holy Spirit, as it is considered to be the work of the devil."[18] Nomatter Sande (supporting this view), argues that rather than helping persons with disabilities, the way Pentecostals preach and pray for healing impacts negatively on people as they are not healed, especially those with a disability.[19]

This chapter argues that this attitude by Pentecostal churches demonstrates their failure not only to understand but also to accept the fact that disability does not call for healing. Therefore, trying to heal persons with disabilities shows that able bodied people are not ready to accept or embrace the otherness of PWDs

Charles Drum et al, writing from a public health point of view, challenge the church to "recognize the fact that disability will always be with us."[20] We affirm this and contend that this implies that disability does not need any healing. R. Damon, speaking on BBC, formulated this clearly:

---

[17] Marno Retief & Rantoa Letšosa, "Models of Disability: A Brief Overview," *HTS Teologiese Studies/Theological Studies*, 2018, 74(1), 2.

[18] Nelly Mwale & Joseph Chita, "Religious Pluralism and Disability in Zambia: Approaches and Healing in Selected Pentecostal Churches," *Studia Historiae Ecclesiasticae*, 42(2), 2016, 53-57.

[19] Nomatter Sande, "Pastoral Ministry and Persons with Disabilities: The Case of the Apostolic Faith Mission in Zimbabwe," *African Journal of Disability* (Online), 2019/8, 1-8.

[20] Charles E. Drum, Gloria L. Krahn & Hank Bersani, *Disability and Public Health: American Association on Intellectual and Developmental Disabilities*, Washington, D.C.: APHA Press, 2009, 1.

Stop trying to heal me – Like countless persons with disabilities, I am frequently approached by Christians who seek to pray for me to receive healing. Much as they may be well-intentioned, these experiences time and again leave me feeling judged … So, I set out to realize what Christianity has to render persons with disabilities beyond promises of miracle cures.[21]

The story Rose Damon presents in this article depicts the pain of many persons with disabilities who feel spiritually abused as the church fails to comprehend that disability is not a tragedy that needs to be undone.[22] According to Thomas Reynolds, "the medical model of defining disability represents an inability, abnormality, or disadvantage calling for management and corrections to restore proper functioning. Moreover, the medical model reduces disability to a problem requiring diagnosis and treatment, a broken object that needs to be mended."[23] According to Edwin Etieyibo and Odirin Omiegbe, Aristotle and Plato suggested getting rid of all children considered to be imperfect as they were considered non-sturdy people, including those with different forms of disabilities, as they were regarded as standing in the way of the perfect world.[24]

This chapter argues that it seems that society determines who is a human being and who is not, and that embracing such beliefs indicates the lack of understanding that disability can be both congenital and acquired in the process of life. The chapter further

---

[21] Rose Damon, "Stop Trying to 'Heal' me," *British Broadcasting Corporation News*, 28 April, 2019, www.bbc.com/news/uk-48054113.[7.9.2019].

[22] Ibid. – For a similar full life testimony see: Sebenzile Matsebula, "Inclusion and Participation: A Success Story and Convictions of a Person with a Disability," in James Amanze & Fidelis Nkomazana (eds), *Disability is not Inability. A Quest for Inclusion and Participation of People with Disability in Society*, Mzuzu: Mzuni Press, 2020, 171-178.

[23] Thomas E. Reynolds, *Vulnerable Communion: A Theology of Disability and Hospitality*. Grand Rapids: Brazos Press, 2008, 25.

[24] Edwin Etieyibo & Odirin Omiegbe, "Religion, Culture, and Discrimination against Persons with Disabilities in Nigeria, *African Journal of Disability*, 5(1) 2016, 4.

questions whether society (people), as created beings, have the right to determine the humanity of another created person. Thomas Reynolds hints at the need to have a positive Christian understanding of disability, and poses the question, "Is disability a tragedy to be undone?" He further maintains that this aspect renders the coupling of Christianity and disability problematic.[25] Jennifer Fitzgerald argues that these religious constructions of disability in most instances also operate to define and confine the spiritual journey of people with disability.[26]

Because of the above, Black inquires: "what effect do these contradictory descriptions have on the way persons with disabilities view themselves? How do these descriptions affect how other people treat PWDs in our churches and society?"[27] Laurent Magesa remarks that disability is thought of as an affliction, which means an abnormality that represents a diminishment or destruction of the force of life; thus, something must be done to restore it.[28]

Cultural Myths and Beliefs on Disability

African countries, including Zambia, have people with different forms of disabilities, and the experiences of people with disabilities seem to be the same due to cultural beliefs. These are commonly embraced for generations, thereby producing negative societal attitudes towards PWDs. In addressing cultural myths and beliefs on disability,

---

[25] Thomas E. Reynolds, _Vulnerable Communion: A Theology of Disability and Hospitality_. Grand Rapids: Brazos Press, 2008, 25.

[26] Jennifer Fitzgerald, "Reclaiming the Whole: Self, Spirit, and Society," _Journal of Disability and Rehabilitation_, Vol. 19, no. 10, 1997.

[27] Kathy Black, _A Healing Homiletic: Preaching and Disability_, Nashville: Abingdon, 1996.

[28] Laurent Magesa, _African Religion: The Moral Traditions of Abundant Life_, New York: Orbis Books, 1997, 173.

it is imperative to understand what culture means in the context of this study:

> Culture can be considered as a construction of a revocable reaction. Culture constructs us, and we, in turn, construct it. Cultural construction implies that not all thoughts, feelings and human activities are natural, but they are the result of historical encounters that become an indispensable part of the culture.[29]

The chapter argues that if culture is a construction of a revocable reaction, then these cultural beliefs of disability can be revoked or deconstructed to create a cultural atmosphere that is inclusive and can embrace the otherness of people with disabilities. In discussing disability from a cultural perspective, Patrick Devlieger asks, "What does disability mean in a particular culture? How is the status of a person with a disability determined by the culture in which he/she lives?"[30] Hebron Ndlovu argues that "indigenous African beliefs about disability and persons with disabilities are contradictory because they render disability and persons with impairments nega-tively."[31] According to Edwin Etieyibo and Odirin Omiegbe, many people in Nigeria acquire beliefs through an indirect approach. They further maintain that

> our experiences concerning disability and our actions towards persons with disability in Nigeria suggest that people who acquire their beliefs through

---

[29] M. Eskay et al, "Disability within the African Culture," *Contemporary Voices from the Margin: African Educators on African and American Education*, 2012, 474.

[30] Patrick Devlieger, "Why Disabled? The Cultural Understanding of Physical Disability in an African Society," in Susan Whyte and Benedicte Ingstal (eds), *Disability and Culture*. Los Angeles: University of California Press, 1995, 93.

[31] Hebron L. Ndlovu, "African Beliefs Concerning People with Disabilities: Implications for Theological Education," *Journal of Disability & Religion*, 20(1-2), 2016, 29-39.

direct approach are more sympathetic than those with an indirect approach.[32]

Some people assume that

disability is a punishment or bad fortune in the family, which is caused by ancestral spirits and witchcraft — however, these stories cause some families to hide away persons with disabilities as indicated by the Ministry of Community Development and Social Welfare National Policy on Disability.[33]

The study disagrees with these negative cultural beliefs, which for a long time have dehumanized people with disabilities. Thus, the study calls for transformed cultural attitudes which are life-affirming towards PWDs. Theresa Abang subscribes to this argument and concludes that

[t]he majority of Nigerians view disability and disabled people as a judgement or curse from God who repays everyone following his or her deeds; this belief is mainly seen in the manner in which a disabled child is treated in most families.[34]

Micheline Kamba Kasongo agrees with Theresa Abang's argument and affirms that

[i]n Africa, disability is not only considered as a tragedy that requires sympathy and charity; however, at times, it evokes condemnation; that is

---

[32] Edwin Etieyibo & Odirin Omiegbe, "Religion, Culture, and Discrimination against Persons with Disabilities in Nigeria," *African Journal of Disability*, 5(1) 2016, 5.

[33] Ministry of Community Development and Social Welfare, "National Policy on Disability Launched," 2016, p. 8, www.mcdsw.gov.zm/?page_id=5266. [25.10. 2019].

[34] Theresa B. Abang, "Disablement, Disability, and the Nigerian Society," *Disability, Handicap & Society*, 3(1), 1988, 71-77.

cultural beliefs present disability as a curse, bad luck brought by Satan because of sin.[35]

On the other hand, the observation is that "if a child with disabilities was allowed to live, he or she would never get the same treatment as the other members of the community."[36] The word disability usually presents with it negative connotations. Loeb *et al* also note that "among the Shona-speaking Zimbabweans, the word disability translates as non-human, and in certain cultures, disability is alluded to as punishment for transgressions committed in previous lives."[37] We want to argue that these cultural conclusions related to the humanness of people with disabilities are very derogatory and offensive to them. According to Bjorn Franzen,[38] in some communities in Kenya and Zimbabwe, a child born with a disability represents a curse befalling the entire family. Hence, such attitudes harm the growth of the child as less care, attention, education and other essentials of life are given to them. In short, although they exist, they are rejected. The study notes with sadness that such an attitude represents the hidden and unspoken pain that many people with disabilities are exposed to throughout their lifetime. Building on this argument, the Union of the Physically Impaired Against Segregation [UPIAS] maintains that:

---

[35] Micheline Kamba Kasongo, "Mission to Persons with Disabilities: A Transforming Love for Justice in 1 Samuel 9: 1-11," *International Review of Mission*, 108(1), 2019, 18-24.

[36] Theresa B. Abang, "Disablement, Disability, and the Nigerian Society," *Disability, Handicap & Society*, 3(1), 1988, 71-77.

[37] M.E. Loeb, A.H. Eide, and D. Mont, "Approaching the Measurement of Disability Prevalence: The Case of Zambia," *Alter*, vol. 2, no. 1, 2008, 32-43.

[38] Bjorn Franzen, Attitudes Towards People with Disabilities in Kenya and Zimbabwe," MA module, School for International Training, Nybro, 1990, 21-26.

Disability is forced on top of our impairments by the way we are avoidably isolated and excluded from full involvement in society. Persons with disabilities are thus an oppressed category of people in society.[39]

The chapter affirms this argument and remarks that indeed, with such beliefs and attitudes, PWDs are an oppressed group of people. Desmond Tutu articulates that Africans are known to be social beings that are in constant communion with one another in an environment where a human being is considered as a human being only through their relationships to other human beings.[40] Following these arguments, we want to argue that it seems that there is a social construction of who a human being is in African society. This social construction is not only associated with disabilities but also the description of one's humanness stands out as a challenge even with the social construction of mental disability – _ishilu_. Aud Talle subscribes to the fact that:

> The moral code of the Maasai people of Kenya firmly holds that impaired children should be cared for in the same way as other children without discriminating against them – a child is a child whatever it looks like. It is wrong to kill or mistreat deformed or impaired children because they are the same blood, meaning that they are human beings.[41]

The study affirms such cultural beliefs which are inclusive and endeavour to embrace the otherness of persons with disabilities. However, contrary to Talle's argument, is that "if a child was born deformed, it was suffocated before the midwife announced to the

---

[39] Union for the Physically Impaired Against Segregation, _Fundamental Principles of Disability_, London: The Union of Physically Impaired Against Segregation, 1976, 14.

[40] Michael Battle, _Reconciliation: The Ubuntu Theology of Desmond Tutu_. Cleveland: Pilgrim Press, 1997, 39-43.

[41] Aud Talle, "A Child is a Child: Disability and Equality among the Kenya Maasai," in Susan Whyte and Benedicte Ingstal (eds), _Disability and Culture_. Los Angeles: University of California Press, 1995, 67.

people that it was a stillbirth; such a child was put in a pot and disposed of immediately."[42] Given this line of argument, Etieyibo and Omiegbe conclude that disability is a curse and people with disabilities are hopeless. Besides the ancient local myth concerning disability, there is a belief that People with Disabilities (PWDs) are outcasts serving retribution for the sins of their forefathers.[43] Sensokhuhle Doreen Setume, writing on African beliefs and myths, argues that:

> African belief systems, like any human endeavour to present both negative (in myths) and positive (proverbs) disposition towards people with disabilities. Myths explain the causes of the occurrence of disability. Thus, as long as the myths make meaning and enable the explanation of a disability, such will prevail. Therefore, education is a key to new ways of explaining disability that can be availed to some African communities.[44]

African Worldviews on Mental Disability/Illness

The African worldviews on the social construction of *ishilu* are very stereotypical and pose a danger to the lives of such people, in the way society treats them as outcasts. Mental illness or disability is a culturally loaded experience, and different cultures have peculiar ways of constructing mental illness.[45] Annabelle Opare-Henaku and Utsey,[46]

---

[42] Theresa B. Abang, "Disablement, Disability, and the Nigerian Society," *Disability, Handicap & Society*, 3(1), 1988, 73.

[43] Edwin Etieyibo & Odirin Omiegbe, "Religion, Culture, and Discrimination against Persons with Disabilities in Nigeria, *African Journal of Disability*, 5(1) 2016.

[44] Sensokhuhle Doreen Setume, "Myths and Beliefs about Disabilities: Implications for Educators and Counsellors," *Journal of Disability & Religion*, 20(1-2), 2016, 62-76.

[45] Annabelle Opare-Henaku and S.O. Utsey, "Culturally Prescribed Beliefs about Mental Illness among the Akan of Ghana," *Transcultural Psychiatry*, 54(4), 2017, 502-522.

[46] Ibid.

Adiibokah & Nyame[47] and Kwasi Wiredu,[48] reveal that the Akan of Ghana interpret mental illness in terms of spirit agency. The belief is that mental illness is regarded as the same as a loss of social status by others, thereby implying the loss of a person's essential humanity, and it carries a moral charge.[49] According to Hebron Ndlovu indigenous African religions depict people with mental impairments as victims of either witchcraft or ancestral anger due to their moral indiscretion.[50] Laurent Magesa also maintains that:

> Indigenous African religions interpret mental illness as an affliction that can best be contained by diviners or mediums who can establish the cause of the affliction and also advise on what steps must be taken to obtain healing.[51]

Hebron Ndlovu concludes that:

> Indigenous African beliefs portray virtually all types of physical and psychological impairment as an affliction that must be counteracted with all means of traditional therapies for mental illnesses ranging from social stress, anxiety, depression, schizophrenia, and insanity.[52]

---

[47] Edward Adiibokah and S. Nyame, "Local Suffering and the Global Discourse of Mental Health and Human Rights: An Ethnographic Study of Responses to Mental Illness in Rural Ghana," _Global Health_, Oct 14, 2009, doi: 10.1186/1744-8603-5-13.

[48] Kwasi Wiredu (ed), _A Companion to African Philosophy_, Oxford: Blackwell, 2005.

[49] Hebron L. Ndlovu, "African Beliefs Concerning People with Disabilities: Implications for Theological Education," _Journal of Disability & Religion_, 20(1-2), 2016, 29-39.

[50] Laurent Magesa, _African Religion: The Moral Traditions of Abundant Life_, New York: Orbis Books, 1997, 214.

[51] Ibid.

[52] Hebron L. Ndlovu, "African Beliefs Concerning People with Disabilities: Implications for Theological Education," _Journal of Disability & Religion_, 20(1-2), 2016, 29-39.

Social Construction Stereotype on Women with Mental Disability in Zambia (*Ishilu*)

The study observes that Zambia has adopted the social model of disability enshrined in the Constitution and in the Persons with Disability Act of 2012. The social model of disability was developed by Mike Oliver as a disabled activist. Oliver argues that "there is a need to focus on the social facets of disability, primarily on how the physical and social environment imposes restrictions upon a specific class of people."[53] Molly Haslam agrees with Oliver and concludes that:

> The problem identified which is associated with this model, is not the particular characteristics of an individual but rather the socially constructed stereotyping elements that act as barriers keeping persons with disabilities from attaining status as equal citizens in society.[54]

This chapter affirms Molly Haslam's line of argument and contends that one of the reasons why there seems to be a negative response to sexual abuse of women with mental disability in Zambia is the social construction and stereotyping element evident in the name-calling of these people as *ishilu.*

Peter Berger and Thomas Luckman, in their book *The Social Construction of Reality*, argue that "the sociology of knowledge concerns itself with the social construction of reality."[55] Following this line of argument, Conrad and Barker highlight that "social constructionism is a framework with an emphasis on the cultural and historical elements of phenomena widely thought to be exclusively natural.

---

[53] Mike Oliver, "A New Model of the Social Work Role in Relation to Disability," In Jo Campling (ed), *The Handicapped Person: A New Perspective for Social Workers*, London: Radar, 1981, 19–32.

[54] Molly C. Haslam, *A Constructive Theology of Intellectual Disability: Human Being as Mutuality and Response*, New York: Fordham University Press, 2012, 11.

[55] Peter L. Berger and Thomas Luckman, *The Social Construction of Reality: A Treatise in the Sociology of Knowledge*, New York: Open Road Media, 2011.

Besides, the emphasis is on how meanings of phenomena do not necessarily exist essentially in phenomena themselves but develop through interaction in a social context."[56] Donilen Loseke and Joel Best assert that

> constructionist perspectives focus on how people create and respond to conditions, how we categorize and typify, how the meaning of problems is instinctively constructed, and how our constructions influence how we act toward those conditions.[57]

The study agrees with the argument that the sociology of knowledge concerns itself with the social construction of reality and maintains that the social construction of *Ishilu* presents a negative stereotype of the attitude of society's perception of mental disability. Tobin Siebers affirms this line of argument concerning disability and articulates that often disability poses a challenge in the way the body is represented.[58] Tobin Siebers further contends that people with disabilities provide insights into and a clear understanding that all bodies are socially constructed.[59]

According to Amos Yong, there is a need to recognize the broader social context within which disabilities are constructed as this highlights the importance of understanding disability perspectives from cultural and social criticisms.[60] Vivian Burr points out that

---

[56] Peter Conrad and Kristin K. Barker, "The Social Construction of Illness: Key Insights and Policy Implications," *Journal of Health and Social Behaviour*, 51(1_suppl), 2010, S67-S79.

[57] Donilen R. Loseke and Joel Best, *Social Problems: Constructionist Readings*, London: Routledge, 2017, 4.

[58] Tobin Siebers, "Disability in Theory: From Social Constructionism to the New Realism of the Body," *American Literary History*, 13(4), 2001, 737-754.

[59] Ibid.

[60] Amos Yong, *The Bible, Disability, and the Church: A New Vision of the People of God*, Grand Rapids: Eerdmans, 2011, 102.

language continually influences the construction of how disability is understood and perpetuated in society.[61] Louise Kretzschmar, writing in *The Church and Disability*, observes that "the proper use of language about disability remains a complex matter."[62] Vivian Burr, writing on language as a pre-condition for thought, argues that "our way of understanding the world does not come from objective reality but from people, both past and present."[63] Amos Yong affirms this and maintains that "the language about the disabled is also designed to remind us about the subtle yet undeniable ways that persons with disabilities continue to be objectified and thereby experience the world through discrimination at the hands of the non-disabled."[64] Following these arguments, Berger and Luckman remark that

> language is capable not only of constructing symbols that are highly abstracted from everyday experience but also of 'bringing back' these symbols and presenting them as objectively real elements in everyday life.[65]

Chris Hermans *et al* illustrate that "on the one hand, no social reality exists unless it has a linguistic meaning. On the other hand, this does not insinuate that all social reality may be limited to language."[66] On the contrary, those cultural beliefs influence how people construct reality concerning mental illness according to Vivian Dzokoto and

---

[61] Vivian Burr, *An Introduction to Social Constructionism*, London: Routledge, 1995.

[62] Louise Kretzschmar, *The Church and Disability*, Pietermaritzburg: Cluster, 2018, 4.

[63] Vivian Burr, *An Introduction to Social Constructionism*, London: Routledge, 1995, 7.

[64] Amos Yong, *The Bible, Disability, and the Church: A New Vision of the People of God*, Grand Rapids: Eerdmans, 2011, ix.

[65] Peter Berger and Thomas Luckman, *The Social Construction of Reality a Treatise in the Sociology of Knowledge*, New York: Open Road Media, 2011.

[66] Chris Hermans et al (eds), *Social Constructionism and Theology*, Leiden: Brill, 2002, xvi.

Glen Adams.[67] Given this argument, to address the socio-cultural construction of mental disability in Zambia, language plays a significant role. This is commonly observed in the usage of the word _ishilu_, which is a very derogatory word that devalues, demeans, and takes away the dignity and humanness of someone, thereby, rendering them useless. In the Zambian context, _ishilu_ is not used only regarding people with mental illnesses but even to those without mental disability if someone does what is viewed as abnormal and unpleasant in society.

The phrases like, '_Uli shilu_ or _cili shilu ci_, or _bushe batuntulu aba, bacitafya ifya bushilu,_[68] are commonly spoken even to people without mental disability. The socio-cultural construction of _ishilu_ demonstrates how people, through language and social context, have created a negative image and how this has influenced their response to mental disability. Given this view, we find the terminology of _ishilu_ very problematic due to the negative image it creates. It gives birth to barriers that make society fail to respond to the challenge of sexual abuse of this key population of women in this study.

Susan Wendell, referring to the cultural construction of disability, argues that culture makes significant contributions to disability. This includes not only the lack of disability experiences in cultural representations of life in society but more so, the cultural stereotyping

---

[67] Vivian Afi Dzokoto and Glenn Adams, _Understanding Genital-Shrinking Epidemics in West-Africa: Koro, Juju or Mass Psychogenic Illness, Culture, Medicine and Psychiatry_, 2005, 29, 53-78; see also Glen Adams and Phia S. Salter, "Health Psychology in African Settings: A Cultural-Psychological Analysis," _Journal of Health Psychology_, 12(3), 2007, 539-551.

[68] These phrases portray one as not being normal but having a mental issue, and their behaviour resembles those with mental disability.

of persons with disabilities.[69] She further notes that the selective stigmatization of physical and mental limitations and other differences has negatively contributed to the adverse treatment of people with disabilities in society.[70] M.A. Devine remarks that people always construct knowledge, which is assumed to be a reality; but social behaviour, language, and attitudes are merely social constructions of society.[71] Given this argument, Vivian Burr indicates that "each different construction also brings with it a different kind of action from human beings; therefore, such descriptions or constructions of the world support some patterns of action and prohibits others."[72] This chapter affirms Vivian Burr's argument and remarks that this is the lived reality of *ishilu*. This social construction of mental disability has created patterns of action and societal attitudes of stigma, discrimination and marginalization, thereby socially excluding PWDs.

The chapter agrees with these arguments and asserts that this socio-cultural construction of *ishilu* has influenced how gender activists, the government through the Ministry of Gender, and the church through the three ecumenical bodies engage in the fight against SGBV. The ecumenical bodies are theologically better positioned to understand these women as the image of God, which should encourage their response to the sexual abuse of women with mental disability. Although PWDs generally are exposed to stigma, marginalization, and discrimination, it is imperative to understand that those with mental illness experience this more than any other category of disability. This, therefore, implies that although this category of people may be

---

[69] Susan Wendell, *The Rejected Body: Feminist Philosophical Reflections on Disability*, New York: Routledge, 1996.

[70] Ibid.

[71] M.A. Devine, "Inclusive Leisure Services and Research: A Consideration of the Use of Social Construction Theory," *Journal of Leisurability*, 24(2), 1997, 1-9.

[72] Vivian Burr, *An Introduction to Social Constructionism*, London: Routledge, 1995, 5.

under the same condition, the masculine and feminine elements in them still play a significant role.

The masculine aspect in men with mental disabilities still leaves them with power, while the feminine aspect for women makes them more vulnerable. For instance, when one meets a man with mental illness, automatically the conscience tells one to keep away; hence, for the most part, we find ourselves avoiding them by all means. However, this is different for women. Feminine vulnerability subjects women with mental disabilities to sexual abuse. The question to ask is, "Is it easy (or possible) for a woman to sexually abuse a man with mental illness?" The social construction of mental disability in Zambia causes persons with mental illness to be stigmatized, marginalized, and discriminated, leading to rejection even by their families.

Kurt Danziger in _The Varieties of Social Construction: Theories in Psychology_ contends that in psychology, social constructionism functions as a critique.[73] According to Vivian Burr, critical psychology focuses on how a person is placed within society; that is, it is about difference, gender, sexuality, inequality, and power.[74] In light of these arguments, the social constructionist approach is ideal in challenging how persons with disabilities have been located as the 'other' in Zambian society, especially women with mental disability. Furthermore, the unexceptional oppressive and discriminatory practices of the socio-cultural construct of _ishilu_ in Zambia as well as this gendered crime needs to be voiced out. In addition, the ecumenical bodies' response to women with mental disabilities who are also victims of sexual abuse, who have not yet embraced GBV activism, is another factor worth noting. Furthermore, this socio-cultural construction of

---

[73]   Kurt Danziger, "The Varieties of Social Construction," _Theory & Psychology_, 7(3), 1997, 399-416.

[74]   Vivian Burr, _An Introduction to Social Constructionism_, 1995, 16.

mental disability means that both society and the church contribute to perpetuating and entertaining violence against these women.

Thus, the term of *ishilu* has a robust social construction that has adversely influenced or caused a lack of inclusiveness in the fight against sexual gender-based violence, as the focus centres more on able-bodied women and girls than on those with disabilities. This socio-cultural construction of *ishilu* creates a barrier that makes gender activists and the church, through ecumenical bodies, fail to embrace the otherness of women and girls with mental disabilities. Does this mean that this key population of women is not among the vulnerable who fall prey to SGBV? In addressing the lack of response of the ecumenical bodies to the sexual abuse of women with mental disabilities, the study engages Chris Hermans *et al's* work in social constructionism and theology since these are theologically grounded organizations.[75] Chris Hermans *et al*[76] define practical theology as an action science: it is empirically-oriented and uses the theological theory of mediation of the Christian faith within the praxis of modern society.

Concerning this definition, Gerben Heitink further speaks about two types of praxis, namely; the mediation of the Christian faith as praxis and the context of the modern society as praxis. The first praxis points to the fact that the typical object of practical theology is the transformation of the intentional actions of persons or groups.[77] Micheline Kamba Kasongo, an African feminist theologian living with a disability, writes in *"A Mission to PWDs a Transforming Love for Justice"* that "the love of God should put us in a place where we can consider the others, despite their otherness, as the image of God

---

[75] Chris Hermans et al (eds), *Social Constructionism and Theology*, Leiden: Brill, ix.

[76] Citing Gerben Heitink, *Practical Theology: History, Theory, Action Domains, Manual for Practical Theology*, Grand Rapids: Eerdmans, 1993.

[77] Ibid.

created to live alongside other human beings."[78] She further argues that the mission to PWDs is a transformational mission of love that focuses on actions of justice.[79] This line of argument challenges the ecumenical bodies in Zambia to reflect theologically on the importance of pastoral theology and seeks intentional actions toward the sexual abuse of women with mental disabilities. The praxis task is to take transformative action against the dominant assumption that is levelled against persons with disabilities and should be part of their agenda of inclusiveness.

Stigmatization and Discrimination of Persons with Disabilities

Stigma and discrimination are profound in African society, and different issues attract how one is subjected to such. For example, areas of stigma and discrimination include being barren, unmarried, or uneducated, to mention a few. However, the stigma and discrimination against persons with disabilities undermines their human dignity. According to Djoyou Kamga, central to the discourse on disability is the question of systemic disadvantage, characterized by the discrimination, and often complete exclusion, of persons with disabilities in society.[80] Etieyibo and Omiegbe contend that religious and cultural beliefs have contributed and supported the discrimination of persons with disabilities, thereby violating their human rights. PWDs have been subjected to stigma and discrimination based on their

---

[78] Micheline Kamba Kasongo, "Mission to Persons with Disabilities: A Transforming Love for Justice in 1 Samuel 9:1-11," _International Review of Mission_, 108(1), 2019, 18-24 [1].

[79] Ibid.

[80] Djoyou Kamga, "Call for the Protocol to the African Charter on Human and Peoples' Rights on the Rights of Persons with Disabilities in Africa," _African Journal of International and Comparative Law_, 21(2), 2013, 219.

physical and mental disability. Although stigma remains a challenge in the way people with mental and physical disabilities are perceived,[81] Lars Jacobsson observes that traditional societies seem to stigmatize and discriminate less towards the mentally ill.[82] Hebron Ndlovu disagrees with him and argues that the tendency of indigenous African beliefs to stigmatize mental illness and people with mental impairments goes beyond other forms of disabilities, such as blindness, paralysis, and albinism.[83]

The chapter maintains that the experiences of stigma, discrimination and marginalization are the lived reality of people with disabilities. However, it is essential to understand that disability is not inability; for instance, there are people with disabilities who are renowned and better placed in society than some able-bodied. Samuel Kabue and Micheline Kasongo Kamba, though visually and physically disabled respectively, are well placed academically and have gained international recognition through their works. Kelsey Koszela argues that "the primary reason that causes stigmatization of persons with disabilities in the African context, is the lack of education about disability and lack of realization about the needs of PWDs."[84] Lars

---

[81] Edwin Etieyibo & Odirin Omiegbe, "Religion, Culture, and Discrimination against Persons with Disabilities in Nigeria, *African Journal of Disability*, 5(1) 2016.

[82] Lars Jacobsson, "The Roots of Stigmatization," *Journal of the World Psychiatric Association* (WPA), 1(1), 2002, 25.

[83] Hebron L. Ndlovu, "African Beliefs Concerning People with Disabilities: Implications for Theological Education," *Journal of Disability & Religion*, 20(1-2), 2016, 34.

[84] Kelsey Koszela, "The Stigmatization of Disabilities in Africa and the Developmental Effects," *Independent Study Project (ISP) Collection 1639*, 2013, 2, https://digitalcollections.sit.edu/isp_collection/1639.[20.6.2019].

Jacobsson, writing in _The Roots of Stigmatization_, remarks that stigma and discrimination against the mentally ill is always a complex issue.[85]

Given this fact, Julio Arboleda-Flórez and N. Sartorius affirm that "stigmatizing of, and discrimination against, people with mental disorders (physical disabilities too) is as old as humanity, hence the fact that stigma and discrimination exist is not in question."[86] Thornicroft _et al_ bring out four key aspects concerning stigma:

> first, the labelling of personal characteristics conveys that there are some essential differences. Second, stereotyping links present these differences and create undesirable characteristics. Thirdly, there is a definite distinction between the regular group and the one that is labelled as in some respects, which are different. Moreover, lastly, loss of status and discrimination: results in devaluing, rejecting, and excluding the labelled group.[87]

So, the _ishilu_ concept as a social construct stands out as the labelling of personal characteristics that presents essential differences. This highlights the typical experience of _ishilu_ whose human status seems to be lost.[88]

The study affirms that the stigma illustrated in these points is a reminder that, although many people are educationally enlightened in modern times, there remains an element of being illiterate in the way society treats PWDs, even by those who seem to be exposed to

---

[85] Lars Jacobsson, "The Roots of Stigmatization," _Journal of the World Psychiatric Association_ (WPA), 1(1), 2002, 25.

[86] Julio Arboleda-Flórez and N. Sartorius, _Understanding the Stigma of Mental Illness: Theory and Interventions_, Chichester: John Wiley & Sons, 2008, ix.

[87] G. Thornicroft, E. Brohan, and A. Kassam, "Public Attitudes and the Challenge of Stigma," in Michael Gelder, Juan López-Ibor, and Nancy Andreasen (eds), _New Oxford Textbook of Psychiatry_, Oxford University Press, 2009.

[88] E. Adiibokah and S. Nyame, "Local Suffering and the Global Discourse of Mental Health and Human Rights: An Ethnographic Study of Responses to Mental Illness in Rural Ghana," _Global Health_, October 14, 2009.

education. Given this line of argument, Koszela asserts that "in educating communities concerning the causes of disabilities, the rights and needs of persons with disabilities are critical in creating a society that is stigma-free and inclusive of persons with disabilities."[89] The study observes that, unfortunately, stigmas are created out of a lack of understanding; hence, addressing the knowledge gap and helping all people to have a better understanding of disabilities helps the process of acceptance, although with challenges. On the contrary, Theresa Abang disagrees with Koszela and argues that "even literate parents whom one expects to know much about disabilities and the various causes, would rather hide their disabled child than expose the child to friends and neighbours for fear that they might consider him or her to be wicked, thus paying for some misdeeds."[90]

A Postcolonial Feminist Critique of *Ishilu*

The social construction of *ishilu* can be traced back to the problematic British Colonial Mental Disorders Act of 1951, in which the derogatory name-calling of persons with mental disorders was presented with terms such as, "mentally defective," "idiots," "feeble-minded," "imbeciles" and "moral imbeciles." According to Mental Disability Advocacy Centre (MDAC)[91] and Mental Health Users Network of

---

[89] Kelsey Koszela, "The Stigmatization of Disabilities in Africa and the Developmental Effects," *Independent Study Project (ISP) Collection 1639*, 2013, 2, https://digitalcollections.sit.edu/isp_collection/1639.[20.6.2019], 10.

[90] Theresa B. Abang, "Disablement, Disability, and the Nigerian Society," *Disability, Handicap & Society*, 3(1), 1988, 71-77.

[91] Mental Disability Advocacy Centre and Mental Health Users Network of Zambia, "Human Rights and Mental Health in Zambia – Mental Disability," September 4, 2014, www.mdac.org/sites/mdac.info/files/zambia_layout_web 4.pdf [7.2.2019].

Zambia (MHUNZA),[92] the Zambian laws affecting the rights of people with mental health issues include the Mental Disorders Act of 1951, the 1996 Constitution, the Health Profession Act of 2009, the PWDs Act of 2012, and the Medicines and Allied Substances Act of 2013. Catalina Devandas-Aguilar affirms this and concludes that the British Mental Disorders Act of 1951 has discriminatory provisions against persons with psychosocial disabilities and is outdated; there-fore, does not align with the Convention but continues to be in effect and is being applied by national authorities.[93] Moreover, Mental Disa-bility Advocacy Centre [MDAC] and Mental Health Users Network of Zambia [MHUNZA] indicate that the Mental Disorders Act of 1951 is a piece of legislation from colonial times. It labelled people as

mad, disregarding their views about how they wanted to conduct their lives. This law uses the offensive (and legally meaningless) terms "mentally defective," "idiots," "feeble-minded," "imbeciles" and "moral imbeciles," all of whom can be lawfully detained against their will in *their* own and society's best interests.[94]

The British Colonial Act of 1951 had some elements of the socially constructed *ishilu,* and thereby built barriers of stigmatization, marginalization, and discrimination. This is manifested even in this present time in the way people with mental disorders are treated in society.[95] When a person has *ubushilu* (mental disability) their human

---

[92] "Human Rights and Mental Health in Zambia – Mental Disability," September 4, 2014.

[93] Catalina Devandas-Aguilar, "Report of the Special Rapporteur on the Rights of Persons with Disabilities on her Visit to Zambia," 2016, www.medbox.org [20.10.2019].

[94] "Human Rights and Mental Health in Zambia – Mental Disability," September 4, 2014, 20.

[95] Mental Disability Advocacy Center and Mental Health Users Network of Zambia, *British Colonial Mental Disorder Act,* 2014, www.mdac.org/sites/mdac-.info/files/zambia_layout_web4.pdf [7.2.2019].

dignity is stripped by society, as seen in their treatment. Jackson's book, *Surfacing Up: Psychiatry and Social Order in Colonial Zimbabwe, 1908-1968, – the Birth of Asylum in Africa*, remarks that:

> The first European lunatic asylum in Africa was established as part of the general infirmary at Robben Island in the Cape colony in 1846; before this, the island was used as a convict station and farm. Furthermore, like most asylums, the one at Robben Island was considered an advance over the earlier practice of keeping the unruly insane either with the infirmed in a place like at Somerset hospital in Cape Town or with criminals in prisons and put in chains.[96]

According to Lynette Jackson, in 1908, the British opened a lunatic asylum on the outskirts of Bulawayo in Matabeleland region of Southern Rhodesia, the first to be built in British Central Africa.[97] The second one was built in Nyasaland, now Malawi. Following this, in 1964, Chainama Hills Hospital was opened in Northern Rhodesia (Zambia).[98] This institution is currently running as a psychiatric [mental health] hospital. In the traditional African context, persons with mental disability or illness were never institutionalized or excluded from the community, even in the process of seeking healing solutions, as Hebron Ndlovu indicates.[99] The idea of excluding PWDs can also be associated with the changing paradigms in the understanding of family structures.

---

[96] Lynette A. Jackson, *Surfacing Up: Psychiatry and Social Order in Colonial Zimbabwe, 1908-1968 – the Birth of Asylum in Africa*, Ithaca: Cornell University Press, 2005, 24.

[97] Ibid.

[98] Ibid.

[99] Hebron Ndlovu, "African Beliefs Concerning People with Disabilities: Implications for Theological Education," *Journal of Disability & Religion*, 20(1-2), 2016, 29-39.

Conclusion

The problem of gender-based violence among people with disabilities is one area of research that has not yet received a lot of attention, especially in the work of the Circle of Concerned African Women Theologians. Although there seem to be studies undertaken on disability, most of them have focused on conceptualizing disability and not so much on the challenges faced by people with disabilities. The concept of stigma and name calling as reflected in this chapter is one aspect that has contributed to trivializing the challenges faced by people with disabilities. From such name-calling as *ishilu*, the institutionalization of persons with mental disabilities is upheld and they are misunderstood, overlooked, and discriminated against. They are by some even seen as not being the image of God.

Chapter Five

Speaking One Voice against Gender Based Violence: Perspectives from the "Thursdays in Black" Campaign

Cynthia Kabanda &
Sylvia Mukuka

Introduction

To acquire a clearer perspective of gender-based violence, certain critical questions are inevitable, such as why there is a high prevalence of violence in our societies. Paula Gilbert wonders why people are so fascinated with crime and violence, such that, in the contemporary society, this fascination takes the form of public obsession with forensic culture.[1] Not only this, Gail Mason also questions what triggers violent reactions by individuals both in private homes and in the society. These are serious questions that society should be asking to address issues of violence.[2] Moreover, Gail Mason wonders as to whether violence is a form of power. She sees the oppression of violence which is found in the ability of the act itself to repress the way in which victims act and experience their lives,[3] while questioning who exerts more power in the event of violence.[4] A response to such

---

[1] Paula R. Gilbert, *Violence and the Female Imagination: Quebec Women Writers Reframe Gender in North American Cultures*, Montreal: McGill-Queen's University Press, 2006, 13-14.

[2] Gail Mason, *The Spectacle of Violence: Homophobia, Gender and Knowledge*, London: Routledge, 2002, 117-126.

[3] Ibid, 120.

[4] Ibid.

questions, as Gail Mason argues, is that violence is actually oppressive, and as such, it is imperatively necessary that this phenomenon is clearly defined within the context of patriarchal power. Apparently, today there are very heartening and inspiring responses from women who no longer endure violence in silence, and who have come out to expose the effects of violence outside their confinement.[5]

Patrizia Romito acknowledges that there is no longer secrecy surrounding violence against women. In the new millennium, violence is no longer considered a secret that victims have to live with, live without hope.[6] Besides, Patrizia Romito underscores the fact that society today is more aware of the frequency and consequences of domestic violence, rape, harassment at work and sexual child abuse, phenomena, for most of which there was not even a name until the 1970s.[7] These views are further acknowledged by Morrison and Orlando, who admit that "gender-based violence is undoubtedly one of the most common forms of violence in the world."[8] More so, Lara Fergus and Rogier van 't Rood have distinctly defined gender-based violence as acts of physical, sexual, and psychological violence directed at individuals or groups because of their biological sex and/ or their specific gender role in society.[9] In

---

[5] Ibid, 122.

[6] Patrizia Romito, *A Deafening Silence. Hidden Violence against Women and Children*, Bristol, UK: Policy Press, 2008, 1-2.

[7] Ibid.

[8] Andrew R. Morrison and M.B. Orlando, "The Socio-economic Costs of Domestic Violence: Chile and Nicaragua," in A. Morrison and Mariah L. Biehl (eds), *Too Close to Home: Domestic Violence in the Americas*, Washington DC: Inter-American Development Bank, 1999, 3.

[9] Lara Fergus and Rogier van 't Rood, *Unlocking the Potential for Change; Education and Prevention of Gender-based Violence*, London: Rochester Publications, 2013.

this context, gender-based violence primarily affects women and girls and is usually perpetrated by a male known to the victim, although it is not disputed that men and boys can also fall victim to gender-based violence. However, rape is very much perpetrated against women and girls, often in conflict settings.[10] In this perspective, gender-based violence may include physical, emotional, sexual, and economic violence.

In view of the widespread gender-based violence worldwide, Zambia not excluded, this chapter hopes to analyze the effectiveness of "Thursdays in Black" as a tool to address violence against women. The chapter will also analyze the effects of gender-based violence using the concept of Speaking One Voice.

Methodology and Framework

This is a qualitative study that engages with literature and narratives as well as different media as the sources of information. It takes an example from the narrative process of the Cinderella of Serenje and the disillusionment of a Sesheke family who underwent serious experiences of abuse. Fourteen women, aged 19-50 years, all married, from different sectors who were victims of violence, were interviewed in Serenje and Sesheke districts of Zambia. The aim of the research was to expose the extent of GBV and rape in the two areas. The reality of the narratives told by the women, as Andrew Lester puts it, often helps them to redefine themselves.[11] Narrative theory, constructed within the context of pain and suffering due to trauma and abuse,[12] creates an enabling space within which women can express their feelings and maybe find healing. Besides, the narrative

---

[10] Ibid.

[11] Andrew D. Lester, *Hope in Pastoral Care and Counselling*, London: John Knox Press, 1995.

[12] Ibid.

structure is a meaningful principle for understanding human behaviour, as it provides a background and a context within which human experiences are better expressed.[13] In addition, narratives by women set an impetus for the assessment and effectiveness of how the ideology of the "Thursdays in Black" Campaign can be used as a tool to speak as one voice about gender-based violence. "One voice" implies that everyone must be an advocate for a world without rape and violence. This is a serious commitment that calls for a society to stand together in solidarity against violence.

Gender Based Violence

The United Nation's first internationally accepted definition of violence against women in 1993 suggests that such violence can be perceived as

> any act of gender-based violence that results in, or is likely to result in, physical, sexual or psychological harm or suffering to women regardless of where it is perpetuated, whether occurring in public or private life.[14]

Gender-based violence is an act of aggression, which has left painful scars in many people's lives. In all societies, many women and girls have fallen victim to violence due to their vulnerability and their physical nature. Gender-based violence is a worldwide evil reality that contravenes human rights, and it is a major social crisis.

Gender-based violence against women is a serious human abuse and health hazard. Jalna Hanmer, who analyzes gender-based violence from a social perspective, argues that, although men are violent, it is

---

13 Ibid.

14 United Nations, _Declaration on the Elimination of Violence against Women._ United Nations General Assembly Resolution 48/104, New York: United Nations, 1993; See also United Nations Population Fund (UNFPA), _Ending Widespread Violence against Women_, 1998, www.unfpa.org/gender/violence.htm. [29.2.2020].

not every male who is violent, but men are violent with relative impunity, if they so wish.[15] It can therefore be suggested that gender-based violence is sometimes regulated by the pattern of gender relations and norms which guide the allocation of resources and power at household levels. Patriarchy ensures and maintains the status quo of 'power over' orchestrated by the cultural set up in terms of gendered roles and division of labour, where male authority and power are dominant.[16]

Patriarchy can be perceived within the context of social relations whereby men feel superior by holding a dominant position over women.[17] Patriarchy is a system of social stratification and differentiation based on gender which provides material advantages to males while simultaneously placing severe constraints on the roles and activities of females.[18]

Traditionally, in many societies, the problem of gender-based violence is triggered by several factors, such as the empires that come out of the wider realm of patriarchy. Men and boys are considered the protagonists who head households as breadwinners in the private and public domain, while women and girls are only valued in relation to their ability to organize household social reproduction efficiently.

---

[15] Jalna Hanmer, "Men, Power and the Exploitation of Women," *Women's Studies International Forum*, 13(5), 1990, 443-456.

[16] Ibid.

[17] Patriarchy is often defined as 'the rule of fathers,' but today's male domination goes beyond the 'rule of fathers' and includes the rule of husbands, of male bosses, of men running most societal institutions, and of men in politics and economics.

[18] Cheris Kramarae, "The Condition of Patriarchy," in Cheris Kramarae and Spender Dale (eds), *The Knowledge Explosion: Generations of Feminist Scholarship*, London: Athan Series, Teachers College Press, 1992; Olabisi I. Aina, "Women, Culture and Society," in Sesay Amadu and Odebiyi Adetanwa (eds), *Nigerian Women in Society and Development*, Ibadan: Dokun Publishing House, 1998, 6.

It is, however, within that very same family context that most gender-based violence occurs.[19]

Patrizia Romito argues that, though not all men are violent, all men are the beneficiaries of patriarchy in the sense that even those who are not violent receive at least some of the dividends from a patriarchal system, gaining from the violence committed by some.[20] She observes that males are associated with violence as sometimes, at the mention of the word male, the adjective male is added to the word violence, so that "men are associated with a punch in the stomach."[21]

Sydney Mwaba suggests that gender-based violence is a widespread problem, and that women stand a high chance of falling victims to gender-based violence, but that single women are somewhat less prone to be victims of violence than married women.[22] He also notes that gender-based violence has been on the increase in Zambia,[23] as statistics from a 2010 UN special rapporteur on violence against women showed that the causes and consequences of violence against women were disheartening to Zambian women.[24]

---

[19] Muriithi Muthoni, Chioma Ukuwagu, Saskia van Venn, Anneli Verkade, *Breaking a Culture of Silence: Social Norms that Perpetuate Violence against Women and Girls in Nigeria*, Oxford: Oxfam, 2018.

[20] Patrizia Romito, *A Deafening Silence. Hidden Violence against Women and Children*, Bristol: Policy Press, 2008, 1-2.

[21] Ibid.

[22] Sydney O. Mwaba, "Gender-based Violence: The Zambian Situation. Studies in Social Sciences and Humanities," *Research Academy of Social Sciences*, vol. I, 4(2) 2020, 105-118, ideas.repec.org [23.5.2020].

[23] Ibid.

[24] United Nations, *Declaration on the Elimination of Violence against Women*. United Nations General Assembly Resolution 48/104, New York: United Nations, 1993.

Therefore, in the final analysis, gender-based violence is one of the major contributing factors of ill health internationally, in terms of female morbidity and mortality and as leading to psychological trauma and depression.[25]

Gender-based violence is not just violence against individuals, but violence against a society. It is a serious human rights abuse that threatens the very moral fibre of the society. It is also a public health problem that negatively impacts the well-being of families, individuals, and the society at large. Therefore, women must begin to challenge the patriarchal ideologies embedded in the cultural (patriarchal) belief systems that injure women in our societies.[26]

Factors Influencing Gender Based Violence

It has been observed that the causes of gender-based violence are multiple and complex, and that gender-based violence is a phenomenon that has been in existence for a long time and which can be located within individuals, families and at all societal levels. It has been argued that one of the common acts of gender-based violence is rape, which is often committed during times of war, but also within homes and in the community.[27] Rape is one of the extreme and

---

[25] Christopher Murray and Alan Lopez, *The Global Burden of Disease: A Comprehensive Assessment of Mortality and Disability from Diseases, Injuries and Risk Factors in 1990 and Projected to 2020*, Global Burden of Disease and Injury Series, vol. I, Cambridge, 1996; Liz Kelly, "Wars against Women: Sexual Violence, Sexual Politics and the Militarized State," in Susie M. Jacobs, Ruth Jacobson and Jen March Bank (eds), *State of Conflict, Gender, Violence and Resistance*, New York: Zed Books, 2000.

[26] Lilian C. Siwila, "In Search of a Feminist Cultural Analysis Model for Effective Dialogue on Harmful Cultural Practices," in Isabel A. Phiri & Sarojini Nadar (eds), *Journal of Gender and Religion in Africa, Publication Information*, vol. 18, no. Special Issue, 2012, 106-112.

[27] Liz Kelly, "Wars against Women: Sexual Violence, Sexual Politics and the Militarized State, State of Conflict Gender," 2000, 7-11

effective forms of patriarchal control which has negatively been associated with sexual violence in many different contexts.[28]

Liz Kelly contends that it is the role of feminists to pay attention to every day violence by questioning it and making the distinction between rape that occurs during military conflicts and rape that is committed during so called peace time.[29] Madelaine Morris points out that military culture is detrimental to the well-being of women.[30] She argues that

> the military culture itself encourages higher incidences of rape, in the sense that its culture is often built on standards of masculinity that emphasizes dominance, assertiveness, aggressiveness, independence and self-sufficiency, and its features present a greater propensity for sexual promiscuity, which generally accepts violence against women.[31]

Therefore, violence presented in such a context can be considered within a military perspective which suggests that violence committed against women, whether in the context of war or during peace time, is directly linked to patriarchal domination.[32] Furthermore, Madelaine Morris argues that, "in reality, the violence continuum that goes back and forth between gendered public and private violence is therefore visible during both war and women's everyday life in militarized states."[33] Amina Mama underscores the repressive domestication of patriarchal violence, that it combines European models of violence against women with models of patriarchal oppression that existed

---

[28] Ibid.

[29] Ibid.

[30] Madeleine Morris, "In War and Peace: Rape, War, and Military Culture," in Ann Llewellyn Barstow (ed), *War's Dirty Secret, Rape, Prostitution, and Other Crimes against Women*, Barstow, Cleveland OH: Pilgrim Press, 2000.

[31] Ibid.

[32] Ibid.

[33] Ibid.

both before and after colonization.[34] She further argues that colonization humiliated African women not simply as "colonial subjects," but specifically as women.[35] Ultimately, in considering the extent and gravity of violence against women, societies have come up with different approaches and mitigation strategies against violence. This implies that violence should be condemned and not condoned, particularly in the case of patriarchal societies where violence against women is permissible.

Thursdays in Black Campaign as a Tool to Fight Gender Based Violence

The call for a just and peaceful society cannot be overemphasized. As a result of the atrocities committed against women, various strategies and mitigating efforts against gender-based violence have been put in place. Today many voices call for a peaceful society that is free of violence and injustice. One of the schemes is the concept of dressing in black on Thursdays.

Dressing in Black on Thursday is not a new phenomenon, but a movement that advocates for freedom of expression by the victims of abuse in ensuring that women and men speak out against violence so that the society can be transformed into a safer place in which people can live.

"Thursdays in Black" as a movement draws a long history as far back as the 1970s and 1980s. It started as an Argentinian Movement by the "Mothers of the Plaza de Mayo," referring to the mothers who protested against the policy of having dissidents "disappear" (a term

---

[34] Amina Mama, "Sheroes and Villains: Conceptualizing Colonial and Contemporary Violence against Women in Africa," in M. Jacqui Alexander and Chandra Talpade Mohanty (eds), *Feminist Genealogies, Colonial Legacies, Democratic Futures*, New York: Routledge, 1997.

[35] Ibid.

used to describe people killed by the ruling regime). The mothers assembled in the Plazo de Mayo in Buenos Aires every Thursday to register their protest with the authorities against the disappearance of their children and all related forms of oppression.[36]

Similar protests from different countries arose against rape and sexual assault which were used as weapons of war in Rwanda and in Bosnia. Other women opposed the Israeli occupation of the West Bank and the abuse of Palestinians.[37] In South Africa, the Thursdays in Black campaign was also used as protest against apartheid and the use of violence against black people.[38] The same movement was also revived by a student-led group who campaigned against the rape of a female university student in 2015. Their aim was to raise awareness and educate students about sexual violence and how to tackle rape-supportive cultures that pervade university campus life.[39]

In this campaign, the colour Black was chosen as a symbol of resistance and resilience. "Thursdays in Black" originated from the World Council of Churches' (WCC) Decade in Solidarity with Women (1988-1998) and later became a widespread movement following an increasing number of reported rapes during wars, cases of gender injustice, abuse, violence and many other violent acts

---

[36] Thursdays in Black, "Towards a World without Rape and Violence," World Council of Churches, 2013, www.oikoumene.org>get-involved [6.10.2020].

[37] Thursdays in Black, "World Federation of Methodist and Uniting Church Women," 2020, www.lutheranworld.org.

[38] Thursdays in Black, "Towards a World without Rape and Violence," 2013; See also Marguerite Guzmán Bouvard *Speaking Truth to Power. Madres of the Plaza de Mayo*, 1994, www.womeninworldhistory.com.

[39] Harriet Winn, "Thursdays in Black: Localized Responses to Rape Culture and Gender Violence in Aotearoa New Zealand," in: C. Blyth, E. Colgan & K. Edwards K. (eds) *Rape Culture, Gender Violence, and Religion. Religion and Radicalism.* Palgrave Macmillan, Cham. https://doi.org/10.1007/978-3-319-72224-5_4, (2018).

against women which became increasingly visible, especially during conflicts. In effect, the World Council of Churches (WCC) re-invigorated their involvement in these campaigns for a peaceful society at the General Assembly in Busan, 2013.[40] The World Federation of Methodist and Uniting Church Women discovered that gender-based violence was a reality. Thus, the Thursdays in Black movement has broadened its activities and is not confined to focus on victims of war. It is a campaign that focuses on understanding domestic violence, sexual assault, rape, incest, female murder, infanti-cide, female genital mutilation, sexual harassment, gender discrimi-nation and sex trafficking which ultimately is described as sexism.[41] In their quest to be in line with the movement's ethos, the Lutheran World Federation supports and encourages congregants to dress in black on Thursdays as a global support for gender justice. The violation of women as sexual objects has even been included in church sermons.[42]

The Thursdays in Black campaign focusses on ways in which individuals may challenge attitudes that cause rape and violence. According to a UN report, one third of women globally have experienced physical or sexual violence at some point in their lives. More than 125 million girls and women alive today have been subjected to female genital mutilation in countries in Africa and the Middle East. It is against this background that a mass campaign has emerged to raise awareness, to educate and to engage in activities that mitigate the effects of gender-based violence.[43] This campaign acknowledges the fact that there are links between gender-based

---

[40] Thursdays in Black, "World Federation of Methodist and Uniting Church Women," 2020, https//www.lutheranworld.org. [28.5.2020].

[41] Ibid.

[42] Ibid. [23.9.2020].

[43] United Nations, *Declaration on the Elimination of Violence against Women*. United Nations General Assembly Resolution 48/104, New York: United Nations, 1993.

violence and patriarchy. Gender-based violence can largely be seen as a result of inequalities against women, and the associated violence and harmful beliefs of patriarchy embedded in many traditional and cultural beliefs.[44] Violence against women is deeply embedded in the patriarchal belief that men are superior to women and as such, dominating women is man's prerogative. Thus, educating women is the main tool to build a society where gender-based violence would not be tolerated.[45] Apparently, the response by both genders has been very positive as many have committed themselves to becoming ambassadors for peace by wearing black on Thursdays. This act of wearing black is an outward symbol of courage and strength, of solidarity with women who have experienced some form of violence, and mourning, especially for those who have died because of gender-based violence, even within their own homes.[46] This is a powerful call for a world that is free of rape. As such, both women and men in black stand in solidarity for supporting such women, as they try to make a difference in society. Today this campaign is a worldwide movement which has the support of churches, commercial organizations and many Non-Governmental Organizations (NGOs).

Speaking with a Gendered One Voice

Speaking with a Gendered One Voice is a reaction prompted by the current trends of gender-based violence in Zambia. This response to gender-based violence has led the public to rise up by teaming together for urgent action. Through Gendered One Voice, the Zambian society has pledged to rise up in solidarity with the survivors

---

[44] UN Women, "Patriarchal Culture," 2019, https://eca.unwomen.org [29.5.2020].

[45] Ibid.

[46] Thursdays in Black, "Christian Aid," 2020, https//christianaid.org.uk. [28.5.2020].

of sexual and gender-based violence. This demands affirmative action against sexual atrocities perpetrated against women which are used to oppress them. The Gendered One Voice advocacy against gender-based violence demands a change in attitudes by a society that blames and victimizes the survivors and not the perpetrators; which also is a key concept of Thursdays in Black. Gendered One Voice demands greater protection of communities at risk. Above all, it demands that survivors are listened to and taken seriously by first listening to their needs. The concept of Gendered One Voice Against Violence is a belief that a single voice can be heard in curbing gender-based violence making the world a safer place for all through the Thursdays in Black campaign movement. The Gendered One Voice concept is against keeping silent by the women who experience violence. Similarly, Christine Mushibwe and Lilian Siwila bemoan the culture of silence among women, which is a common scenario in most African communities and which has contributed to the oppression and suppression of women.[47] It has been observed that oftentimes women opt to keep silent as a result of shame, which according to Fast is considered as the "master emotion" and its existence is rarely acknowledged and many people are unaware of it even when they experience it.[48] It is women who sometimes prefer to keep silent even when they are under pressure. Patrizia Romito suggests that those women who have suffered sexual violence remain deeply wounded, their trust in the world is undermined to such an extent that they are often forced to change their attitudes, it being irrelevant whether the

---

[47] Christine Mushibwe, "What are the Effects of Cultural Traditions on the Education of Women (The Study of the Tumbuka People of Zambia)," PhD, University of Huddersfield, 2009, 109; Lillian C. Siwila, "In Search of a Feminist Cultural Analysis Model for Effective Dialogue on Harmful Cultural Practices," in Isabel A. Phiri and Sarojini Nadar (eds), *Journal of Gender and Religion in Africa*, vol. 18, Special Issue, 2012, 106-112.

[48] Jonathan Fast, *Beyond Bullying: Breaking the Cycle of Shame, Bullying and Violence*, New York: Oxford University Press, 2016, 9-16.

rape was committed by a man they knew or did not know, whether or not it was accompanied by physical violence and whether or not the victim defined it as rape.[49] Jonathan Fast further notes that shame is "hard wired" in human beings and truly is the secret agent of emotions which exerts pressure, for instance, if shame is used intentionally to injure a person's self-concept, then it should be considered 'a weaponized shame,' which is considered as gender-based violence.[50] It is as a result of such experiences that Gendered One Voice through Thursdays in Black was initiated. Those that have chosen to speak up have started supporting each other by encouraging survivors to speak up through creating awareness, providing support for survivors, and educating the masses about what it will take to end this violence. Many concerned people, among them the religious fraternity, have come on board becoming part of the worldwide movement which advocates for a peaceful and free society. Gendered One Voice speaks against pain and anger caused by rape and other forms of violence by seeking action by all concerned. Through the Thursdays in Black campaign, it exposes the patriarchal propensities that lead to the discrimination and oppresssion of women in many sectors and often result in rape, abuse, and many other forms of violence against them.

The Narratives by the Cinderella of Serenje and the Disillusionment of Sesheke

Domestic violence is generally perpetrated by male partners. Too often, such behaviour is met with silence that is tolerated by men themselves. It has been observed by Luis Martin-Cabrera that,

---

[49]   Patrizia Romito, *A Deafening Silence. Hidden Violence against Women and Children*, Bristol, UK: Policy Press, 2008.

[50]   Jonathan Fast, *Beyond Bullying, Breaking the Cycle of Shame Bullying and Violence*, New York: Oxford University Press, 2016, 6-7.

"Silence is the best friend of impunity and it needs to be broken."[51] Abuses were recorded in Sesheke; the Ministry of Women Affairs reported a case involving a man who continuously sexually abused his own biological children and ultimately impregnated one of his daughters.[52] Other cases were reported by Cinderella narratives of the survivors of gender-based violence. Among the many stories was one by a 35-year-old woman who lives in Serenje District , who narrated how she was repeatedly beaten by her husband with whom she has six children. Despite reporting her husband to the authorities several times over his behaviour, he has never been arrested. Despite the abuse, the woman said that she has nowhere else to go since her husband is the sole breadwinner. These were her words:

> I am scared that one of us will be badly injured if we continue to fight. Sadly, my family do not seem to care, they have given up on us and have washed their hands off our problem, after seeing that we have not tried to resolve the problem. The cause of our fights is poverty. Many of the fights start when he can't get his preferred relish.

This abuse even attracted the neighbours' attention who have urged them to stop fighting and have tried as much as possible, to talk to them about the dangers of gender-based violence. The narratives of the women of Cinderella of Serenje and the families of Sesheke are some of the realities of violence in a society. These stories have helped us to conceptualize the extent of GBV in the Zambian context as the women exposed their personal experiences. We have understood the extent of violence that women must endure within households and within society. More so, the Cinderella project strives to

---

[51] Martin Luis, "Radical Justice: Spain and the Southern Cone beyond Market and State," Lewisburg: Bucknell University Press, 2011, http://epaper.daily-mail.co.zm/ [3.5.2020].

[52] Ministry of Women's Affairs, *Restoring Soul: Effective Interventions for Adult Victims/Survivors of Sexual Violence*, Wellington: MWA, Google Scholar, 2009.

expose the power of patriarchy as an empire and how the weak and underprivileged in a society are abused.

At the same time, the stories have helped to understand that one cannot continue living a life of oppression. It is argued that, if the solutions to the violence against women have to be found, then patriarchy as an empire must be exposed. Patriarchal gender constructions contribute to violence against women. Such violence has its roots in political and economic inequality, but it also stems from gender identification in terms of masculinity and femininity. Patriarchy is an expression of identity and the way in which identity is constructed and reconstructed by society.[53] Thus, situating gender-based violence within the human rights discourse, Rico Nieves attempts to describe GBV within households where human rights are violated, such as the right to identity. GBV reinforces and reproduces the subordination of women to men, thereby leading to a distortion of human nature in terms of the right to affection.[54] In fact, violence in a marriage can be explained within what we may phrase as the "Chameleon theory." The Chameleon theory refers to the changing faces of the empire in a marriage. This is where the husband, wife, children, relations, and relatives may be the sources of gender-based violence, and that each person may be blaming the other for their violent acts. For example, a husband may attribute his violent behaviour to poor cooking by his wife, or to lack of sex in the conjugal relationship. At the same time, a wife may declare her behaviour as "enduring violence, just for the sake of the children," as the cases have always been. Thus, the Cinderella and Sesheke stories show that violence is strongly

---

[53] Graeme Simpson and Gerald Kraak "The Illusions of Sanctuary and the Weight of the Past: Notes on Violence and Gender in South Africa," in _Development Update 2: The Right to be: Sexuality and Sexual Rights in Southern Africa_, 1998, 1-10.

[54] Rico Nieves, " Gender Based Violence: A Human Rights Issue," _Women and Development Unit_, Mujer Y. Desarrallo, 1997, 13-16.

influenced by communities' social values and norms regarding the use of violence, and how they are resolved. Oftentimes, such norms conflict with women's positions in challenging traditional gender roles by supporting sexism.[55] Gender-based violence is culturally patterned and prevalent in societies with rigid gender roles or in patriarchal communities in which male dominance is ingrained in a masculine identity.[56] Although Zambia is seen to be a tolerant nation in as far as gender roles are concerned due to the presence of matrilineal societies, the reality on the ground is different, as matrilineal sies . The country still experiences patriarchal tendencies that are oppressive to women even in the so-called matrilineal societies.

Conclusion

It is clear that rape and other forms of sexual violence are a violation of human rights. It is a well-known fact that the atrocities committed through gender-based violence have a devastating impact on the lives of the people. Society today can witness the negative impact of violence through the survivors of these horrific acts which are both physical and psychological. Too often, these acts of violence are committed with the intent to de-humanize and degrade one's identity and personality. Inasmuch as violence is being exposed today, there are other serious violations that are hidden. Therefore, with the introduction of the Thursdays in Black movement, it is hoped that the ills of gender-based violence shall be a thing of the past because societies will be exposed to such hidden practices both in homes and in society. It is the wish of the movement that every concerned

---

[55] R. Jewkes, "Intimate Partner Violence: Causation and Primary Prevention," *Lancet*, 2002, 1423-1429.

[56] L. Heise, "A Global Overview of Gender-based Violence," *International Journal of Gynecology and Obstetrics*, vol. 78, supplement 1, 1998, 262-290. www.oikoume-ne.org/en/get-involved/thursdays-in-black [4.4.2020].

member of society will be a part of the process to sensitize others, even as the movement continues to strive for a peaceful and loving society where everyone will feel respected and loved, making the world a safe place for all. Through the Thursdays in Black campaign, many survivors will be given opportunities to speak out as they will also be creating awareness and providing support for other survivors through education and public advocacy.

Chapter Six

Penetrating the Cracks of Patriarchy: Perspectives on Gender and Leadership in the Church

Peggy Mulambya-Kabonde

Introduction

While there is a recognition in churches of the need for greater equity, there is a deep concern that the policies, strategies and instruments are being determined by men, and that women are required to respond to these rather than setting the agenda themselves. The most important reason why women's issues are overlooked is usually because needs assessment is not carried out, although this can be explored further. The stage, therefore, is set for the formulation of a project or a book publication, which underpins the position of women in all aspects.

Women need the space and the resources to enable them to establish their own priorities and determine how they wish to pursue these priorities. However, women have been treated like perpetual infants or minors who will never grow up and decide what they want to do. As Emmanuel Mveng outlines, the association [of men] should cease forthwith to pretend to speak in our name, to represent us, to take up collections for us, as if we had no mind of our own.[1] Therefore, those who wish to take women seriously will dialogue with women

---

[1] Engelbert Mveng, "Third World Theology – What Theology? What Third World? Evaluation by an African Delegate," in Virginia M.M. Fabella and Sergio Torres (eds), *Irruption of the Third World: Challenge to Theology*, Maryknoll: Orbis, 1983, 201-221.

and not with intermediaries, especially unauthorized intermediaries.[2] On the one hand, Emmanuel Mveng is saying it is time men stopped behaving as intermediaries, speaking on behalf of women, to stand for women and collect everything that belongs to women as if women were not there.[3] On the other hand, Mveng is cautioning the women to be mindful of 'men's associations' that do not wish to give women their own voices.[4] Like Mercy Amba Oduyoye,[5] Mveng calls men to include women in setting the agendas, to dialogue with the women and form a community of justice, participation, inclusiveness and ministry which are the most frequent concepts that generate discussion of the church's self-understanding among African women.[6]

My wish with this chapter is to create gender awareness in the church. It is my belief that the church has never seriously engaged in such an exercise before. The lack of adequate female representation and highly developed women leaders has been taken for granted. For example, in the United Church of Zambia Synod minute book of 1999, the roll call records that there were only six women present against thirty-seven men. It seems as if the church was generally saying that a sufficient number of women had not come forward, and yet no serious attempt was made to consider removing various impediments placed in the way of women. Mercy Amba Oduyoye observes that

> [r]esponding to a question on the participation of women in church practices and the place of their special needs and concerns in the agenda of

---

[2] Ibid, 219.

[3] Ibid.

[4] Ibid, 201-221.

[5] Mercy Amba Oduyoye, _Introducing African Women's Theology_, Sheffield: Sheffield Academic Press, 2001, 85.

[6] Emmanuel Mveng, "Third World Theology- What Theology?" 1983, 219.

the church, women are very much concerned about the church, but the church is not so much concerned about women.[7]

Women, just like men, are human beings, created in the image of God, but, in many cases, women are treated like objects. For instance, whenever the church wants to use them, they are called upon. After accomplishing what they have been asked to do, the women are forgotten. This trend emanates from the home and social context and extends into the Church.

For many men, the idea of women in church leadership is still a hindrance to women's participation. Mercy Amba Oduyoye asserts that within the church structure

[t]he question a feminist ecclesiology has to answer is not whether or not women ought to 'leave' or 'stay', but how it is possible to rethink what it means to be church within a theology paradigm which aims at reconsidering the basics of Christian theology and practice in feminist terms.[8]

The notion of who should do 'a rethinking of what it means to be church' should be considered by both women and men. Drawing from Oduyoye's view above, African Women Theologians advocate that whatever impacts negatively on the well-being of women is not uplifting but tends to dehumanize. To this end, this chapter argues that women fully participate in the church and are not spectators or passengers to be carried like little children.

Because of the above discourse many feminist scholars argue that the aim should be "partnership with men, not the emphasis on differences."[9] The following section illustrates the result of gender disparities in the church and society.

---

[7] Mercy Amba Oduyoye, *Hearing and Knowing*, Maryknoll: Orbis, 1986, 124.

[8] Mercy Amba Oduyoye, *Introducing African Women's Theology*, Sheffield: Sheffield Academic Press, 2001, 4.

[9] Ibid, 24.

Gender Disparities

Central to what was agreed at the World Council of Churches (WCC) Women's Decade Festival in Harare, was the approach of deliberate organization, which affords an opportunity for women to share views and analyze their situation and its underlying causes. Women's partners [who are men] should support them so that women can expand their choices and opportunities. M. Jennings suggests:

> [i]f a positive impact is to be made ... then women's existing power, resilience, roles and work must be recognized and enhanced while the constraints they face must be addressed ... If women are engaged in the process of decision-making and implementation, they themselves will guide and lead development efforts in the way that is most beneficial for them.[10]

Jennings is of the view that in all institutions it is important that women are included in decision-making so that the gap between women and men is removed. This will promote the equal participation of women and men in many activities in all spheres of life. For Jennings, the gender disparities in the church and in societies that are experienced by women due to unequal power relations have contributed to the vulnerability of women. These have resulted in some women acquiring infectious diseases such as HIV and AIDS. The constraints women face need to be addressed, and women need to be included in all agendas and at all levels so as to pave way for processes of development that will be beneficial to women.[11] This brings me to discuss briefly the feminist ecclesiological theoretical framework that is used in this chapter.

---

[10] M. Jennings, "Communities in Development: The Theory and Practice of Gender," in Mary van Lieshout (ed), *A Woman's World beyond the Headlines*, Dublin: Attic Press, 1996, 107-117.

[11] Ibid.

The Feminist Ecclesiological Theoretical Framework

Feminist ecclesiology searches for "counter-patriarchal and subversive readings of traditional ecclesiology,"[12] as a tool that is liberating and gives life in its fullness to both women and men. All forms of oppressive language used to describe the church, including texts that describe institutions which oppress and marginalize women and exclude them from all essential processes of representation and self-definition, will be critically scrutinized by feminist ecclesiology.[13]

The goal of the feminist ecclesiological theoretical framework is to equip scholars in the field of gender and religion with appropriate tools to engage the existing church traditions and structures. This is rooted in the strong desire among women to make the church a place where justice is done and right relationships are formed in a "framework of interconnectedness and participation."[14] Therefore, I employ the feminist ecclesiological theoretical framework to assess the unequal partnership between women and men, as I explore the relationship between gender and leadership in the church in Zambia. Before I examine the historical background of the feminist theory, I will briefly define two crucial concepts.

Equity and Equality

The feminist ecclesiological theoretical framework is of great importance to this chapter because it provides a platform for a

---

[12] Natalie K. Watson, *Introducing Feminist Ecclesiology*, Sheffield: Sheffield Academic Press, 2002, 3. See also Susan Rakoczy, "Living Life to the Full: Reflections on Feminist Spirituality," in Celia Ellen Teresa Kourie and Louise Kretzschmar (eds), *Christian Spirituality in South Africa*, Pietermaritzburg: Cluster, 2000, 69-91.

[13] Natalie Watson, *Introducing Feminist Ecclesiology*, 2002, 109.

[14] S. Longwell, *Gender and the Media: Issues for Media Personnel*, Lusaka: ZARD, 1993; Natalie Watson, *Introducing Feminist Ecclesiology*, Sheffield: Sheffield Academic Press, 2002, 109.

theology of equity and equality with particular reference to gender and a theological understanding of partnership. To better understand the two concepts, I will provide brief definitions of the words, equity and equality, with regard to the way I will use them in this chapter. While the word 'equity' is often used in finance to describe 'ownership of assets', I utilize the word *equity* in this chapter to mean 'fairness and justice in the way women are treated in the church'. *Equality* would then mean "a situation in which men and women, people of different races or religions are all treated fairly and have the same opportunities."[15] These two concepts, equality and equity, will thus form the basis of the chapter and elucidate the following question: *What is the wholistic understanding of the words "equality and equity" from a theological and gender perspective?* The following section discusses the equity approach.

The Equity Approach

Equity and equality are two distinct terms: Equity is giving everyone what they need so that they are successful. Mercy Amba Oduyoye observes that a move towards sharing power entails an aspiration towards the sharing of skills, knowledge and abilities as well as the equal participation of all members for the common good.[16] Fairness in sharing power and knowledge will enhance the sharing of skills and abilities in the church. This may not only be done in the church, but it will start from the home and the community, and in the church equal participation and justice will be adhered to. To this end, for any

---

[15] United Church of Canada, "Gender Justice and Partnership Guidelines," February, 1998, www.ucc.home.page [20.3.2020].

[16] Mercy Amba Oduyoye, "Reflections from a Third World Women's Perspective Women's Experience and Liberation Theologies," in Virginia Fabella & Sergio Torres, *Irruption of the Third World: Challenge to Theology,* Maryknoll: Orbis, 1983, 244-250.

project to be undertaken within the church, community or group, it ought to begin with an assessment of the needs of the target group, both by considering the needs which are felt needs in the women's situation and by asking them their priorities. This is where the concept of equity promotes fairness and justice in the way women or other members of the society may be treated.

The Equality Approach

Equality is treating everyone the same. Equality aims to promote fairness, but it can only work fairly if everyone starts from the same place and needs the same help. Because this chapter deals with issues of gender imbalances in the church, the term inter-sectionality has been accepted as the most significant contribution in women's studies. Kathy Davies refers to inter-sectionality

> as the interaction between gender, race, and other categories of difference in individual lives, social practices, institutional arrangements, and cultural ideologies and the outcomes of these interactions in terms of power.[17]

For Kathy Davies, the interaction of intersectionality includes class, ethnic groups, disciplines, religions, and government policies. All these dimensions are intertwined with issues of power.[18] In James Scott's terms, this is the power that lies within the public transcript and in the hands of the dominant groups.[19] According to Scott the capacity of dominant groups to define what may be called public transcripts and to maintain that which is hidden remains in their

---

[17] Kathy Davies, "Intersectionality as Buzzword: A Sociology of Science Perspective on what Makes a Feminist Theory Successful," in *Journal of Feminist Theory*, vol. 9(1), 2008, 67-85.

[18] Ibid.

[19] James C. Scott, *Domination and the Arts of Resistance: Hidden Transcripts*, New Haven: Yale University Press, 1990.

power to control. This struggle between the dominant and dominated groups is one of the common conflicts that exist in our daily lives.[20]

This is the reason why Mercy Amba Oduyoye advocates for transparency, a world where trust, love and justice prevail and create a peaceful home for us.[21] She states that we can meet the challenge that we have by admitting and embracing our differences, admitting that we can learn from each other, and that "the other is worthy. The goal of reaching towards universality, even as we live out our particularity, is that of achieving mutual spiritual enrichment."[22] All these scholars, Kathy Davies, James Scott, and Mercy Amba Oduyoye, emphasize the concept of equality between men and women in church and society. For the equality approach to exist, there ought to be mutual understanding and equal sharing of gifts among human beings regardless of differences between races, genders, classes, ethnic groups, disciplines, religions, and government policies, for peace to prevail. The following section highlights the historical background of the feminist theory.

Historical Background of Feminist Theory

Feminist theory requires a critical analysis of structures and ideologies that rank people as inferior or superior according to "various human natures."[23] For example, Michelle le Doeuff contends that the

---

[20] Ibid, p. 14.

[21] Mercy Amba Oduyoye, "African Culture and the Gospel: Inculturation from an African Woman's Perspective," in Mercy Amba Oduyoye and H.M. Vroom (eds), *One Gospel—Many Cultures: Case Studies and Reflections on Cross-Cultural Theology*, Amsterdam/New York: Editions Rodopi, 2003, 54.

[22] Ibid, 54.

[23] D. Louw, "From Phenomenology to Ontology in the Gender Debate," in S. Pillay, S. Nadar and Le Bruyns (eds), *Rag Bag Theologies: Essays in Honour of Denise M. Ackermann: A Feminist Theologian of Praxis*, Stellenbosch: SUN Press, 2009, 95-102.

generation and production of knowledge has been an important part of feminist theory. This debate proposes such questions as, "Are there 'women's ways of knowing' and 'women's knowledge'?" and, "How does the knowledge women produce about themselves differ from that produced by men and what is to be done?" Feminist theorists have also proposed "feminist standpoint knowledge," which attempts to replace "the view from nowhere" with a model of knowing that expels the "view from women's lives." A feminist approach to epistemology seeks to establish knowledge production from a woman's perspective. [24] Le Doeuff asserts that feminists need not reject a feminism of difference because history may be repeating itself by replicating the very structures against which it is protesting. For instance, in the 19th and early 20th centuries women struggled for the right to vote and own property in their own name, but somehow, it soon went into oblivion.[25]

This, therefore, requires changes in the deep structures of the church and of social life, and collective action, not simply individual action. It requires profound changes in the way that cooking and serving food during meetings is integrated, so as to make women's partici-pation autonomous. If women have been doing most of the work in the church, like cooking and serving food, while men are going on with the business affairs of the church, is this a way to eliminate or downplay their potential influence? Are women in the church only for domestic work, or are they partners in the running of and in the on-going life of the church? This is what is meant by social

---

[24] Michelle le Deouff, "Women and Philosophy," in T. Moi (ed), _French Feminist Thought: A Reader_, Oxford: Basil Blackwell, 1987, 182.

[25] Sarah Bentley, "The New Feminism in the USA," in _Sexism in the 1970s: Discrimination against Women: A Report of a World Council of Churches Consultation West Berlin 1974_, Genève: World Council of Church, 1975, 20-23; see also Annie Clifford, _Introducing Feminist Theology_, Maryknoll: Orbis, 2001, 9-13.

constructed roles, which we have imported into the church of Jesus Christ. Henrietta Moore argues:

> The difference between men and women can be conceptualized as a set of opposed pairs, which resonate with other sets of oppositions. Thus, men may be associated with 'up', 'right', 'culture', and 'strength', while women are associated with their opposites, 'down', 'left', 'low', 'nature', and 'weakness'. These associations are not inherent in the biological or social nature of the sexes, but are cultural constructs, which are powerfully reinforced by the social activities, which both define and are defined by them. The value of analyzing 'man' and 'woman' as symbolic categories or constructs lies in the identification of the expectations and values which individual cultures associate with being male or female. Such analysis provides some indication of the ideal behaviour of men and women in their different roles, which can then be compared with the actual behaviour and responsibilities of the two sexes.[26]

An analysis of the above quotation on who does the construction, identification and expectations of what, who, and which individual or gender plays a particular role in the home, in church or in the society lies in the power that is within the public transcript. The dominant group of human beings that inherits these power structures of construction, identification and expectations are usually men, and women are always found in the hidden transcripts. The church has inherited these social constructs from the cultural milieu and tends to give women particular types of jobs, usually those low in status. Haralambos and Holborn state that "some explanations for these inequalities concentrate on characteristics of women and men. They generally see the inequalities in the labour market as stemming from women's role in the family."[27]

---

[26] Henrietta L. Moore, "Gender and Status: Explaining the Position of Women," in Henrietta L. Moore (ed), _Feminism and Anthropology_, Cambridge: Polity Press, 1988, 12-30.

[27] M. Haralambos and M. Holborn, _Themes and Perspectives_, London: Harper Collins, 1995, 619.

Origin of these Social Constructs

It is in this sense that we could understand some of the ideas that Paul expressed in 1Timothy 2:1-13: 'Let a woman learn in silence with all submissiveness. I permit no woman to teach or to have authority over men' (RSV). While I am dealing with Paul, I wish to point out something about the way in which the apostle Paul typically argues his case. Unlike the other passages where Paul says, 'yet not I but Christ in me', this particular passage emphasizes the subjective 'I', pointing to some personal or cultural bias on the part of the apostle. Indeed, this personal bias is further developed when the apostle Paul argues that it was the woman, Eve, who was the transgressor, and not the (male) man, Adam. This seems to conflict with God's idea of a salvation that is without distinction, without regard for who did or did not sin first. Yet, this is not a contradiction; it is a pointer to the fact that, although 'inspired', the Biblical writers were individuals who were products of a Jewish religious system that had less regard for women than for men.[28] As Africans, we bring a similar cultural bias to our interpretations of the Bible. Our culture has enslaved us so much that sometimes we even forget what the Bible is saying to us; time and again, as Christians, we are being challenged by what our leader, the Lord Jesus Christ, did. Instead, we have been doing things contrary to His example. He crossed the man-made barriers and violated their oppressive rules.

---

[28] For an interpretation that sees Paul's gender theology in a positive light, see Lazarus Chilenje, *Paul's Gender Theology and the Ordained Women's Ministry in the CCAP in Zambia*, Mzuzu: Mzuni Press, 2021. For the possibility of translating the injunction as: "I do not want a woman to teach and to make sexual advances to men" (cf. Jezebel in Rev 2:20) see: Rachel NyaGondwe Fiedler, Johannes Hofmeyr and Klaus Fiedler, *African Feminist Hermeneutics. An Evangelical Reflection*, Mzuzu: Mzuni Press, 2016, 115.

Our task is to identify those values which found their way into the Scriptures so that ordinary people may not mistake them for God's final say on matters of gender. Karen Jo Torjesen has argued:

> Consequently, although women's words, achievements, and women's lives were an integral part of the fabric of every Christian community, women's contributions to formative Christianity have been largely suppressed or ignored. Although women such as Mary Magdalene were prominent in an early tradition, their importance was muted through the ongoing process of reworking those traditions to make them conform better to contemporary beliefs about gender.[29]

In this situation then, Biblical scholarship should push texts back to their social-cultural base before turning them into any dogma.

Violet Sampa-Bredt, the first female minister in the United Church of Zambia, suggested that it is important to have a gender-based approach on the role of women in the church that may result in equitable outcomes if the church cultivates the following:

1. An awareness of its members' values and those of the environment in which they work;

2. An understanding of how these values influence their decision-making;

3. Sensitivity to gender issues in general;

4. A deliberate effort to change the structures that oppress women and replace them with those that are sensitive to the needs of women.

Writing from women's perspective, Violet Sampa-Bredt realized that members of the United Church of Zambia in particular, should be taught the gender-sensitive approach wherever they are, in their homes, in the community and in the church. The members should

---

[29] Karen Jo Torjesen, "Reconstruction of Women's Early Christian History in Searching the Scriptures," in Elisabeth Schüssler Fiorenza (ed), _A Feminist Introduction_, vol. 1, New York: Crossroads, 1993, 291.

understand the values of the gender-based approach so that decision-making in homes and churches should be made together by both women and men. Violet Sampa-Bredt cautioned authorities of the church to examine the structures that oppress women and replace them with those that are calling for equity and equality. Exploring these values and perceptions may help to sharpen awareness of factors that are important to the process of arriving at a gender policy that better addresses the needs of women in an ever-changing Church of Zambia.

Awareness of Gender Issues

Neither male nor female is our ultimate basis for identification of gender to be illustrated in this section. Nevertheless, history has made sex an important issue of identification for those who have been oppressed on the basis of sex. It is therefore encouraging to note that women have done many important projects that have been respected by men. An example of such a project is the forming of the Circle of Concerned African Women Theologians by African women in 1989.[30] It is important for those women who feel alienated from men to recognize that our forebearers, who first knew Jesus Christ has risen, were not men. Many women have felt alienated from the church because of men's interpretation of the Bible and because of the cultural biases against women's equal participation in the church.[31]

---

[30] For more information about the Circle of Concerned African Women Theologians, see Mercy Amba Oduyoye, Musimbi Kanyoro, Nyambura Njoroge, Musa Dube, Isabel Apawo Phiri, Rachel NyaGondwe Fiedler and others. *Botswana Daily News*, 3rd July, 2019, www.dailynews.gov.bw/news-details.php?nid=50159. [4.4.2020]. For Circle's history see: Rachel NyaGondwe Fiedler, *The History of the Circle of Concerned African Women Theologians, 1989-2007*, Mzuzu: Mzuni Press, 2016.

[31] For an example of such alienation (and how it was overcome) see: Phoebe Faith Chifungo, "Women in the CCAP Nkhoma Synod. A Practical Theological Study

Many Zambian women, particularly in the United Church of Zambia, have felt frustrated in the church because of men who think that they are the ones who possess the ability and knowledge to run the church effectively. Some women are tired of living in the confines of the oppressive systemic structures. For many years, women have been dehumanized in the name of culture. It is written in the Bible that Jesus said, 'Father, let them be one, just as you and I are one' (Jn 17:21). This in itself was an earnest prayer. Time and again, we have been caught in a culture that dominates and oppresses women. The former South African President, Thabo Mbeki, in his statement on the adoption of the Constitution said that it

> seeks to create a situation in which all our people shall be free from fear, including fear of the oppression of one sex group by another, the fear of the disempowerment of one privileged group by another, the fear of the use of power to deny anybody their fundamental rights.[32]

This statement aims to open doors so that those who were disadvantaged can assume their place in the church as equals with their fellow counterparts. Similarly, Molefi Asante argues:

> I like to call the product of this bias of categorization, which divides people into teachers and those taught, sinners and saved, black and white, inferior and superior, weak and strong, one can add male and female. Out of this bias have developed the catastrophic disharmonies that we experience in our world today.[33]

---

of their Leadership Roles," PhD, Stellenbosch University, 2014. Related publication forthcoming.

[32] Tabo Mbeki, "The Deputy President's Statement, on Behalf of the African National Congress," At the adoption of South Africa's 1996 Constitution Bill, Cape Town, 8 May 1996, on the theme "I am an African," 4.

[33] Molefi Kete Asante, *The Afrocentric Idea*, Philadelphia: Temple University Press, 1986, 184.

Molefi Asante refers to the social construct of women and men as 'the product of this bias of categorization...' In Asante's view, this 'product of categorization' has continued to divide people according to their social status, such as engineer, teacher, short, tall, black, white, holy or sinner. To Asante, these are the dividing lines that give people identities.[34] As Harrow Mudimbe suggests, the women must burst out of the metaphorical elevator and permit themselves to repossess the power of speech and work out of a discourse that would lead African (women) to positively engage "others" in an inter-subjective dialogue.[35] In fact, it is this very close association of the church with oppressive secular colonial institutions that alienated some women. When they are praised for having male characteristics to help in the running of the church, it can be argued that women do not want to work in isolation; certainly, they will always have something to learn from others even while theorizing their own experiences from within. Rubem Alves observes that:

> We need a fresh start. We need to rebuild civilization upon a new foundation. It is not enough that we become fatter. Our world needs a new body; it must be regenerated in the etymological sense. The old body must die if life is to be preserved in a new one. For man's body is much more than his own limited organism; it is the whole civilization we have created in order to make existence possible. Biblical language affirms that for life to be preserved, the body, which has grown old and senile – which has ceased to be an instrument for the expression of life and now functions to repress it – must be dissolved. It has to die. This is what gives life a chance to create a new body for itself. It is then resurrected in another form. Society, organization, civilization, and culture; these are our limbs, the extensions of our biological structure. They have become oppressive and repressive ... This body must be dissolved, if life is to have a chance to create a new one. We have to go through death and resurrection. We need to be again. To let this body die is to dissolve the rules of life as they have been established by

---

[34] Ibid.

[35] Harrow K. Mudimbe, "The Power of the Word," in Stephen Arnold (ed), *African Literature Studies: The Present State*, Washington DC: Three Continents Press/African Literature Association, 1985, 91-100.

past generations. The dead must not rule the world of the living and only beyond the dissolution of the old, now hopelessly enmeshed in its internal contradictions, can a new synthesis be created.[36]

Rubem Alves' suggestion is that we need to revisit our history and work out a shared and common identity, where all of us can make this world a better place to live in, in the church and in society.

Let me point, in general terms, to some of the areas in which women have been marginalized. As discussed earlier, the concept of gender introduces us to the difference in the roles of men and women in relation to work; to sharing the world's resources and benefits; to human rights; and to culture and religion. This entails that men and women have roles in the domain of production and public life from the community, the church, through to government level. With reference to the world's resources and benefits, gender inequality still holds true, as stated in a paper presented at the Beijing Conference in 1995. The Development Alternatives with Women for a New Era (DAWN) statistics commented on women becoming owners of properties and leaders. Thus, although women are engaged in many productive activities, they still work in an environment that militates against them in terms of the following factors:

5. The non-involvement of women in mainstream production;

6. The lack of access for women to own property and receive financial loans;

7. The down-grading of women as potential candidates for high religious offices in the church;

8. The lack of church-will to involve women in the development process in general.

The above is in line with what Jennings suggests, that

---

[36] Rubem Alves, *Tomorrow's Child: Imagination, Creativity, and the Rebirth of Culture*, London: SCM Press, 1972, 64.

the majority of development assistance still fails to reach women and there is a call for a more holistic gender approach rather than a Women in Development (WID) approach. To achieve this, projects must focus their analysis on those whom unequal power relations suppress mostly.[37]

These unequal power relations suppress mostly women because they are always at the receiving end and not included in the decision-making agendas as stated in the beginning of this chapter.

This chapter wishes to address this inequality, of men having the best and women being given the worst. This kind of inequality has been inherited from the gender-insensitive political structures of wider society, which have found their way into the church of God. The church today is caught up in a pot of mixed loyalties. Most African mainline churches and even the African Initiated/Independent Churches (AICS) are to some extent linked both in doctrine and structure, to what may be called their Eurocentric counterparts in the west. Charles Villa-Vicencio argues that "the liberal consensus is not thin at all but thick with white, male, Eurocentric particularisms deceptively sold in the name of value – free common sense and universal realism."[38] There have been some changes in perception of gender issues in some of these Eurocentric churches. Some AICs also have been including women in the decision-making and some mainline churches such as the Presbyterians and the United Church of Zambia have been ordaining women and including them in the decision-making agendas.

However, a certain fear of the unknown seems to characterize the African church's outlook on gender-related matters. It seems as if

---

[37] M. Jennings, "Communities in Development: The Theory and Practice of Gender," in Mary van Lieshout (ed), _A Woman's World beyond the Headlines_, Dublin: Attic Press, 1996, 107-117.

[38] Charles Villa-Vicencio, "Difference and Belonging," in J. Witte and van der Vyer (eds), _Religious Human Rights in Global Perspectives_, The Hague/Boston/London: Martinus Nijhoff, 1994, 517-553.

culture has its roots in the life and work of the church. Because of culture, the church is afraid to come out in the open to address the issues pertaining to women head on. Charles Villa-Vicencio further writes:

[c]ulture is being … to an extent that the person is alive, responding to new challenges, ready to engage the other in dialogue, culture is dynamic. Culture is enroute because people are enroute."

These are the equity and equality approaches. The following section will discuss gender equity and equality with a view to using the feminist ecclesiological theoretical framework lens.[39]

Towards Gender Equity: Using the Feminist Ecclesiological Theoretical Framework

Elizabeth Schüssler Fiorenza contends that "one must also consider that women, even more than men, have internalized cultural-religious feminine values and they consequently tend to reproduce, uncritically, the patriarchal 'politics of submission and otherness' in their speaking and writing."[40] With this view in mind, coupled with the feminist ecclesiological theoretical framework that undergirds this chapter, women should start identifying themselves as closely with God as men do, because women, too, are created in the image of God. Even though some feminists implicitly reject this understanding, as for them God is a 'male figure', it is the duty of the women to engage in biblical teachings to liberate their fellow women in the church and in the community. Women should insist on a wider way of thinking that has its roots in the Bible and traditions of the church, but it has only really developed to full maturity in recent

---

[39]   Ibid.

[40]   Elisabeth Schüssler-Fiorenza, _Discipleship of Equals_, New York: Crossroad, 1993, 142.

years: the view that God is neither female nor male but transcends these human divisions, so that all humanity can fully identify with God.

Therefore, justice and partnership in its entirety must be problematized in light of our cultural-religious structure, especially in the Bible as part of it. This is the goal of the feminist ecclesiological theoretical framework that can equip scholars in the field of gender and religion with appropriate tools to engage the existing church traditions and structures. This will uproot the selfish attitude that has been ingrained in many men that they are better than women. A culture of inclusiveness should now start taking root in the church to make it a place where justice is done, and healthy relationships are formed in a "framework of interconnectedness and participation."

We can harness cultural existence for the benefit of women. Therefore, the church can also start the process of inclusiveness. The church can start recognizing the gifts of women and men and engage them in its affairs allowing women's voices to be heard. The church must avail itself of the many developments yet unrecognized, and the untapped activities in which women are engaged, such as economic production (for example, farming). This will be in line with Villa-Vicencio's aforementioned idea. Additionally, the value of women's work is shown when even the Apostle Paul speaks of Phoebe, the deaconess:[41]

> I commend to you our sister Phoebe, a Deaconess of the church at Cenchrea, that you may receive her in the Lord as befits the saints and help her in whatever she may require from you, for she has been a helper of many and of myself as well (Romans 16:1-2).

---

[41] The translation "deaconess" can be misunderstood. The Greek word is of male gender (*diakonos*), so the meaning is not that she holds a specific female office ("Order of Deaconesses"), but is a Deacon of the church who is (incidentally) female.

In the same vein, the Apostle Paul was moved to speak of sisters Euodia and Syntyche:

> And I ask you also, true yokefellow, help these women, for they have laboured side by side with me in the gospel together with Clement and the rest of my fellow workers, whose names are in the book of life. (Philippians 4:1-3)

It is certainly interesting to note that Paul uses the expression 'side by side with me' in his recommendation of Euodia and Syntyche. This expression is an elevation of women in the Lord and, by implication, in the Lord's Church. This brings us to explore some elements of equality.

Elements of Equality

Drawing on Villa-Vicencio's point of "culture is being," the spiritual culture contains elements of equality, so we can as well use them in our present context. As long as we are still living, we do respond to new challenges in our daily dialogue. A woman must be treated as working 'side by side with' and not 'behind' a man.[42] This is not a statement of feminist theology; it is a humble acceptance of the view of a God who cuts across sexual, racial, age and other barriers in the execution of His eternal plan of salvation, a plan which culminated in the death of our Lord at Calvary. It is a realization of the cutting edge of the Cross—in all cultural settings. It is a submission to the Lordship of a Christ who came, not to enslave anyone to tradition, but to liberate everyone to a life of complete human dignity and respect. Musimbi Kanyoro writes:

---

[42]   Charles Villa-Vicencio, "Difference and Belonging," 1994, 517-553.

> African women theologians have come to realize that as long as men and
> foreign researchers remain the authorities on culture, rituals and religion,
> African women will continue to be spoken of as if they were dead.[43]

As long as we stand up and realize who we are, created in the Image
of God, we should not allow our men to speak on our behalf as if we
had no voice. Instead, we must partner with the men and come to
agree about what must be on the agenda. Mercy Amba Oduyoye has
observed that:

> [t]he person who sleeps by the fire knows best how intensely it burns; (so
> runs an Asante's proverb). The irruption of women in the church and
> society is an integral part of the voice of the earth's voiceless majority that
> is beginning to penetrate the atmosphere and disturb the peace of the
> principalities and powers that hold the structure of our so-called one world
> in their hands.[44]

This brings me to discuss the wholistic understanding of the words
equality and equity from a theological and gender perspective.

The Wholistic Understanding of "Equity" from a Theological and Gender Perspective: Galatians 3:28

"There is neither Jew nor Greek, slave nor free, male nor female, for
you are all one in Christ Jesus." Paul identifies three major divisions
in society, and then says, "you are all one in Christ Jesus." Paul is
referring here to the community of the baptized, the group that
represents the new people of God on earth. Within the group, there
is no one who is different from anyone else. Our common
relationship with Christ is more important than anything that divides

---

[43] Musimbi Kanyoro, "Introduction," in Musimbi Kanyoro and Mercy Amba
Oduyoye (eds), *The Will to Arise: Women, Traditional and the Church in Africa*, Maryknoll: Orbis, 1995, 1-8.

[44] Mercy Amba Oduyoye, "Reflections from a Third World Women's Perspective
Women's Experience and Liberation Theologies," in Virginia Fabella & Sergio
Torres, *Irruption of the Third World: Challenge to Theology*, Maryknoll: Orbis, 1983, 244-
250.

us at a human level. This is important because there are some passages attributed to St Paul which are heavily used by those who think that God has decreed an inferior role for women in the church.

The above passage from Galatians is universally accepted as coming from St Paul himself. It reflects a theological position on the relationship that men and women have in God's kingdom. The text must be interpreted according to its context, and the context here refers to the teaching that, through faith, we are heirs of the promise, and that without distinction of gender. Thus, we can see that St Paul, too, thinks that in the kingdom, men and women stand on an equal footing and should not be divided from each other by their differences of gender.

Gender justice is an important aspect of wider change, which this chapter envisages as a movement towards systemic justice. There are all sorts of unfair imbalances in relationships, caused by various differences in humanity: wealth, education, class, race, ethnicity, age and so on. But of the most important ones, perhaps the most crucial is the difference between women and men. It is important, because it underlies or adds to other imbalances in relationships. God's royal rule is expressed through the creation and strengthening of transformative relationships.[45]

This means that God's Kingdom demands an end to the oppressive relations that characterize patriarchy. Gender justice is to be understood as the alteration of the very nature of relationships between men and women so that they are no longer in a power struggle but have a relationship where neither partner is subordinate to the other. This is just part of the transformation of all human relations which needs to happen as we move towards the Kingdom

---

[45] United Church of Canada, "Gender Justice and Partnership Guidelines," February, 1998, www.ucc.home.page [20.3.2020].

of God, so that no one relational structure gives one person dominance or privilege over another, but practices equality in their relationships with each other.

Rosemary Radford-Ruether writes that "baptism signifies our disaffiliation from patriarchy and all its claims to social necessity and divine legitimacy, and our commitment to a new order."[46] The church of Jesus should be understood in the light of a theology, which recognizes both the objective and the subjective side of baptism. The objective side is God's liberating love, which is given to both men and women as an unmerited gift from beyond our historical nature and which transforms the self into a new being in communion with God. The subjective side is the process of personally examining baptism by making this journey of metanoia and transformation meaningful in one's own life.[47] The church must work towards the disaffiliation of patriarchy, which holds the power of corruption of our humanity, and turns males into instruments of domination and shapes women into tools of submission.

Conclusion

Firstly, let me say a few things concerning how members of the Church ought to approach gender partnership. I suggest that we need to establish right from the start that we all have a responsibility to ensure that church politics, programmes and legislation are equitable for both women and men. To fully discharge these responsibilities, those involved in policy development and analysis should have an understanding of gender issues.

---

[46] Rosemary Radford Ruether, *Women-Church. Theology and Practice of Feminist Liturgical Communities*, Eugene: Wipf & Stock, 1985, 125.

[47] Rosemary Radford Ruether, *Women-Church. Theology and Practice of Feminist Liturgical Communities*, 125.

Secondly, I wish to suggest that gender-policy discussions in the church be to a large extent about values. The concept of gender was first used in the 1970s by Ann Oakley and other feminist theorists, and describes those characteristics of men and women that are socially determined, in contrast to those that are biologically defined. Thus, gender roles can, and often do, change over time, according to changing social and cultural factors. Therefore, anyone participating in such policy discussions must necessarily contend with their own values, shaped by their ways of working, knowledge base, information sources, contacts, culture and life experiences, that will influence the way they perceive the gender-policy issue and the approach they take. The values of the system in which they will work also influence their gender policy-making, and we must understand, therefore, that gender-sensitive policy may sometimes conflict with the 'public dominant' values around which our church is organized.[48]

---

[48] James C. Scott, *Domination and the Arts of Resistance: Hidden Transcripts*, New Haven: Yale University Press, 1990.

Chapter Seven

Remembering the Silent Liberationist Political Hero! Mama Betty Kaunda, the Mother of the Nation

Judith Lubasi Ziwa

Introduction

The 1960s brought great changes to Africa. A strong spirit of nationalism swept through Africa as more and more African countries gained their independence. Women joined the ranks of nationalists in ever-growing numbers. Fighting side by side with men, they played an invaluable role in the armed revolutionary struggle. Women realized that their contribution was crucial in the struggle in order to get rid of the tyrannical colonialism in Africa. This contribution of women in the liberation struggle has not been as well researched and recorded as that of men. Regardless of this scholarly gender inequality, uncoordinated electronic media literature on Zambia's political history indicates notable social and political reformation activities spearheaded by women such as Mama Julia Chikamoneka, Princess Nakatindi Nganga Yeta and Mama Chibesa Kankasa, who contributed to the development of the nation. In this chapter, the focus is on Beatrice Kaweche Banda, popularly known as Mama Betty Kaunda. The chapter will focus on her contribution towards Zambia's independence both as a politician and as a church woman. The chapter argues that even though women contributed significantly to the fight for the freedom of African nations, the political public space says little or nothing about the contribution of women freedom fighters, demonstrating the gendered nature of the political public space. Data used in this chapter was collected through interviews with one of Betty's sons and one of her granddaughters. This provided validity to the data collected. I also partly relied on the review of different literature and of resources posted on the internet.

To sufficiently understand Betty's contribution towards Zambian political and social development, the following part gives her brief life history as given by the participants during interviews.

Background of Mama Betty Kaunda

According to Kaweche Kaunda,[1] Betty was born on 17 November 1928 in the Eastern Province of Zambia in Jumbe Chiefdom, Mambwe District. Soon after she was born her parents moved to Mpika where she grew up.

Betty was the second born daughter to John Kaweche Banda and Milika Sakala. Her birth name was _Mutinkhe_, which literary means "you will get annoyed."[2] Later, she was named Beatrice. During her childhood she was briefly called 'Biti', the local Kunda name for Beatrice. This resulted into her being called Betty, which famously became her name. Apparently, this is the reason the name "Betty" did not appear in her family lineage, instead the name "Beatrice" existed. Mama Betty had her early education in Mpika at Mbereshi Girls' School and she later underwent a Women's Training Programme at Mindolo Ecumenical Foundation and worked as a teacher in Mufulira.[3] Betty married Kenneth Kaunda in 1946, who was involved in the freedom struggle at the time, and later went on to become the first President of independent Zambia in 1964. As the

---

[1] Kaweche Kaunda is the sixth born son of Mama Betty Kaunda. The family regards him as the family historian. He was interviewed on 9.9.2017.

[2] The name, _Mutinkhe_, was chosen due to circumstances that surrounded the parents before her birth.

[3] Edith Dahlschen, _Women in Zambia_, Lusaka: Kenneth Kaunda Foundation, 1970.

First Lady of Zambia, Betty Kaunda was largely valued and honoured by all male and female Zambians; she was considered the national mother of Zambia, hence she is commonly referred to as "Mama Betty Kaunda." After suffering from diabetes for many years, Mama Betty Kaunda died in September 2012 at the age of 83. The informants further narrated the kind of life Mama Betty lived and how it was ingrained in their minds as presented below.

The Legacy behind Betty Kaunda's Life

In an interview conducted with the son of Mama Betty, Kaweche described Betty as the backbone to Kenneth Kaunda who was in the forefront of the freedom fighters. By using the phrase "behind every successful man there is a woman", Kaweche described Betty as the secret behind President Kaunda's courage. She was a source of support and advice to her husband, the freedom fighter, as she would give him timely advice and encouragement. In other words, Kaweche's comment suggests that without Betty's encouragement and support, Kenneth Kaunda's success would have been almost impossible. Kenneth Kaunda touched on this point in his book *Letter to my Children* when he acknowledged that Betty was the strength behind him all through their relationship as she took care of the children in his absence.[4]

Kaweche further indicated that he remembered Betty as a generous woman who had the zeal to uplift the living standards of the vulnerable people. "She, at different times, donated to the poor, though in most cases, she did not invite print and electronic media to cover such gestures," Kaweche lamented. According to him, this was one example of the humble personality she possessed. She liked working from behind the scenes.

---

[4] Kenneth Kaunda, *Letter to my Children*, Lusaka: Longman, 1973, 12-15.

It was also learnt, during the interview with Kaweche, that Mama Betty Kaunda loved and embraced Zambian traditional culture. Kaweche explained this point by referring to how his mother managed to run the affairs of the State House family and of those of her own family in a traditional manner. This was also evidenced by the traditional names she gave her children which were Panji Tushuke, Wazamazuma, Tilyenji Chandakunda, Masuzyo Malume Ngwembe, Kaweche, Musata, Cheswa and Kambarage (the twins) and Chola.

In Kaweche's view, Betty Kaunda's traditional lifestyle led many Zambians to respect and trust her. It also compelled women from various parts of the country to visit her at State House for advice and counsel on various issues. This traditional form of education offered by Mama Betty did not only help to strengthen marriage relationships and foster respect for the dignity of all individuals but also helped needy couples with shelter and food. Where there is respect, virtues such as honesty, hard work, trust and forgiveness are flourishing. "Through providing counselling to women, Mama Betty contributed to the development of the nation," Kaweche emphasized.

Her granddaughter Musata[5] gave a similar account of Betty as she acknowledged her as a real African woman whom she had a good relationship with and who was for her a reliable source of advice as she narrates:

> Education was key for my grandmother. Most grandparents focused on marriage, but for her, school was more important than anything else. She used to say: *kumulu ku kalepa, pashi pa kakosa*, heaven will be very far and the earth will be hard to live on. This showed how my grandmother valued

---

[5] Musata Kaunda started staying with her when she was 5 years old upon losing her father to death. She was, perhaps, the closest granddaughter to Betty. It was therefore appropriate that I took time to gather information from her. At the time of the interview, 9.9.2017, Musata owned a law firm in Lusaka.

education. Without education, you cannot do much on earth, and try to go up, it will be too far.

My grandmother taught me not to love money but responsibility and hard work. She used to say "money is like cassava; it melts when you need it." So, I was told that my grandfather, Dr. Kenneth Kaunda, would not leave me money but a good name, as the Bible says: a good name is better than fine perfume (Ecclesiastes 7:1). My grandmother was a holder of information and offered advice to the needy and those who approached her. She was approachable and created an enabling environment to the visitors. Our home was their home too.

At the time Musata grew up with her grandmother, it did not make sense what life would be like for her. However, when she grew up, the relationship had a lot of meaning. She became a capable, typical African wife because her grandmother helped her to understand what it meant to be an African. "I care for my daughter and husband and I know how to cook. I also like to hold parties for my family members and friends," she concluded.

Going by the above presentation of the findings, it can be said that, as a woman who had to fulfil the role of first lady and spouse, Mama Betty Kaunda combined her traditional Victorian housewife role with that of the former. Equally important to mention, being married to Kaunda did not only offer Betty the privilege to be a companion and friend of one of Africa's best known freedom fighters, but also a platform to showcase her political and social development schemes she had for Zambia as later presented in this chapter. At this point, however, it is worth looking at the broader picture on how women unexpectedly responded to prevailing political and social developments in Zambia and across Africa from the early 19th century.

Women's Participation in Political, Economic and Social Development in the 19th Century

In pre-independence African societies, women faced both traditional and colonial systems that prioritized male dominance, confining women to customary domestic activities. Colonial authorities, traditional chiefs and religious leaders created an atmosphere in which women's participation in political, social and economic development was undermined.[6] It is not clear whether the authorities consciously put in place such policies with a view to sideline women from reaching social, political and economic emancipation. What is clear, however, is that they all played a role.[7] The colonial authorities indirectly supported the system as they sought to strengthen their relationship with chiefs as partners in government by setting native tribunals and treasuries on a firm foundation, so that they could assume some of the responsibilities of the local government. In their agenda to recreate African families and to encourage African participation in politics as a civilizing influence, missionaries instilled the concept of individualism and fathers secluded women in the domestic domain under the Christian discourse of respectability.[8]

Furthermore, Parpart asserted that in the process of implementing new systems, African chiefs and male elders argued alongside missionaries and colonial officials that African women did not need to go to urban areas in search of an improved life. As such, strict surveillance programmes were set by village chiefs and elders to

---

[6] Emmanuel Akyeampong and Hippolite Fofack, *The Contribution of African Women to Economic Growth and Development: Historical Perspectives and Policy Implications Part I: The Pre-colonial and Colonial Periods*, Policy Research Working Papers, April 2012, doi: 10.1596/1813-9450-6051.

[7] Ibid.

[8] Ibid.

prevent women from getting to town, especially if they were not married.[9] Those who sneaked into town were labelled prostitutes and were punished by colonial officials. And married women in town were confined to domestic and reproductive duties only.[10] Such was considered the model of a Christian woman. In simple yet clear terms, colonial official's and missionaries' patriarchal assumptions enabled African chiefs and male elders to orchestrate a social coup that systematically subordinated women and became routinized in colonial and missionary education.

African feminist scholars have referred to the aforementioned collaboration as the "patriarchal alliance."[11] It was an alliance that institutionalized male dominance and superiority over females, an alliance that brought about negative perceptions towards women who had a desire to develop themselves and society.

Despite this phenomenon, there is the recognition that women out of their "stubbornness" played a significant role in the liberation movements and the economic and social life of their communities, though often presented as that of men.[12] In Uganda, for instance, it was women farmers who first started cotton cultivation. Yet, in 1923, the British administrator in charge of agriculture declared that cotton

---

[9] Jane L. Parpart, "Where is Your Mother? Gender, Urban Marriage and Colonial Discourses on the Zambian Copperbelt, 1924-1945," *International Journal of Historical Studies*, 27(2), 1994, 241-271.

[10] Ibid.

[11] Lilian Cheelo Siwila, "Reconstructing the Distorted Image of Women as Reproductive Labour on the Copperbelt Mines in Zambia (1920-1954)," *Journal for the Study of Religion*, 30(2), 2017, 75–89, http://dx.doi.org/ 10.17159/2413-3027 /2017/v30n2a3/.[11.4.2020].

[12] Donald B. Freeman, "Survival Strategy or Business Training Ground? The Significance of Urban Agriculture of the Advancement of Women in African Cities," *African Studies Review*, 36/3, 1993.

growing could not be left to women and old people, hence men took over even though female labour remained crucial.[13]

Similarly, in West Africa women farmed cotton and indigo, spun, wove and dyed cotton textiles for centuries and their commitment resulted in the commercialization of the textile manufacturing industry, male dominated.[14] While women in textile manufacturing had a long history in the area that became the Sokoto Caliphate, the imposition of an Islamic caliphate introduced new restrictions on the female dominated industry, as women were barred from training as tailors and garment embroiders to make the most luxurious and profitable men's robes.[15]

Polly Hill has documented how Krobo and Akuapim farmers of the Gold Coast migrated in search of farm land for cocoa, propelling the economic revolution that made the Gold Coast the world's leading producer of cocoa in 1911.[16] Women's contribution to this feat was fundamental, but the cash went into the pockets of men.[17] Such scenarios prompted Asante women of modern day Ghana to create their own cocoa farms instead of working for their husbands, often precipitating a crisis in marriage.[18] Others went to court to challenge

---

[13] Ibid.

[14] Colleen Kriger, _Cloth in West African History_, Lanham: AltaMira Press, 2006.

[15] Ibid, 2006.

[16] Polly Hill, _The Migrant Cocoa Farmers of Southern Ghana_, Cambridge: Cambridge University Press, 1963.

[17] Christine Okali, _Cocoa and Kinship in Ghana: The Matrilineal Akan of Ghana_, London: Kegan Paul, 1983; Gwendolyn Mikell, _Cocoa and Chaos in Ghana_, New York: Paragon, 1989; Gareth Austin, _Labour, Land and Capital in Ghana: From Slavery to Free Labour in Asante, 1807-1956_, Rochester: University of Rochester Press, 2005.

[18] Jean Allman, "Rounding up Spinsters: Gender Chaos and Unmarried Women in Colonial Asante," _Journal of African History_, 1996, 37(2), 195-214.

the rules of matrilineal inheritance that excluded them from the benefits of their labour.

In Zambia, though the patriarchal alliance did not permit women to go to town, when they did move there first, their presence boosted industrial production in the mining industry to an extent that administrators deemed it necessary to allow women into the mining towns. Companies that were preoccupied with their labour needs and the financial implications of a world depression adopted a laissez-faire approach to married women in the labour force.[19] While initially only single women were employed in the mine compounds, the mine officials soon discovered that married workers were more reliable and productive than single workers. As a result, the companies gradually increased the percentage of married workers on the mines.[20]

Women boosted production in the mines. Their inputs enabled the Copperbelt mine companies to compete with others on the African continent. However, scholars like Lilian Siwila and others have bemoaned the lack of acknowledgement of women's contribution towards the labour economy in Zambia. Women were not recognized and honoured as part of the developing industrial production complex on the Copperbelt.[21] Sadly, peripherization of women in the continues even modern-day global market economy.[22]

---

[19] Jane L. Parpart, "'Where Is Your Mother?': Gender, Urban Marriage, and Colonial Discourse on the Zambian Copperbelt, 1924-1945." The International Journal of African Historical Studies 27, no. 2 (1994): 241–71. https://doi.org/10.2307/221025.

[20] Ibid, 248.

[21] Lilian Cheelo Siwila, "Feminist Critique of the Education Model of Mabel Shaw Girls' Boarding Mission School in Zambia 1915-1940 and its Effect on the Education of Girls," *Scriptura 116*, 2017, 1-12, http://scriptura.journals. ac.za [11.4.2020].

[22] Ibid.

Politically, women's contribution towards the nationalist movements in Africa during the colonial era cannot be emphasized enough. Though not all women can be brought into the limelight in terms of their contribution, there is wide acknowledgement that women's involvement in the struggle against the colonial authorities can be traced back to the early 19th century.

In the pantheon of Zimbabwe's struggle icons, one woman stands out: Mbuya Nehanda, a powerful spiritual leader of the Shona people and the spirit of the original Nehanda, who is said to have been a princess of the Mutapa Empire. Nehanda Charwe Nyakasikana stirred her people into rebellion against the increasing number of British settlers in their territory.[23] So Mbuya Nehanda contributed strongly to the first Chimurenga, the first liberation struggle in Zimbabwe. Mbuya Nehanda has acquired near mythical status and has been respected and admired for generations. Unfortunately, the same respect and recognition has not been extended to the majority of women who joined the fight for independence.[24]

Like elsewhere in Africa, Zambian women contributed significantly towards the struggle for freedom. One of the most dynamic personalities was Mama Betty Kaunda, who was one of the privileged few young women to complete a teacher's training course, which was a rare achievement at that time.

In her endeavour to contribute to the socio-political development of Zambia, Mama Kaunda did not work alone. One of her friends was Mrs. Julia Mulenga, popularly known as 'Mama Chikamoneka' or

---

[23] Mark Mathabane, *African Women, Three Generations*, London: Penguin Group, 1994.

[24] Mako Muzenda, "The Invisible Trauma of Women in Zimbabwe's Liberation Struggle," 2019, https://thisisafrica.me/politics-and-society/the-invisible-trauma-of-women-in-zimbabwes-liberation-struggle [11.4.2020].

'Mama UNIP'. Mama Chikamoneka was a rare example of a brave, proud and fearless person. She could stand and argue with a white man or woman, when it was taboo for a black person (especially a woman) to do so.[25] This was so because many African societies promoted patriarchy: the "rule of fathers," a political system in which women have inferior social and political rights.[26] Mama Chikamoneka was extremely competent at recruiting female members and sensitizing them about the discrimination and ill treatment by Europeans. While running her small food-shop, she would organize women and map out protest marches. In this way, women showed their total support for the male freedom fighters.[27]

Other methods adopted by Zambian women in the struggle for independence were blocking roads using logs for stopping police and soldiers from entering and disrupting their public meetings, demonstrating while half naked before the colonial authorities, civil disobedience and fighting against discrimination. When the men burnt their *chitupas* (identity cards), the women also burnt their *imichato* (marriage certificates) to show their dislike and displeasure towards the colonial masters.[28]

---

[25] Edith Dahlschen, *Women in Zambia*. Lusaka: Kenneth Kaunda Foundation, 1970.

[26] Jonathan Kangwa, *Gender, Christianity and African Culture*, Texas: Saint Paul Press, 2017.

[27] Edith Dahlschen, *Women in Zambia*. Lusaka: Kenneth Kaunda Foundation, 1970.

[28] K. Krishna and F.E. Mulenga, "Contribution of Zambian Women and Indian Women to the Struggle for Freedom: A Legend of Courage and Compassion," Paper presented at the *African Renewal, African Renaissance': New Perspectives on Africa's Past and Africa's Present, The African Studies Association of Australia and the Pacific (AFSAAP) Annual Conference*, 26-28 November 2004, University of Western Australia.

This moment marked a paradigm shift on how society looked at who should participate in national, political and social reformation. For example, in 1961 Mama Kankasa was one of the first women to become a regional secretary. In the same line, the zeal by various other women to take part in the political struggle must have provided motivation for Betty to work hard towards Zambia's political liberation. The remaining part of this chapter focuses on specific contributions Mama Betty Kaunda made towards Zambian political and social development.

Betty's Contribution towards the Independence of Zambia from Colonial Rule

Betty Kaunda's contribution towards Zambia's independence began in 1946 when she met and married Kenneth Kaunda who was also a teacher. As a ring leader of nationalists, Kaunda never stayed home for long periods of time. He often traversed the country mobilizing the masses and sometimes he was incarcerated by the colonial government. But what is more important to note is how Betty took responsibility of looking after herself and their children. She did what was within her means to cater for the needs of the children. According to her husband, at one point Betty turned to charcoal burning to ensure that the family had food on the table and that the children were able to attend school.[29] With their agenda to frustrate Kaunda and turn Betty's attention away from supporting her husband, colonial masters tried to bribe her and other freedom fighters' wives with food and money; however; she never succumbed to their enticement. In her own words Betty laments:

> We accepted their food and money but we never submitted to their corrupt motives. We were threatened but we stood firm. The colonial masters

---

[29] Kenneth Kaunda, *Letter to my Children*, 1973.

threatened to send us back to our villages after our husbands were arrested, but we refused.[30]

This shows the spirit of courage, determination and truthfulness Betty demonstrated towards Zambia's political development. This is true in the sense that she had other options to survive whilst Kaunda was committed to his political agenda, which was at the expense of providing for the family. For example, she could have gone to the village and sought comfort from her maternal brothers as it was a common trend during those days among the matrilineal people.[31] Instead, she viewed matters outside the box and sacrificed her comfort for the good of the country. As a youthful educated woman, Betty refused to submit to intimidation and stoically supported the freedom movement while she proved to be a dependable ally of all the nationalists who were fighting alongside her husband to end white minority rule. She joined others with one objective: to usher in a new era of multi-racial politics based on universal suffrage or, as the nationalists put it, "one man, one vote."[32] Mama Chikamoneka and Mama Betty Kaunda mobilized nearly three quarters of the women in the country to take part in the cutting down of trees to barricade roads with.[33] They also prepared meals for freedom fighters to enable them to work hard. Obviously, Mama Betty Kaunda was at the forefront encouraging women to hold politically oriented meetings,

---

[30] "Betty Kaunda: Mother of Zambia, Heroine of the Struggle," *The Herald*, 2020, 2, www.herald.co.zw/betty-kaunda-mother-of-zambia-heroine-of-the-struggle [9.4.2020].

[31] Jane L. Parpart, "Where is Your Mother?" 1994, 248.

[32] Wim van Binsbergen, "Chiefs and the State in Independent Zambia: Exploring the Zambian National Press," *Journal of Legal Pluralism and Unofficial Law*, 10, 1987, https://openaccess.leidenuniv.nl/search [11.4.2020].

[33] Ilsa Schuster, "Zambian Women in Politics, Constraints and Opportunities in Political Participation: The Case of Zambian Women," vol. xxi, no. 2, 2000.

organizing demonstrations and composing tunes for freedom songs and slogans.

Mama Betty was not only an organizer but was also at the forefront of different demonstrations. In March 1960, when Ian Macleod (Secretary of State for the Colonies) visited Zambia, Betty Kaunda and Mama Chikamoneka along with other women demanded immediate independence and self-rule.[34] Mama Betty Kaunda's high spirit and optimism were a great encouragement to everyone during the pre-independence days. The heroism of Mama Betty Kaunda is legendary in the history of Zambia.[35] Many Senior Zambian citizens describe Betty as a woman who demonstrated not only resilience and courage, but also humility, playing the role of husband, wife and mother during the struggle.[36]

As if this was not enough, Betty's lifestyle proved in many ways that she was a "true mother" to many freedom fighters, whom she sheltered and supported during the era of "Cha Cha Cha", the period of heightened civil disobedience in the early 1960s as the independence struggle intensified. It is also worth stating that countless visitors felt welcome at Kaunda's home because of his wife who welcomed them, a woman who shared their political aspirations and their vision of a free and independent country.

In 1964 Zambia got its independence, and Betty, as the wife to Kenneth Kaunda, officially became the First Lady. Although the position of First Lady carries no official duties, every society

---

[34] M. Walubita, in Mbuyu Nalumango and Monde Sifuniso (eds), _Women Power in Politics_, Lusaka: Zambia Women Writers Association, 1988, 38-53.

[35] Ibid.

[36] "Betty Kaunda: Mother of Zambia, Heroine of the Struggle," _The Herald_, 2020, www.herald.co.zw/betty-kaunda-mother-of-zambia-heroine-of-the-strug   gle [9.4.2020].

institutionalizes it which comes with social norms and public expectations of it.[37] She is expected to be the presidential escort, the leader of social protocol and noblesse oblige, a policy maker and a political advisor.[38] Mama Betty Kaunda could not escape these expectations beyond her role as spouse and mother, and she did all she could for the best interests of the country.

Betty's Contribution towards Zambian's Social Development after Independence

As a First Lady, mother, and a Christian, Betty always worked towards ensuring Zambia's social development even after independence. It is important to mention that Betty performed her services to the nation with a high sense of humility whilst maintaining loyalty towards her husband. In his book, "The Long Sunset: My Reflections," Vernon Mwaanga, a veteran diplomat and politician, describes Mama Betty Kaunda as a "true mother of the nation who did not interfere in state affairs."[39] When Vernon Mwaanga speaks of Betty not interfering in the State affairs, it is not as though she was silent in State House. Her biographer admits that Betty rarely issued public statements, but that, whenever she did; there was a lot of substance to them.[40] She was concerned about Zambian society. For example, the time her husband threatened to quit the presidency because of excessive beer drinking in the country by the youth, she was equally concerned as she echoed:

> What is even more worrying is that our politicians encourage the young people to drink beer, especially during campaigns. This is all wrong, there

---

[37] Lisa M. Burns, *First Ladies as Political Women: Press Framing of Presidential Wives 1900-2001*, Maryland: University of Maryland, 2004.

[38] Betty H. Winfield, "The First Lady's Relations with the Mass Media," In Laura Bush (ed), *The Report to the First Lady*, New York: Nova History Publications, 2001.

[39] Vernon Mwaanga, *The Long Sunset: My Reflections*, Lusaka: Fleetfoot, 2008.

[40] Ibid.

has to be dignity even in politics. What kind of a country are we trying to build for ourselves if there is so much beer-drinking among the youths?[41]

Following her sentiments above, it is clear that she was not against the ideology of multi-partyism that had emerged around that period in the country. Betty was, however, concerned with the way mushrooming politicians opted to gain popularity. For her, giving beer to the youth was a threat to social development as well as a decaying agent for national values and norms. In this vein, she courageously took a step further in urging politicians to genuinely assist youths to overcome some of the challenges they faced such as lack of employment and access to education instead of enticing them with beer to win popularity. She further proposed that the illicit strong brew commonly known as _kachasu_ should be discouraged because it was destroying people's lives.[42]

As confirmed by Kaweche, Mama Betty cherished Zambian traditional life of her days which distinctively set a margin between men's and women's roles in society. However, at the same time, she endeavoured to wrestle with negative traditional perceptions which hindered women from taking part in national development. As a lady in the spotlight, she lived by the principle and went ahead to teach others how to be good wives and custodians of homes during conferences she chaired in different parts of the country. Perhaps she was replicating lessons she underwent during her school days at the mission institution, as it has been widely argued by scholars like Lilian Siwila that its syllabus centred on preparing girls for marriage.[43] What

---

[41] "Betty Kaunda: Mother of Zambia, Heroine of the Struggle," _The Herald_, 2020.

[42] Betty Kaunda and Stephen A. Mpashi, _Betty Kaunda: Wife of the President of the Republic of Zambia_, Lusaka: Longman, 1969.

[43] Lilian Cheelo Siwila, "Reconstructing the Distorted Image of Women as Reproductive Labour on the Copperbelt Mines in Zambia (1920-1954)," _Journal for_

was important is that she tried to strike a balance, as can be seen in Betty's 1970 conference held in the Copperbelt province of Zambia themed "Women's Rights."[44] Going by its theme most men raised their eyebrows, but she confidently assured Zambians that there should be no overthrow of male authority. On the contrary, she defined the new role of women as "custodians of happiness and security in the home, the watchdogs of morality in our society."[45]

Besides her effort to put society in a position where modern and traditional life balanced, Betty also promoted Christian values. As a United Church of Zambia member, she demonstrated it practically in her dealings with others. She showed unfailing love, compassion, and fellow feeling towards Zambian citizens regardless of the region they belonged to. One such gesture is her response towards fellow women whose husbands died in the 1967 mine accident. Mama Betty was at the forefront helping to raise funds for the widows as well as to console them.

No doubt the public expects the first lady to fulfil a multitude of roles flawlessly. There is criticism at any departure from perceived standards, with constantly changing criteria for success of a first lady as the public's view of women evolves and develops.[46] This description is prevalent in Zambian society where the first lady is seen as responsible for charity, women's empowerment and gender support, and she has the symbolic role of fostering national values. As the First Lady, Betty Kaunda was part of many diplomatic visits

---

the *Study of Religion* 30, 2, 2017 75–89, http://dx.doi.org/10.17159/ 2413-3027/2017/v30n2a3.[11.4.2020].

[44] Gisela Geisler, "Sisters under the Skin: Women and the Women's League in Zambia," *The Journal of Modern African Studies, 25*(1), 1987, 43-66 [1] [11.4.2020], www.jstor.org/stable/160966.

[45] Ibid.

[46] Lewis L. Gould, "First Ladies," *American Scholar*, 55, 1986, 529.

and a matron of many organizations. As per political observers, she led a very simple life as the First Lady. She was involved in many charitable initiatives and received the Indira Gandhi Non-Violence Award from UNIP for her efforts in 2003 by the Lusaka Province UNIP leadership. This award amplified the zeal she portrayed in her entire life of maintaining peace and harmony in the country. Mama Betty did all she could and within her means to help Zambia realize the philosophy of humanism, justice and peace in the post-colonial era. Her footsteps remain a forever tool of reference to first ladies of modern Zambia and Africa at large.[47]

President and First Lady, Dr Kenneth Kaunda and Betty, were frontrunners in HIV and AIDS eradication in the country. Many Zambians appreciated them for leading the way in the fight against the scourge. This role fits well with the social expectations of first ladies of fostering social values and norms among citizens and promoting the prevention of pandemics, including HIV and AIDS. Through various workshops, meetings and media presentations, first ladies had reached out to many people.[48]

Granted, the position of First Lady carries no official duties, so each one serves her nation according to her own wishes and interests. Some have played an active role in policy making, some have devoted themselves to humanitarian and charitable work and others have focused on family and social responsibilities. Mama Betty Kaunda courageously fought for Zambian freedom, demonstrated love whilst serving as the first lady, and in her wisdom and humility offered the state timely counsel.

---

[47] Lyubov Y. Prokopenko "Development of the Institution of the First Ladyship in Africa," _Journal of Globalisation Studies_, vol 12/1, 2021, 38-60.

[48] Lisa M. Burns, _First Ladies as Political Women: Press Framing of Presidential Wives, 1900 – 2001_, Maryland: University of Maryland, 2004.

The Demise of Mama Betty Kaunda

There was an outpouring of grief on social media networks on Wednesday September 19, 2012 following the news of the death of former Zambian First Lady, Betty Kaunda. Betty had suffered the effects of a stroke since 1991. She died in the early hours of 19 September 2012 in Harare while visiting her daughter. Dr. Kaunda and the other family members left for Harare to receive her body. She was 83 when she died and survived by her husband, eight children, 30 grandchildren and eleven great grandchildren. The whole nation mourned her death and she was given state respect as the First Lady of Zambia. She was a Christian and her final rites were performed based on Christian practices. The service at the Cathedral of the Holy Cross in Lusaka on 28 September 2012 was attended by diplomats, state officials and thousands of Zambians. The government declared three days of national mourning, while television and radio stations played hymns dedicated to her during the morning and evening. Her burial was initially planned at Lubwa Mission,[49] but was moved to the capital city, Lusaka, on account of the family's request.

Mama Kaunda's death was particularly shocking because less than three weeks before her death she and Dr Kaunda, her husband, had celebrated their 66th wedding anniversary. From the collection of condolence messages on social media, here are the selected farewell messages by her followers and family members:

> Dr. Kaunda explained that working together during the struggle for independence was the most difficult time for the family as he had to leave her with the children for a long time amidst the challenges of providing for the family. He further described his late wife as a freedom fighter who led fellow women to strengthen the struggle despite the dangers that came

---

[49] Lubwa Mission became her home after she got married to Kenneth Kaunda. Lubwa Mission is also the place where Kenneth Kaunda's parents and other family members are buried.

along with it. He further stated that Mama Betty's involvement in the struggle was for the love of peace and justice. He attributed his marriage and success with his late wife to a partnership that came through God's divine love.[50] Kaweche Kaunda stated that the death of his 83-year-old mother had deprived the nation and the Kaunda family of a pillar.[51]

Colonel Panji Kaunda wrote that his mother, Mama Betty Kaunda, was a good model whose life should be celebrated. Her daughter, Musata Banda, from Zimbabwe where Mama Betty went to visit and later died, described her mother's death as an unforgettable moment as she hardly knew that her mother visited her for the last time. Mrs. Banda observed that Mama Betty was a preacher of peace, unity and love for all people. She further stated that Mama Betty never got tired of teaching her children, grandchildren and great grandchildren the better ways of life and the importance of justice and harmony among all people. Meanwhile, her granddaughters and grandsons described Mama Betty as a pillar of hope, trust and hard work who always had a heart for people without segregation.[52]

Model Set by Betty towards other Women

From a gender perspective, the life of Mama Betty Kaunda presents a picture of how women can take on various roles. Growing up in the era when women were confined to domestic chores, she managed to become First Lady, a role which came with various social responsibilities. Her life shows the possibility of empowered women and their positive role in social and political development. By combining her traditional roles as a spouse and that of the first lady such as presidential escort, leader of social protocol, noblesse oblige, policymaker, and political advisor, she showed the resilience and astuteness which women have in performing multiple tasks. These are challenging tasks as the public expects the first lady to fulfil a

---

[50] Interview, 9.9.2017.

[51] Book of Condolences for Mama Betty Kaunda, opened on 22.9.2012.

[52] Ibid.

multitude of roles flawlessly, and there is criticism at any departure from perceived standards.[53]

First ladies can be said to be in privileged positions, though with various responsibilities. However, society should focus on nurturing, empowering the girl-child and the women in their daily lives. This also justifies first ladies' involvement in charity and empowerment related activities. First ladies present a model and create in the minds of the girl-child, possibilities of progression and participation in national activities. This has been exemplified by the relationship Musata had with her grandmother, Mama Betty Kaunda.

Finally, interventions and programmes that focus on women empowerment should consider a wholistic approach that is not limited to providing women with financial or material capital. Instead, there is the need for an integrated approach that provides women with the opportunities to have a mental shift from being domestic workers to socio-political decision makers. Traditions and customs should be analyzed to capture and adopt only those that are beneficial to women and the girl child. These should be integrated with contemporary approaches and the human rights framework which considers women as equal participants in the development process.

Conclusion

Gender roles are the activities that societies assign to males and females according to their gender. In response to the socio-economic changes which accentuate their exclusion, women may seek answers in traditions and in modernity. Obviously, not all women react this way, but a great number of them do. This chapter set out to explore the contribution made by the late Mama Betty Kaunda, Zambia's First Lady, between 1964 and 1991. Mama Betty Kaunda gradually started participating with full vigour in the struggle and proved

---

[53] Lewis L. Gould, "First Ladies," *American Scholar* 55, 1986, 529.

worthy. She did not only participate in the freedom struggle of the Zambian nation but also took care of her family and other families she interacted with in different ways. She was a mother, wife, and freedom fighter. Mama Kaunda played these various roles and at the same time, she simultaneously achieved her goal of bringing freedom to the Zambian citizens, against all odds.[54] After independence, other women have been appointed to serve in different political positions. Undoubtedly, Mama Betty Kaunda's contribution fuelled the introduction of women into politics through election and nomination. Indeed, she was a pillar in the socio-political development of Zambia.

Mama Betty Kaunda gradually started participating with full vigour in the struggle and proved worthy. She did not only participate in the freedom struggle of the Zambian nation but also took care of her family and other families she interacted with in different ways. She was a mother, wife, and freedom fighter. Mama Kaunda played these various roles and at the same time, she simultaneously achieved her goal of bringing freedom to the Zambian citizens, against all odds.[55] After independence, other women have been appointed to serve in different political positions. Undoubtedly, Mama Betty Kaunda's contribution fuelled the introduction of women into politics through election and nomination. Indeed, she was a pillar in the socio-political development of Zambia.

---

[54]   Anthony Mukwita, *Against All Odds: Zambia's President Edgar Chagwa Lungu's Rough Journey to State House*, South Africa: Partridge Africa, 2017.

Chapter Eight

Groaning in the Face of Empire: My Journey as the First Woman Bishop in the United Church of Zambia

Sylvia Mukuka

Introduction

Much has been said about the suffering of women, in private homes, in society at large and even in the church. In a quest to have their voices heard, women have taken steps to urgently share their life experiences in whichever way possible, either collectively or individually. Moreover, time has dawned for women from a cross-section of society, and within various sectors, who have courageously emerged from their closets with hidden voices, and have openly shared their experiences through telling their stories. In their argument, women contend that, in order to have a meaningful and tangible development in the church, it is inevitable and imperative that the atrocities perpetrated against women through particular forms of abuse by men are stopped. In fact, it is argued that women narrating their stories is the most powerful and achievable source of healing and known to be a significant approach, as equally affirmed by African Feminist Theologians such as Isabel Phiri, Betty Govinden, Mercy Amba Oduyoye, and Sarojini Nadar,[1] and further supported by Lillian Robinson who also affirms the power in telling

---

[1] Isabel Apawo Phiri, Devakarsham Betty Govinden & Sarojini Nadar (eds), *Her-Stories: Hidden Histories of Women of Faith in Africa*, Pietermaritzburg: Cluster, 2002, 3-12.

stories.[2] Moreover, Christina Landman equally observes that telling stories by women allows the relief of their emotions as a channel for expressing their concerns. Besides, storytelling is a cohesive process among women of faith who are well integrated through creating and reinforcing a path and platform for empowerment and change.[3] Musa Dube attests to the power of storytelling, arguing that, when the ills of oppression are exposed in women's narratives and sharing, society is stimulated to listen to the experiences of women.[4] Lilian Siwila indicates that, in order for women to be liberated from male dominance, there is need to employ a Feminist Cultural Analysis.[5] She further argues that "the feminist analysis of patriarchal ideologies helps us discover how men throughout history have achieved and maintained their domination of women," and she attributes this dominance to the patriarchal ideologies that stem from the traditional cultural belief systems, as well as from how Christianity was introduced.[6] Therefore, it can be argued that, to achieve such a Feminist Cultural Analysis, the process of storytelling will play a critical role, as it calls for serious responses by the listeners.

---

[2] S. Lillian Robinson, "Feminist Criticism – How do we Know when we've Won?" In S. Benston (ed), *Feminist Issues in Literary Scholarship*, Bloomington and Indianapolis: Indiana University Press, 1987.

[3] Christina Landman, "The Implementation of Biblical Hermeneutics," in Nyambura Njoroge & Musa Dube (eds), *Talita Cum! Theologies of African Women*, Pietermaritzburg: Cluster, 2001, 90.

[4] Musa W. Dube, "John 4:1-42, The Five Husbands at the Well of Living Waters: The Samaritan Woman and African Women," Nyambura Njoroge & Musa Dube (eds), *Talita Cum! Theologies of African Women*, Pietermaritzburg: Cluster, 2001, 48.

[5] Lillian C. Siwila, "In Search of a Feminist Cultural Analysis Model for Effective Dialogue on Harmful Cultural Practices," *Journal of Gender and Religion in Africa*, vol. 18, Special Issue, December 2012, 109.

[6] Ibid, 107.

Theoretical Framework

The article presents storytelling about the painful experiences of leadership in the church, and it is positioned within the African Feminist Theology framework. It is constructed within the context of narrative therapy as the most significant expressive paradigm.[7] Within the perspective of storytelling, narrative therapy has proven to be one of the most appropriate and practicable frameworks in the healing process. Andrew Lester holds the view that when stories that are told consciously that had been suppressed, they not only exemplify a person's life by giving clarity, but they also create identities.[8]

In narrative therapy, storytelling is a powerful experience to individuals through which a sense of self-identity is built as pieces that form their experience are transformed and constructed into a narrative.[9] Through the narrative therapy dimension of story-telling women can be helped to refocus and redefine themselves. Narrative theory grants women the power to challenge the tenets of patriarchy. More so, through story telling women can rediscover their identity. Being a powerful, profound, and executable channel it helps to transform women from just being passive observers and victims of patriarchy into participants in the history of humanity.

In the African Feminist Theologians' perspective of storytelling as a narrative therapy, it is believed that women become aware of their needs through a gradual process of interrogation and self-questioning. Within their struggles, women can make a breakthrough in their expression of freedom and in actualizing their dignity as people who share fully in the image of God. Although storytelling

---

[7] Ibid.

[8] Andrew D. Lester, *Hope in Pastoral Care and Counselling*, Louisville: Westminster/John Knox Press, 1995, 29.

[9] Ibid, 30.

has the potential of opening wounds, it is a very powerful means of healing and mending bruised and wounded lives. In the process of telling stories and sharing their experiences, women are engaged in what is called "steaming out." This is one of the most powerful means of achieving relief through releasing the pressure of painful emotions.[10] At the same time, story-telling helps women reshape and reclaim their overshadowed identity as well as recreating their lost images.[11] This is a very powerful therapeutic process that leads to healing and a powerful, profound, and executable channel, wholeness.

Besides, the process of storytelling helps to free women from the painful experiences of sexism in the church. At the same time, it is a kind of therapy that permeates into a powerful method of charting a way forward for women themselves,[12] so that women live with a history which is not just about the past, but which goes beyond the present. Therefore, as women share and narrate their stories, their focus goes beyond the now. It is a lasting and powerful experience, which provides qualitative change for women by acquiring a heightened understanding of their being. In this process the society is also transformed into valuing the nature of women as human beings who equally share the image of God. Therefore, narrative therapy in the form of storytelling is the only way in which women's experiences can be respected. As their stories are heard and shared, society can in turn create a different perspective in the way women are valued and treated.

---

[10]   Isabel Phiri, Betty Govinden, Sarojini Nadar (eds), *Her-Stories: Hidden Histories of Women of Faith in Africa*, 3-9.

[11]   Ibid, 1-12.

[12]   Ibid.

Narrating my Story

I am an African woman and an ordained Minister in the United Church of Zambia. I am one of the few women who have broken the barriers of patriarchy in the ecclesiastical setup, being the first female Bishop in the United Church of Zambia, 37 years after the church's inception. My election to this position came with enormous challenges, which I count today as setting up an impetus and pathway to my personal development and life achievement. My election has also opened a path for other women to attain leadership positions in the church.

My calling on the Christian journey started very early in life. Out of the nine members of my family, I was the only child who took up the path of following Christ at a very tender age. This was perhaps due to the neighbours that lived close to our family, who were very committed to their Christian faith as Roman Catholics. This family lived according to Christian principles and values. Family virtues are a primal space for understanding faith, as the family unit is the fundamental building block of society,[13] and a Christian home is the best space for the nurturing, training, and moulding of young people for succeeding generations.[14]

Before my mature understanding of spiritual matters, however, the excitement of following this family to church intrigued me very much. In my perspective, it was the kind of parenting process that parents missed in the context of the Christian faith and obligation, the failure to introduce me to Christ, as they were not Christians then. Besides, it was a failure to understand the very fact that children were loaned to parents by God, that parents have an obligation of nurturing children into the Christian faith. A Christian home is a

---

[13] Kenneth Boa, "Perspectives on Parenthood," 2016, https://bible.org/article/perspectives-parenthood [18.2.2018].

[14] Ibid.

laboratory for the application of biblical truths in a rational setting, and that "the home is an ideal place and training ground for imparting of values for healthy relationships and the well-being of humanity."[15]

Yet, in spite of that, the doors were slowly and steadily opening for me to knowing the Lord. At the age of nine, and following in the "footsteps" of this family, they took up the responsibility of becoming my godparents during my baptism. In the process, one of their daughters and I, were introduced to an elderly choir under the guidance of one of the Catholic Fathers at _Mungwi_ Catholic Parish. As a young girl with yet limited knowledge about Christ, all I knew was that it was the rightful thing for me to do, since everyone went to church, and sang in the choir. It was fine, and so it was with me.

It was several years later, after entering full time ministry, that the revelation of God's plans and purpose over my life began to unfold. I agree with Rick Warren that as Christians we are not on earth by accident.[16] Rick Warren sees every person as being destined for something which must be completed. And that God is not taken aback by events in our lives, because he is the author of life, who knows every soul in his creation.[17] Each person is destined to do something in life, known even before creation. Life's events are accomplished by every person. This includes ambitions, aspirations, desires and drives to a particular role in history.[18]

---

[15] Ibid.

[16] Rick Warren, _Purpose Driven Life: What on Earth am I Here for_, Grand Rapids: Zondervan, 2014, 234-235.

[17] Ibid.

[18] Ibid.

Academic, Marital, and Spiritual Life

After completing my junior and secondary education, I was employed by the government in the ministry of agriculture in which I worked in various positions. Years later, I got married and I was blessed with three children, two girls and one boy, *Mujinga, Kasoka* and *Kamau*. My spiritual journey continued steadily following my confirmation to full communicant membership in the United Church of Zambia, having entered the church with a Catholic background. My faith was kept steadily aglow, especially after my involvement in various church activities, such as youth programmes and the teaching of Sunday School, Girls' Brigade, and later, the Women's Guild known as the Women Christian Fellowship (WCF).

The Life of Widowhood

In life there are positive and negative experiences that people must grapple with. Sometime later, I lost my husband in a car accident, which I admit, nearly crippled my life. The experience of widowhood in most cases leaves people disorientated and devastated, as the pain of losing a spouse is so incomprehensible. This is because death is a very difficult phenomenon which can hardly be explained. Just as Fulata Moyo observes, "the loss of a beloved husband is a crushing experience that leaves a person emotionally desolate and drained."[19] More so, death disrupts the normal psychological functioning of an individual due to its painful pangs, no matter how faithful and strong an individual may appear to be. When death occurs, it leaves a huge vacuum that is both devastating and psychologically traumatic. Its impact is so immense that an individual is often left with more

---

[19] Fulata Lusungu Moyo, "Singing and Dancing Women's Liberation: My Story of Faith," in Isabel Apawo Phiri, Devakarsham Betty Govinden & Sarojini Nadar (eds), *Her-Stories: Hidden Histories of Women of Faith in Africa*, Pietermaritzburg: Cluster, 2002, 398.

questions than answers. Death is the final cessation of human life here on earth.[20] However, though the Scripture also offers hope in death,[21] when it strikes, it never occurs to people that indeed death is inevitable in our lives. The experience of death naturally raises such serious questions as to why such loss occurs. Why have individuals to face death, and why are some people left widowed at a very tender age? Most often, death does not make sense to people and neither did it make sense to me.

According to Gersie Alida, bereavement is the most painful experience in one's life. This is the kind of pain which emanates from acknowledging the very fact that an important bond to a loved one is terminated by death and unavoidably altered by that prolonged absence.[22] So, "death is the great expected unexpected, it is an anticipated yet unknown journey," which means that life is spoiled and wasted.[23] Gersie Alida points out that according to an Anglo Saxon's interpretation, when a loved one dies, it is like leaving a person standing naked before life, when the clothes and the armour of protection are forcibly removed.[24] In fact, when people hold such views about death, many find it to be very frightening, such that it is not at all a pleasant subject that can be discussed. More so, death is a

---

[20] "By the sweat of your brow you will eat your food until you return to the ground, since from it you were taken; for dust you are and to dust you will return" (Genesis 3:19) and John 11:25. _Holy Bible: New International Version_, Toronto: International Bible Society, 1984.

[21] "Jesus said to her: I am the resurrection and the life. He who believes in me will live, even though he dies" (John 11:25).

[22] Gersie Alida, _Story Making in Bereavement. Dragons Fight in the Meadow_, London: Jessica Kingsley, 1992, 29-32.

[23] Ibid.

[24] Ibid.

phenomenon that arouses a whole range of emotions such as fear, sorrow, resignation and helplessness.

In my comparative study on bereavement, many of those interviewed shared their experiences. Some admitted that death brought relief, freedom and triumph depending on their circumstances, while for many others, death brought pain, fear, and loss of interest in life.[25] Similarly, Elisabeth Kübler-Ross affirms the effects of mourning by noting that the loss of a loved one leads to anger, pain, and frustration due to the failure to hold on to the deceased. As a result, there is a projection of anger towards God. In her view, the process of bereavement takes several stages, such as denial, bargaining, anger, depression and acceptance.[26] Admittedly so, I experienced these practical psychological emotions during my bereavement process, although it can be mentioned here that the process of bereavement sometimes does not occur in the same sequence.[27] Thus, bereavement stages often vary depending on the emotional strength of an individual.[28]

My understanding of bereavement was based upon the very fact that death is one of the most powerful forces in the human history, which gives no warning to its impending occurrence. Thus, death comes when it is neither expected nor wanted. In fact, no human being has

---

[25] Sylvia Mukuka, "A Critical Comparative Study of Experiences of Bereavement in the Western and African Contexts with Implications for Pastoral Care," MA, University of Aberdeen, 2001, 4-10.

[26] Elizabeth Kübler-Ross, *Death the Final Stages of Growth*, Hoboken, New Jersey: Prentice Hall, 1975.

[27] Skinner A. Cook and Daniel S. Dworkin, *Helping the Bereaved, Therapeutic Interventions for Children, Adolescents and Adults*, Harper Collins, Basic Books, 1992, 16.

[28] Hasila Leda Limann, "Womanhood Rites and the Rites of Women in Africa, The Ugandan Experience," LLM (Human Rights and Democratization in Africa), Makerere University, Kampala, 2003, 27-30.

control over death, either to resist or even to ward it off. It is understood that death shall always remain a mystery and will always be part of the human condition, which simply suggests that it will always remain a big puzzle to humanity.[29]

During bereavement, what scares most people is the thought of remaining alone, especially if there are little children to look after, as was the case with me. Because of that, I entered the stages of bereavement saturated by emotions of anger, denial and depression. My anger was expressed towards everyone, including my friends and relatives. In fact, the deep sense of loss generated huge emotions of anger in me, so much, so that I asked God why my husband had died. At the same time, the anger was towards my husband, as I questioned why he had to leave. This kind of experience can create feelings of hostility, suspicion, distrust and social withdrawal, which are common emotions of bereavement,[30] and in extreme cases of bereavement it is observed that there is, "anger towards a husband that the deceased has left them with the task of rearing young children

---

[29] Sylvia Mukuka, "A Critical Comparative Study of Experiences of Bereavement in the Western and African Contexts with Implications for Pastoral Care," MA, University of Aberdeen, 2001, 4-10. Similar views are held by Onukwugha who argues that, "despite the religious knowledge and hope, the unpredictability and inevitability of death fascinates and frightens a whole range of humanity, hence, the fear of death is quite enormous" (Gerald Onyewuchi Onukwugha, "Death and Dying in the African Context, Chicken Bones," *Journal for Literary and Artistic African American Themes*, 2016, www.nathanielturner.com/deathanddyingafrican.htm [17.2.2018]).

[30] Sheila Payne, Sandra Horn and Relf Marilyn (eds), *Health Psychology. Loss and Bereavement*, Buckingham: Open University Press, 2000, 25.

alone, also anger expressed towards an 'unfair God,' with unanswered questions such as "why it has to be me."[31]

In fact, Trish Walker suggests that anger is the most normal, innate and constitutive element of grief which varies in its manifestations for each individual.[32] Similarly, Colin Parkes, suggests that

> [i]t is important that mourning is encouraged in order to facilitate a release of emotions. Grief is, after all, a normal response to dealing with bereavement. It is a normal response to death, which, when blocked, may result into a serious emotional breakdown. Grieving, it is observed, is a price that is paid for loving our spouses and a cost for commitment.[33]

Moreover, anger is a response and the safest way of releasing emotions; if not released they can be extremely harmful in an individual's life. It is also suggested that

> [f]ailure to mourn through the release of anger can be extremely harmful both to the individual and even to those around the person. In the deep sense of anger, this is a projection towards other people, friends, relatives, even to God.[34]

The Stage of Reorganization

In a positive and healthy situation, mourning must come to an end. A bereaved person must come to terms with the reality of death. For the bereaved new prospects in life cannot be ignored and we cannot hold on to our sorrows, and neither can we cancel the memories and

---

[31] Trish Walker, "Anger in Bereavement: How Counselling Can Help," 2012, www.counselling-directory.org.uk.counseeling-can-help [1.6.2017].

[32] Colin M. Parkes, "The First Year of Bereavement: A Longitudinal Study of the Reaction of London Widows to the Death of their Husbands," London, 1970, *Psychiatry: Journal for the Study of Interpersonal Processes*, 33(4), 444–467 [444]

[33] Ibid.

[34] Trish Walker, "Anger in Bereavement: How Counselling Can Help," 2012, www.counselling-directory.org.uk.counseeling-can-help [1.6.2017].

think about all that we did or did not do.[35] And so, after the period of mourning, it is very important for an individual to reach a point of letting go, by opening oneself up to new opportunities as the phase of mourning ends. Equally, after my phase of mourning, I came to terms with my husband's death and with much grace, I accepted my loss which for me was a greater achievement than continuing to grieve.[36] In the process of reorganizing my life, I reorganized my thoughts and developed a completely new perspective on life. Adapting to life after mourning helps one to rebuild a positive identity and purpose in life as despair becomes interspersed with more positive feelings.[37]

Bereavement as a Tool for Counselling in my Ministry

It has been said that time is the greatest healer, but grief does not have a definite end-point which marks recovery, as people may adopt new roles and adapt to them.[38] In this perspective, the experience of bereavement, and the loss that I experienced, changed my perception about death, as I was never the same again.[39] Moreover, the period *after* mourning is a significant experience, which provides a sense of

---

[35] Cf. Gersie Alida, *Story Making in Bereavement. Dragons Fight in the Meadow*, London: Jessica Kingsley, 1992, 167.

[36] It was a kind of process that Julie Axelrod sees in bereavement, a gift in the power of mourning afforded to individuals. She suggests that "one must understand that failure to mourn may not be considered as a mark of brevity nor power, but a disastrous consequence" (Julie Axelrod, "The Five Stages of Grief and Loss," 2016, https://pyshecentral.com/hb/the-5-stages-of-loss-and-grief [1.6.2017]).

[37] Sheila Payne, Sandra Horn and Marilyn Relf (eds), *Health Psychology. Loss and Bereavement*, Buckingham: Open University Press, 2000, 71-72.

[38] Ibid, 80.

[39] Ibid, 71-72.

pride, personal strength, the ability to cope, and resilience after grieving has come to an end.[40] After my bereavement phase, I realized that I had a new outlook about my image and a new outlook on death. Suffice to say, years later, the "why" questions were turned into a significant and strong anchor for my ordained ministry.

I discovered that my experience as a widow became inevitable in ministry, as it set an impetus and a firm foundation in the area of bereavement counselling to people who struggled with life's challenges during their phases of mourning. My bereavement experience provided the key to an in-depth understanding of the real meaning of empathetic counselling which is also known as "walking into another person's frame, and a person's world of thought."[41] Eventually, the bereavement process offered me a clearer perspective of death, and later it opened wider doors to understanding the role of pastoral care in the church. Today, my pastoral care role is offered on a broader dimension, and has richly been enhanced, as it is practiced from an experiential point of view.[42] In fact, it is based on what John Swinton suggests, that pastoral care is offered out of love, commitment, and understanding, which makes church relevant and caring as it touches the lives of people.[43]

---

[40]   Ibid, 80.

[41]   Ibid.

[41]   Marta D. Gherard, "What is Empathy," 2012, www.counselling.org.uk [26.2.2018].

[42]   Ibid.

[43]   John Swinton, "Friendship in Community, Creating a Space for Love," in David Willows and John Swinton (eds), *Spiritual Dimension of Pastoral Care. Practical Theology in a Multidisciplinary Context,* London: Jessica Kinsley, 2000, 74.

Such an experience of bereavement can be used as a pastoral care tool for encouraging a fragmented social and individual existence.[44] Pastoral care strives to create an enabling environment both in and outside the church, to the effect that everyone may feel a sense of well-being, feel acceptance, wholeness and love.[45] My widowhood experience formed the basis for an enriched ministry, based on putting pastoral care tools to good use as we operate in a particular social context.[46] Although death is painful, the experience of widowhood in the context of pastoral care today may seem inevitable to me, as pastoral care is a spiritual dimension, which is expressed wholistically, physically and emotionally and offered to individuals and communities.[47] Ultimately, it can be explained from the perspective that my widowhood experience taught me very powerful and objective lessons about the values of life and wisdom, especially about how to be a resourceful person to my three little children who entirely depended upon my role as both a mother and father to them. In addition, as a single mother, I was offered a broader perspective on the role of pastoral care to single people who face the challenges of raising children on their own.

---

[44] Stephen Pattison, _The Challenges of Practical Theology. Selected Essays_, London: Jessica Kingsley, 2007, 102-107.

[45] Ibid.

[46] Emmanuel Lartey, "Practical Theology as a Theological Form," in David Willows and John Swinton (eds), _Spiritual Dimension of Pastoral Care. Practical Theology in a Multidisciplinary Context_, London: Jessica Kinsley, 2000, 74.

[47] Herbert Moyo, "The Pastor and the Embryonic Pastoral Identities in Southern Africa in the 21st Century," in Herbert Moyo (ed), _Pastoral Care in a Globalized World: African and European Perspectives_, Pietermaritzburg: Cluster, 2015.

A Call into Ministry

My call into full time ministry followed my enrolment into full time ministerial training at the United Church of Zambia's Theological College. In a class of ten, I was the only female student, and I was appointed the class representative. Throughout the first part of three years in training, everything was smooth. However, towards the end of my training my male classmates all of a sudden began to exhibit a very negative attitude towards me. It was a kind of attitude that I still do not understand. My experience had actually exposed how deeply the patriarchal and sexist practices were embedded in the church. In fact, patriarchy is a hidden and subtle practice which requires a critical eye for it to be detected because of the way in which it is practiced in the church today. Patriarchy is very real and practiced in a very insidious manner. Following the policy of the college, each year the best student was selected to go out of the country for further studies, and I was selected to do just that. Immediately after my ordination, I left for Aberdeen in Scotland for further studies. A year later, I successfully completed a Master's degree in Practical Theology with a major in Pastoral Care and Counselling.[48] Once again, upon my return, I found myself to be the only female among the male ministers in the Presbytery. I once again was elected as the consistory chairperson.

A few months later, and from a very precipitous point, the bishop then, demanded that the position of consistory chairperson be surrendered to a male minister on the basis that I was less effective in the administration of the consistory. I was not moved by that decision, as I saw it forthcoming from their negative attitudes towards me. To that effect, a male minister took over from me

---

[48] My thesis was: Sylvia Mukuka, "A Critical Comparative Study of Experiences of Bereavement in the Western and African Contexts with Implications for Pastoral Care," MA, University of Aberdeen, 2001.

without any elections at all. This is something which I personally thought was not done in good faith. In my view, this action could be perceived in line with what Arnold Glasgow might consider, that "one of the tests of leadership is to recognize a problem before it becomes an emergency,"[49] and this, for me, was indeed a problem. However, I resisted the temptation to make a protest.

Many people think authority is a God given right to rule, and it is only men who possess this right. To be male is to possess authority, and to be female is to possess less authority.[50] Thus, in my opinion, the unfair treatment I experienced was tantamount to intimidation, because at no point had I neglected my work in the consistory. However, despite the frustration and the hurtful experience, my spirit towards work remained very high. My aim was to look beyond what had happened in order to remain focused. In fact, James Kouzes and Barry Posner share encouraging insights in situations such as these, that one should "stand on the personal beliefs and let work itself and commitment to duty speak on your behalf."[51] Thus, the frustrating and disappointing experiences became my stepping-stones, but the women in the consistory were infuriated by the action of the higher office and almost staged a protest. However, this was quickly averted as the women were counselled privately. They were advised to look up to God for his will to be done. From that experience a lesson was drawn in the sense that particular events happen for specific reasons, that is, they tested me psychologically. In such circumstances, one

---

[49] Arnold H. Glasgow, "Greatest Leadership Principle," in Pockell Leslie and Adrienne Avila (eds), _The 100 Greatest Leadership Principles of All Time_, New York: Warner Books, 2007, 17.

[50] Linda L. Belleville, _Women Leaders and the Church. Three Crucial Questions_, Baker Book, 2000, 133.

[51] James M. Kouzes and Barry Z. Posner, _The Leadership Challenges Book_, USA: Jossey-Bass/A Wiley Company, 2003, 11-12.

may be drawn to acknowledging the view of Karl von Clausewitz that, "if the leader is filled with high ambition, and he pursues his aims with audacity and strength of will, he will reach them in spite of all obstacles."[52] I also realized that certain events in an individual's life are sometimes inevitable and helpful in making critical introspection about how challenging issues and situations of life can be handled.

My Experience as the First Woman Bishop in the United Church of Zambia

Barely two weeks after being removed from the consistory office, I was elected as the first female Bishop for the North Western Presbytery. That was exonerating for me, but it came as a big challenge for the male ministers. While some accepted my election, others disputed it and called for its nullification. It was contended that my election was prematurely done, because five years had not yet elapsed after ordination, so that the elections were null and void. Surprisingly enough, my predecessor, the male bishop from whom I was to take over, had been elected just one year after his ordination, and that had never raised any argument or query in any way from the male fraternity, whereas in my case, that election took place four years after my ordination. Those male ministers could not grasp the idea of having a woman bishop who could make such a breakthrough in the church at such a critical moment. Their moves showed that highly patriarchal systems are still deeply embedded within the church structures.

I decided to react as Ray Bradbury later phrased it that "in leadership, when things get tough, you have got to jump off cliffs all the time

---

[52] Karl von Clausewitz, "The Greatest Leadership Principle," in Pockell and Avila Adrienne (eds), *The 100 Greatest Leadership Principles of all Time*, New York: Warner Books, 2007, 72.

and build your wings on the way down."[53] This election only confirmed the faithfulness of God who, in his fairness, searches the deeper motives of people. Besides, in spite of how much people may want to close the doors for one's success and destiny, God is the final authority in his own wisdom on how he directs his will in people's lives. In his own power, He opens the hidden doors wider that people are able to see. In this case, for the door that was closed in the consistory, a bigger and wider door was opened in the Presbytery.

Meanwhile, the women celebrated my election as they saw it as a milestone and a breakthrough for women. My election came as a big challenge, and I placed my leadership perspective upon the advice that "titles are granted, but it is your behaviour that wins respect."[54] In fact, a leader must model effectively as one who believes in something, one who must stand up for his or her beliefs.[55] Thus, as a leader, I stood up for my beliefs and was committed to my duties. James Kouzes and Barry Posner suggest that the commitment you can make as a leader is to find your voice by clarifying your personal values and then expressing them in a style that is authentically your own.[56] However, in spite of such challenges, I did not need an eloquent speech about my personal values as I felt that, "commitment to work is far more important than words or protesting about the occurrence."[57]

---

[53] Ray Bradbury, "The Greatest Leadership Principle," in Pockell Leslie and Avila Adrienne (eds), _The 100 Greatest Leadership Principles of All Time_, New York: Warner Books, 2007, 70.

[54] James M. Kouzes and Barry Z. Posner, _The Leadership Challenges Book_, USA: Jossey-Bass/A Wiley Company, 2003, 11-12.

[55] Ibid.

[56] Ibid.

[57] Ibid.

After a huge debate over my election, my name was endorsed and ratified by Synod, making me duly and legitimately elected. The tenacity of male pride and superiority complexes were expressed by many of my male colleagues by a comment uttered within my earshot,

> *Nomba elyo ulukutalwapwa, bushe nikwisa ulukuta luleya?* (The church is now finished, and where is it heading with this kind of decision?)

Comments like this affirm John Rowan's observation that "there are complex issues associated with patriarchy, for instance, forcefulness is considered normal and natural."[58] Moreover, in the perspective of many men, any woman who ascends to a position of authority in the church is one who oversteps the ecclesiastical limits. Generally, the reaction of men towards women who ascend to such positions is perceived as, "desecrating the male ecclesiastical order which was only the preserve for men."[59]

And not only that, inasmuch as the doors are open to the ordination of women, there are other hidden challenges,[60] and in spite of the hardly fought battle for women's ordination in the church, their struggles are still enormous. The ecclesiastical "victory" that women fight so hard for still remains elusive,[61] and the ordained women have had to continue with their struggle in the fight for proper recognition and against the injustices of patriarchy at new and various levels. Sarojini Nadar lamentably argues that

> women's fight for proper recognition still goes on. Unfortunately, for some who do not have the energy to fight on literally keep quiet, and withdraw to

---

[58] John Rowan, *The Horned God, Feminism and Men as Wounding and Healing*, New York: Routledge and Kegan Paul, 1987.

[59] Hilary M. Lips, *Women, Men and Power*, Toronto: Hayfield, 1991, 167.

[60] Sarojini Nadar, "On Being the Pentecostal Church: Pentecostal Women's Voices and Visions," In Isabel Apawo Phiri and Sarojini Nadar (eds), *On Being Church: African Women's Voices and Visions*, Geneva: WCC, 2005, 18.

[61] Ibid.

their respective corners with their small voices, as they remain powerless and just observe."[62]

In addition, Ezra Chitando argues from the perspective of equality that inasmuch as progress is evident, there is still need for the church to deeply reflect if women are to experience equality. One could argue that more often than not, men want to use their positions to create structural barriers for women simply because of their gender,[63] and in many work places today, women face a number of challenges that tend to keep them marginalized. Men want to make women feel like outsiders in their quest to limit their powers.[64]

These challenges often make me curious so that, when I reflect upon the struggles and challenges in ministry, I am often drawn to many other women who have had similar challenges. One such woman was Bishop Barbara Harris, the first black female Bishop in the Episcopalian Church, elected in 2000.[65] Her experience is rather inspiring and very encouraging to me. Her story provides me with the zeal and fervency to move forward. In spite of men refusing to accept her election, the woman of God soldiered on. Her election raised a lot of resentment, even to the point that the Presiding Bishop (USA) refused to attend her induction, as he and other men were convinced that it was taboo for any woman to enter the sacred ecclesiastical order reserved solely for men.[66]

---

[62] Ibid.

[62] Ezra Chitando, "A New Man for a New Era? Zimbabwean Pentecostalism Masculinities and the HIV Epidemic," *Missionalia*, 35(3), 2007, 112-127.

[63] Ibid, 112-127.

[64] Hilary M. Lips, *Women, Men and Power*, Toronto: Hayfield, 1991, 167.

[65] Ibid.

[66] Ibid.

Sarojini Nadar argues that, "the church has failed, for neglecting its role of granting life and healing to people. Thus, before the church can consider doing this, it has to confess its manifold sin and wickedness, including the sins of discrimination, exclusion, and subjugation."[67]

But there is also progress, as Sarojini Nadar equally mentions Bishop Rubin Phillip, who, in the first instance, disapproved the ordination of women and expressed words such as, "Women priests? Over my dead body!"[68] However, heartily enough, Bishop Rubin Phillip later came to appreciate the ordained ministry of women.[69] And that is the way to go: God gives a variety of gifts, and women possess similar gifts as men, and the only thing the church must do is to encourage women to develop their potential to the fullest. Women must be encouraged to be "all that they can be spiritually, by assisting and encouraging them to adequately prepare through theological training in order to be fully equipped for ministry."[70]

Evidently so, in many denominations, the cultural orientation and tendency is for women to be subjugated and relegated to the background. Thus, in this male perspective, leadership is their domain, and for women it is impossible and unachievable. Moreover,

---

[67] Ibid, 19.

[68] Sarojini Nadar, "On Being the Pentecostal Church: Pentecostal Women's Voices and Visions," *Ecumenical Review*, 2004, 56/3, 354-367.

[69] Ibid. – A predecessor to this change was John Wesley, who, in the beginning, forbade women of the revival to preach, but when they persisted, he began to appreciate their ministry and encouraged them in it (Paul Wesley Chilcote, "John Wesley and the Women Preachers of Early Methodism," PhD, Duke University, 1984). When Wesley, advanced in age, was asked why he, as an Anglican priest, could allow women to preach, he answered: "If God owns them in the conversion of sinners, who am I to hinder Him?"

[70] James R. Berk and Craig L. Blomberg, *Two Views on Women in Ministry*, Grand Rapids: Zondervan, 2001, 78.

Olubanke Akintunde argues that, oftentimes, Paul is quoted as the one who interdicted women from participating in leadership roles in the church, and that men who would want to undermine the credibility of women through subjugation hold such views.[71] In her views, this is detrimental and prejudicial to the women because of the cultural restrictions imposed on them by society at large.[72] It should therefore be admitted that patriarchy is a real phenomenon of the church; for instance, in my experience, through such comments. More so, this problem is attributed to the male ego, for which leadership and authority were conceived as a domain for men only. Having a woman in a leadership position in the church is contended as usurping its original male dominion, because it is argued that a woman's position should always be peripheral. Besides, in relation to female identity, Lavinia Byrne also observes that "women have been forced to define their identity in ways that lead to denying themselves as special people who are also made in the image of God. It is important to understand the fact that God looks at women within his image because he is in the image of a woman too."[73] By and large, it is actually hard to detect the propensities of patriarchy in the church today as the language may seem to be gender neutral and inclusive; however, in reality, there is a totally different image of the church which is still male. Just as Lavinia Byrne observes:

> The language that we use in church is critical to our identity. The church should be seen to be open by portraying the attributes of Christ that embrace everyone, women inclusive. Denying women the full knowledge and participation in the mission of the church is to obscure the will of God through women. The language that is used to women in church fails to

---

[71] Olubanke D. Akintunde, "Partnership and the Exercise of Power, in the Christ Apostolic Church, Nigeria," in Isabel Phiri and Sarojini Nadar (eds), *On Being Church: African Women's Voices and Visions*, World Council of Churches, 2005, 89.

[72] Ibid.

[73] Lavinia Byrne, *Women before God*, London: SPCK, 1988, 7.

appreciate women who also bear the image of God. Hence, women must be allowed to appreciate the image of God in them through celebrating their identity in the mission of God.[74] .

The Authority

Despite facing challenging moments in my position, I had a determination to forge ahead. Besides, it was a known fact that my work was being gauged by society's yardstick, such that there were only two options, that I could either succeed or fail. And so, the impulse to move on was motivated by the fact that I was a pioneer. As a leader, my motivation was to step out into the world of the unknown. My failure to do the work could have meant failing other women as well by closing the doors to their future success, and thereby justifying the fear that men hold for allowing a woman in the position of authority. I was aware that in most cases, women who are in positions of leadership have to work much harder than men.[75] They are expected to produce more and prove their worth and give more of themselves in a male dominated world of professionalism.[76] Women are expected to work even harder, do more, be nicer and show more ability than men. Thus, my success had to be earned, for it did not come easily like the light in the morning, but it came through pain and trials.

I was also aware that "leadership is a difficult task which is obviously associated with obstacles, and that difficulties will always be experienced for anyone who desires to pursue lofty career goals."[77] A good leader should not expect leadership to be easy or like a crystal stair case leading to the top. Yet, leadership is also joyful. In as much

[74] Ibid, 10.

[75] Sandra Lee Gupton and Gloria Appelt Slick, *Highly Successful Women Administrators: The Inside Stories of how they got there*, Thousand Oaks: Corwin, 1996, 6.

[76] Ibid., 6.

[77] Ibid, 43.

as it is difficult, "the path however is not loaded with land mines."[78] Thus, my leadership role can be likened to an investment in a huge business venture whose key is patience and endurance. My struggles were the profits earned slowly, and at the same time constituted a learning process.

Leadership is a superior skill developed on a daily basis as each day presented its own lessons. "Excellence and success in top leadership positions is achieved as a result of hard work and determination, and often against tremendous challenges,"[79] and indeed, the challenges I encountered have today become my anchor and stepping stones. This, for me, is actually the very essence of leadership as, "management is efficiency in climbing the ladder of success, the leadership position determines whether the ladder is leaning against the right wall."[80]

More interesting is that every individual has natural gifts and talents, however, nearly all the skills of leadership are gradually learned and improved upon in the process. And so, my entry into the position of leadership and working under such male scrutiny created in me a mixture of emotions of both frustration and endurance. Over and above, forging a new path where other women had not yet passed was equally a challenging task. As a pioneer, my road was rough and thorny, because my leadership position was an exploration and a path for other women. In fact, my leadership role was based on what Ralph Waldo Emerson suggests in his wise counsel: "Do not go where the path may lead, go instead, where there is no path and leave

---

[78] Ibid.

[79] Ibid.

[80] Stephen R. Covey, "The Greatest Leadership Principles," in Leslie Pockell and Adrienne Avila (eds), _The 100 Greatest Leadership Principles of all Times,_ New York: Warner Books, 2007, 16.

a trail."[81] This is actually true, in the sense that, along my path, there was a great danger of stepping on both "pebbles" and "thorns" which sometimes could leave painful "blisters" on my feet. Nevertheless, I drew my strength and courage from the insight that there is also great benefit in leadership.[82] Thus, leadership is not about expertise, but a learning process. In fact, Winston Churchill once said, "mountain tops inspire leaders, but valleys mature them,"[83] and Norman Schwarzkopf suggests that "leadership is a combination of strategy and character. If you must be without one, be without the strategy."[84]

Ultimately, as I reflect on the past tenure of office and my contribution to church development in the presbytery, it is evident that the North Western Presbytery achieved a lot in terms of staff development and church and infrastructure development during the eight years that I served as the bishop. Today, the North Western Presbytery is one of the best in the United Church of Zambia. This could be attributed to my leadership skills that I acquired in the process, which I strongly feel were the catalyst to successful leadership. I found it inevitable that I should first lead myself before leading others, and this meant building my self-confidence, assertiveness, self-discipline and commitment to duty as a leader.

---

[81] Emerson Ralph Waldo, "The Greatest Leadership Principles," in Leslie Pockell and Adrienne Avila (eds), *The 100 Leadership Principles of All Time*, New York: Warner Books, 2007, 8.

[82] Sandra Lee Gupton and Gloria Appelt Slick, *Highly Successful Women Administrators: The Inside Stories of how they got there*, Thousand Oaks: Corwin, 1996, 6.

[83] Winston Churchill, "The Greatest Leadership Principles," In Leslie Pockell and Adrienne Avila (eds), *The 100 Greatest Leadership Principles of All Time*, New York: Warner Books, 2007, 91.

[84] Norman Schwarzkopf, "The Greatest Leadership Principles," in Leslie Pockell and Adrienne Avila (eds), *The 100 Greatest Leadership Principles of All Time*, New York: Warner Books, 2007, 51.

Today, as I sit back and reflect upon my experience, I can breathe a sigh of relief and give glory to God for his faithfulness. Just as Mahatma Ghandi once said, "We must become the change we want to see."[85] Equally, as Antony Jay has observed, "the only real training for leadership is leadership."[86] Thus, having come from a background of conflict, my journey called for a determination to lead a transparent life so others could follow. Moreover, my consciousness was based on the fact that many people, especially fellow women, had invested so much trust in me by actually desiring to see women succeed. Failure would have meant betraying their trust and closing the doors for other women. As a result of my success, the doors are now open to other women in top leadership positions of the church.

Conclusion

In conclusion, having presented the story of my struggles as a woman in the church, I argue that the only catalyst to attaining a position of authority in today's era is adequate preparation. Women must prepare by developing the necessary skills, qualifications and credentials that would qualify them for positions of leadership. I have certainly achieved this by obtaining my PhD in Practical Theology as a ground for effective ministry. Certainly, this is a very sophisticated era we are living in today where society does not only look at us simply because we are women. And that women must never stop fixing their eyes on their goals, as they must remain true to themselves. Women must remember that those who have made it to the top today should

---

[85] Mahatma Ghandi, "The Greatest Leadership Principles," in Leslie Pockell and Adrienne Avila (eds), *The 100 Greatest Leadership Principles of All Time*, New York: Warner Books, 2007, 25.

[86] Anthony Jay, "The Greatest Leadership Principles," in Leslie Pockell and Adrienne Avila (eds), *The 100 Greatest Leadership Principles of All Time*, New York: Warner Books, 2007, 5

encourage fellow women that they must read and learn, always striving to know more than ever before in order to fit in positions of leadership.[87] As women, we must know that God has endowed us with unique gifts, and that we should be who we are as we value our potential. We must be aware that we have been endowed with a great pool of potential, which can be utilized such as ethics, honesty, courage, integrity, intelligence and many other necessary resources to make us reach the highest summit in our leadership prospects.

---

[87] Sandra Lee Gupton and Gloria Appelt Slick, _Highly Successful Women Administrators: The Inside Stories of how they got there,_ Thousand Oaks: Corwin, 1996, 6.

Chapter Nine

On Being a Single Mother and Clergy: A Call to Create Safe Space for Single Women Clergy in the Church

Hellen Chisanga

Introduction

In this chapter I explore the challenges of female single parents who are clergy in the United Church of Zambia (UCZ). I will centre on my experiences as a single clergy mother, but I will also take into account the experiences of other female single mothers who are clergy.

1. Marriage is Central and Prescribed

In Zambian culture, just like in many other African cultures, every woman is expected to marry and procreate, and to parents and extended family feel concerned to have a daughter who is not married for a long time. Isabel Phiri contends that the pressure to be attached to a man to fulfil a particular goal is often understood as a condition of both culture and religion.[1]

According to Mercy Amba Oduyoye, "the fertility of the woman is the biological foundation of marriage and it governs male-female relations within the institution."[2] Oduyoye advocates for women in African societies and invites us to realize that it is actually procreation

---

[1] Isabel A. Phiri, "Doing Theology in Community: The Case of African Women Theologians in the 1990s," *Journal of Theology for Southern Africa*, 1997, 34.

[2] Mercy Amba Oduyoye, *Daughters of Anowa*, Maryknoll: Orbis, 1995, 141.

that is considered most important in an African marriage.[3] Society strongly believes that procreation is not to be experienced outside the 'institution of marriage,' and the assumption is common that it is actually the biological foundation of the woman that safeguards marriage in African cultures.[4]

In most African societies no woman is to remain single. In my tribe (I am a Bemba) a woman ought to start preparing herself for marriage even when she is still at school. As a young girl, you visit your relatives and there are children younger than you in the house and thus you must behave like an adult. Some of us had to take care of our baby cousins. This means, as a young girl, looking after babies and doing house chores is part of what it takes to become a good mother and housewife. Singleness is a foreign concept.

Marriage in African tradition is highly respected. A woman who is married is treated with a lot more respect than one who is single.[5] Bwalya Chuba states that

> If a person does not marry or gets married at the age they are expected to, the family becomes very concerned and worried, because they believe that an unmarried person in African society is missing some human value. This means that anyone who is not married is not considered a human being and cannot participate and make reasonable decisions on certain matters.[6]

This notion that anyone who is not married is less than human has caused harm when it comes to accepting single clergy mothers. People have a lot of respect for the clergy, but there is, at the same

---

[3] Ibid.

[4] J.K. Oliello, "The Gospel and African Culture: Polygamy as a Challenge to the Anglican Church of Tanzania - Diocese of Mara," MTh, University of KwaZulu-Natal, 2005, 30.

[5] Bwalya S. Chuba, _Choosing a Life Partner for a Christian Marriage and a Christian Home_, Mansa: Book & Stationary Centre, 2005, 1.

[6] Ibid.

time, discrimination against single clergy, right from when they were first ordained, and it is still strong today.

2. Singleness

Before I proceed to outline my personal experiences, let me briefly give a background on singleness in African societies. In our societies a home is supposed to have a husband, his wife and their children,[7] and when there is no marriage, it is not considered a home at all.

Marriage, being one of the rites of passage in African society, is also observed as a channel of socialization for women. It is true to state that even if female clergies can manage their affairs without the help of men, the negative perceptions of them affect them personally as well as their work as ministers.

According to our African customs, there is an age limit within which a woman should get married whether she has an education or not. Historically speaking, we are coming from a culture that maintained that a woman's place is in the kitchen and therefore it is practically impossible for her to contribute positively to any matters that deal with decision making.

Reasons for one to remain a single clergy and mother may vary across nations, ranging from personal choices to involuntary circumstances, but it is a fact that single mothers face discrimination, rejection and sometimes even blackmail from society.

George Mwansa states that "marriage is everything and it should be sought by all cost."[8] This statement is rather impractical as it is not

---

[7] Ibid.

[8] George Mwansa, *Women and Marriage: Why Marriage Means Everything to a Woman*, Lusaka: Zambia Adventist Press, 2012, 52.

always possible to fulfil. Some women are never proposed to and some find the wrong partners all together.

3. Single Motherhood

In many African societies, particularly in Zambia, it is still embarrassing for many women, whether ordained as clergy or not, to have children outside marriage according to Mercy Amba Oduyoye,[9] Isabel Phiri,[10] Rachel NyaGondwe-Banda[11] and Fulata Mbano-Moyo.[12] Having children in an African context is a merit, but having a child when one is not married is a very big concern, or, to some other people, a huge mistake.

A single mother is defined as a 'female' who is bringing up a child or children on her own, without a 'male'.[13] Such 'single mothers' may be widowed, divorced or never married. This is not the traditional African concept of family life. The African traditional concept of a family means that a man ought to be with a wife and children and a man should be the head of the family.

Aadriaan van Klinken indicates that according to many parishioners in Zambia, headship means that the man

> is responsible for the well-being of the family, materially as well as morally and spiritually. Headship is associated with sustaining roles, such as being the breadwinner, providing for the material needs of the family, showing

---

[9] Mercy Amba Oduyoye, *Daughters of Anowa*, Maryknoll: Orbis, 1995.

[10] Isabel Apawo Phiri, "Doing Theology in Community: The Case of African Women Theologians in the 1990s," *Journal of Theology for Southern Africa*, 99, 1997, 68-76.

[11] Rachel NyaGondwe Banda [Fiedler], *Women of Bible and Culture: Baptist Convention Women in Southern Malawi*, Zomba: Kachere, 2005.

[12] Fulata Mbano-Moyo, "A Quest for Women's Sexual Empowerment through Education in an HIV and AIDS Context," PhD, University of KwaZulu-Natal, 2009.

[13] Merriam Webster, *The Webster Merriam Dictionary*, Merriam Webster, 1989.

leadership, providing guidance to the family, and leading the family in prayer.[14]

As stated above, the traditional concept of a family entails a wife, husband and children in a nuclear context, but globally, many families are undergoing transformation from a two-parent family to a single parent family.

This may be a temporary family form that lasts a few months or a few years until a mother remarries thus constituting a stepfamily. A number of single mothers are reluctant to remarry, due to the fact that they are not willing to have their children raised by a step-father.[15] In our African context, a woman who has had a child or children and is not married, is regarded as a second-class citizen, and men are reluctant to marry them.

There has been a major increase in single mother families in African countries such as Zimbabwe, Swaziland, Lesotho and South Africa.[16] This increase can be due the fact that some men do not take responsibility for their children or it could be that they are already married and they do not want to be in a polygamous marriage. It could also be a choice by either of the parents. Some men do support their children, especially when they leave a marriage or relationship, while many others do not support their children even when they are able to do so.

Single motherhood in most cases is regarded as a sin or even a curse. A single woman is regarded as being promiscuous or merely a prostitute. This usually happens in communities. However, it becomes very discriminatory when one experiences rejection from

---

[14] Adriaan S. van Klinken, _Transforming Masculinities in African Christianity: Gender Controversies in Times of AIDS_, Farnham: Ashgate Publishing, 2013, 80.

[15] Michael C. Kirwen, _African Widows_, Maryknoll: Orbis, 1979.

[16] F.M. Kiura, _Unwed Teenage Mothers_, Oxford University Press, 1999.

one's own church. It is the church's responsibility to respond positively to cases of single motherhood, irrespective of the circumstances that may have caused it.

4. Analyzing Single Motherhood

Marriage can be everything to those who have it, but there is no guarantee for those who have no partners not to be discriminated and rejected. Stigmatization should not be tolerated as single mothers are also human beings and they deserve love and support from others.

According to Bwalya Chuba "a home is formed through marriage."[17] He further states that "one sets up a home as soon as he or she marries or gets married."[18] This is true when there is a wife and a husband, but when there is no marriage, it is not considered a home at all. It is commonly believed that a home without a man is like eating *nshima* or *papa* without a relish, meaning a home without a partner is not complete.

According to Alderman Chileshe, "one of these important beha-viours which commanded the greatest respect apart from the birth of a child and death of an individual in the family, is the institution of marriage."[19] For one to be respected in our society she or he must be married; a single person is believed not the have any honour.

Therefore, marriage and childbearing are the focus of life. John Mbiti believes child bearing is associated with marriage and a person cannot

---

[17] Bwalya S. Chuba, *Choosing a Life Partner for a Christian Marriage and a Christian Home*, Mansa: Book & Stationary Centre, 2005, 1.

[18] Ibid.

[19] Alderman Habbock Chileshe, *A Tribute to (the Man), His Life and History*, Ndola: Mission Press, 1998, 52.

procreate if she or he is not married according to the African culture. It is taboo for a person to have children without first being married.[20]

Since the world is becoming dynamic and things are changing, single motherhood is increasing and is found in large and small cities and rural areas. Single mothers are found amongst all ethnic groups of the world. Some studies have indicated that there is not much information available on the percentage or number of single mothers in Zambia. This can be attributed to culture which regards singlehood as an abomination and is therefore not reported.

For me to explain the response of the church towards being a single mother and a clergy, I will give my own experience of being an ordained reverend minister in the United Church of Zambia, who is a single mother.

2. Single Clergy Mothers' Experiences and Challenges

The church is a place where people are supposed to find solace, but unfortunately it is often a place where people are discriminated against and suffer rejection. In many cases, female clergies who are single are looked down upon and are discriminated against as non-performers, simply because they are not married.

A female minister was highly honoured and respected when her husband was still alive. However, it became a different story when her husband died as she was judged and put into a small house with her three children. She was accommodated in a smaller apartment with poor sanitation. Furthermore, she was bluntly told that she was

---

[20] John S. Mbiti, *African Religions and Philosophy*, Nairobi: East African Educational Publishers, 1999, 106.

not going to be given the same reception that she received while the husband was still alive.[21]

Despite the harsh conditions that this clergy woman had to go through, she never gave up and continued with her ministry, and she is such an inspiration to many who think they cannot make it without a man. Her perseverance is a true testimony of how women suffer discrimination *and* overcome challenges by making a positive change in life.

One of the first challenges an unmarried woman minister meets is that, when it comes to counselling married couples and those that are about to get married in the congregation, many couples wrongly feel that single women clergy cannot perform these duties simply because they do not have the experience of being in marriage. A single clergy reported that she was not consulted on matters to do with marriage, and that some congregants would rather seek counsel from older women than from a single woman clergy as they believed that a single [female] clergy cannot provide any advice. They see her as *"Chipelelo,"* meaning (in Bemba) someone who has no moral standing and knows nothing about marriage. Even beyond counselling, some congregants do not show respect because they feel that a person who is not married is inexperienced and cannot offer any a tangible solution to anything.

Such rejection and discrimination is not only experienced by female clergy, but even by her children. They need to display the highest standard of morals as society will judge them saying "What do you except of a child without the counsel of a father." This statement is rather abusive to any single mother, and even more so to a female pastor. The child of a single clergy is judged in the same manner as a minister.

---

[21]   *Women of the Collar.* Council of Churches in Zambia, 2015, 14.

An additional challenge is that it is extremely difficult for a single clergy to confide in other clergies or any other person in times of crises. Female clergies are limited with whom they can share their struggles and grievances with.

With reference to all the testimonies and stories given on the challenges of single mother clergies, it is evident that single mothers who are clergies are often rejected and discriminated against. In view of this, they need the congregation's support spiritually, emotionally, financially and physically. This is to ensure that they do not go into isolation, resign from the ministry and go astray or even fall into depression contemplating suicide.

By listening to the testimonies and stories told by the single women, it is evident that indeed single clergy mothers suffer discrimination and rejection in the social, cultural and religious spheres of their daily lives. Although these women have experienced such horrific treatment, they have become strong and have moved forward in life. It has also been discovered that the single mothers still offer very good leadership skills in various congregations they are assigned to, and the good thing is that all the ordained women have managed to overcome the challenges and are still in ministry.[22]

My Own Experience

This is an account of my own experience as a clergy who has been in ministry for a period of 5 years. I am a single mother of two children, 16 and 14 years, my husband died before I went into ministry. I have

---

[22] To compare: Mercy Chilapula, in her study of the female ministers of CCAP Blantyre Synod that all 18 female ministers ordained since the beginning 2001 are still in the Church's ministry (Mercy Chilapula, "A Cry for Inclusion – Experiences of Women Clergy in the Church of Central Africa Presbyterian (CCAP) Blantyre Synod," PhD [submitted], Mzuzu University, 2021).

suffered at the hands of both male and female parishioners, and of both male and female clergies.

Coming from a patriarchal background, I should explain that, as a single mother, I had no place in the church because a woman in most cases is regarded as a non-performer. Some male lay leaders in the church may take up a leadership role leaving the female minister out of any decisions, keeping the upper hand and disregarding her. This means that I had to push my way through for my voice to be heard. As a consequence, some members [women and men] walked out of the church.

I also experienced that people have more respect for male clergy than for female clergy. Even the way they would address a female minister is different from how they would address a male clergy. Sometimes women will treat you with more disrespect than men as they would expect you to cook and clean when there are church meetings and even want you to sleep at a member's funeral, which is never the case with a male clergy.

I was informed that some members, especially my fellow women, were very uncomfortable when they learnt that in their congregation a female minister was succeeding a male minister. When some big assignments came, they preferred to hire a male minister for fear of their female minister mismanaging the congregational funds. To the female members, a male minister could do the job better than a female. When I insisted on my involvement, some women hoped the project would fail.

I give a practical example of how I was viewed immediately after I arrived at my first station in my ministry. Some members of the congregation went as far as shunning me, saying, "*I naturally hate or dislike female ministers, especially that she is single and has no husband. We need to safeguard our husbands.*" Such comments came from fellow women and congregants who believed that I had actually been stationed there to have intimate relationships with their husbands. This was really hurtful, but I knew God had placed me there for a purpose, maybe to listen to what some people were really thinking about me, and such words were even said before they had ever met me.

My experience as a single clergy has been very painful in the sense that there are times where people would slander my name without them even confronting me on the issues or finding out the truth of whatever they suspected. This was painful, considering that many single mothers who are not even ordained clergies go through the same kind of ill-treatment.

The biggest challenge that I encountered as a single female clergy were speculations from church members when I was given a lift by any male members, as by the end of the day the news would spread that I, the minister, was having an affair with whoever assisted me with a lift. It seems like a single clergy can go out with anyone in the congregation.

The other experience I encountered was that I was always being monitored, and that my character as a single minister was always questioned by members. Some congregants even thought I was promiscuous and stated that I was free with all men because of being single.

Single women are vulnerable in the sense that there are men who really want to take advantage of them regardless of what status and position they hold in the society. There are men who treat women as pieces of trash. Some men will never offer assistance without making demands and receiving something in return. From experience, there are men who have no respect for women which can be attributed to the social, cultural or even religious influences of society.

I even experienced blackmail as men tend to take advantage of a woman's vulnerability. One example was when I had asked for some financial support for the church and this man promised to assist us as a church, but only if I submit myself to his demands of sleeping with him. When I declined his proposal, he openly refused to assist the church. Afterwards, I thought that if I had submitted myself to his demands, he would have destroyed my reputation as a clergy and the good name of the church.

I also experienced that a female clergy has no privacy in the sense that she is always monitored. Some church members call at any time after hours only to check on the female clergy, and they would want to visit even after hours in the night. Some seemed to think that I should work without ever resting. Sometimes I questioned whether they would be checking up on me and had such expectations if I had been married.

A single clergy mother is the subject of much gossip and conversation amongst church and community members. A female minister should never dress smartly or wear make-up. Some church members feel threatened by the way I dress, starting with my hair style, cosmetics and the accessories I wear. Some members even want to prescribe the type of clothes that are permissible for a female minister. People forget that clergies are drawn from all walks of life and abrupt change is not easy and it is up to people to accept the way clergy dress. It is imperative to note that the world is dynamic and everything in fashion is moving with time.

The other challenge that I faced was to counsel couples who were having marital disputes as they didn't want to consult with me on any of their problems. The most common responses I got were: "She has never been married before [not even true in my case], what is she going to tell us? What right does she have to interfere in our own marital problems?" These were some of the responses from the congregants of the UCZ members at the first station where I worked as a single mother and clergy.

I would not take offense at people's reactions but attributed them to our Zambian culture which does not recognize someone who is single as being qualified enough to give any kind of counsel to those who are married.

In many cases, married women who are supposed to support single women are actually the ones who discriminate against them, as they are insecure about their husbands. For example, one of my roommates at college avoided introducing me to her husband because I was single and she gave the excuse that her husband dislikes single ladies. We stayed in the same room for two years and she didn't allow her husband to set eyes on me.

Conclusion

It is worth noting that most single mother clergy have really made it in terms of education and putting food on the table for their families. The Church, particularly our United Church of Zambia, which is one of the largest denominations in the country, should embrace widows and single mothers. However, the church cannot do this on its own, and since the UCZ has the most organized structures, sections, congregations, consistories, presbyteries and the Synod, she should engage in teachings of how our Lord Jesus embraced women in the Bible. This is not to say that the UCZ should embrace or condone pregnancy outside of marriage, but the church should involve the youth in leading sectional services or any other projects that the youth may want to take ownership of. The youth and widows should be encouraged to be proactive in all church matters.

Single motherhood should be studied, especially since it is so prevalent. I wish to stress that if people come across this chapter, they may conclude that it is coming from a bitter heart or out of insecurity from those who are married, but this is not the case. It is simply to highlight some of the challenges that single mothers who are clergy go through. Single mothers are discriminated and rejected, but they deserve support in the cultural, social and religious spheres.

Chapter Ten

Re-writing the Story of Ordination of Women: My Story as the First Ordained Woman in the Reformed Church of Zambia

Rose Mulowa

Introduction

Ordination and theological education for women in Africa is one of the main issues that the Circle for Concerned African Women Theologians has been addressing since its inception.[1] Although this battle has essentially been won, in most of the churches the process has been slow and painful. For example, the Reformed Church of Zambia only accepted women for ordination in 2000, a hundred years since the church's establishment. While this can be celebrated as a victory for women and the church, the struggle to belong is still far from over for these ordained women. In this chapter, I have chosen to tell the story of my journey to ordination. Women's experience is the starting point for gender analysis both in the church and in society.[2] Hence, sharing this story in this book is another journey that I hope will be shared with many African women theologians struggling in the world of patriarchy.

---

[1] For its history see: Rachel NyaGondwe Fiedler, *The History of the Circle of Concerned African Women Theologians, 1989-2007*, Mzuzu: Mzuni Press, 2016.

[2] Pamela D. Young, *Feminist Theology/Christian Theology: in Search of Method*, Minneapolis: Fortress, 1990.

Proposals for the Ordination of Women in the Reformed Church in Zambia

In 1999 the Reformed Church in Zambia celebrated 100 years of its existence. During that year several activities were planned to celebrate this event and it included an extraordinary synod held at Katete Boarding High School. For a long time, the church faced a number of challenges which included that no women were being ordained as pastors. A submission came through synod on whether time had not come that women should be ordained as pastors. A committee was elected to debate the issue and bring a report during the plenary. Having attended that synod, I remember during plenary when the report was read and how the delegates felt it was not the right time for women to be ordained as ministers of the word and sacrament. One male clergy stood up and said:

> If we have no more issues to discuss on the agenda, let us close the meeting and disperse. We did not come here to discuss kitchen work and may I add *iyo funso isakabwelenso* (that question should not be allowed again to synod). We say no to women's ordination.

Synod is the highest body which comprises of delegates chosen by a congregational elders' council. Each congregation sends one elder who should actively be in charge of a section. He, together with the minister of a congregation, most of whom are male, attends the synod meeting which meets once every two years. Its main objective is to make resolutions on the running of the church and to discuss issues relating to the constitution and policies of the church. Keeping up with change, the Reformed Church constitution was under evaluation by 1999. At that synod there were no female elders, thus the synod only comprised of male delegates.

When I was trying to ask why this was so, one of the ministers, who was once a moderator of the Reformed Church in Zambia, told me that it was unheard of for a woman to attend synod. He gave an example of one synod meeting of 1985, when the council suspended its discussions because a female representative had attended as an observer. The meeting only resumed after this woman was asked to leave the meeting. The woman was working as a lecturer at Justo Mwale Theological College. Susan Rakoczy argues that:

> The exclusion of women from ministry and decision making in most of the churches represents the power of the Christian tradition's teachings that women are not fully the image of God, they lack true equality with men, are seductive and dangerous, weak on intellect and will. These teachings have provided the basis for the denial of women's gifts for ministry and leadership in the church.[3]

Susan Rakoczy continues by saying for the church to be the body of Christ it needs to be all embracing, otherwise it remains only _looking_ like the body of Christ.[4]

The System Challenged

In 1994, women were allowed to become elders and deacons after the issue had been under discussion for many years. Before then, women were restricted to church women's groups known as Chigwirizano cha Zimai mwa Ukristu (Unity of Women in Christ). Their presence could only be seen by their uniforms. Even after the resolution to include women in leadership, the church was often still not happy to elect them to become elders or deacons. Often men were preferred since they were said to have a better ability to lead than women. It took time for the church to start accepting women leadership in the church. As Isabel Phiri states, the negative responses towards women leaders by both men and women are based on

---

[3] Susan Rakoczy, _In Her Name: Women Doing Theology_, Pietermaritzburg: Cluster, 2004, 199.

[4] Ibid, 199.

people's ideas of the image of women in Christianity and culture, both of which have been shaped by patriarchal ideas.[5]

Some of the identified barriers that restrict the enhancement of women include socially and culturally constructed ideas that are embedded both in Christian traditions through the teachings of the early fathers such as that women are seen as weaker than men, misinterpretation of biblical texts, stereotype views such as that women are less dedicated to their careers than men and that they are unwilling to make tough decisions. Church members also felt that women were less skilled than men and that they were too emotional. These are some of the ideas that need to be challenged as Mercy Amba Oduyoye says "God cannot be said to have brought into being one variety of humanity that is inherently not up to the mark."[6]

By the year 2000, the topic on women's ordination became a hot debate. Proposals to allow women into ministry were sent to synod. The women's fellowship, Chelston Presbytery in Lusaka, was one of the groups of women that moved the motion. After careful debate and reflection, with a majority vote, the 21st synod conference at Mphangwe congregation held 21st-25th of August 2000, took up the challenge of allowing women into the ministry of word and sacrament. I remember being at Kabwata Presbyterian Church where I was doing my practical work when the news reached me. Reverend Edwin Zulu, the then vice principal of Justo Mwale Theological College, announced the news to me. I was overwhelmed with excitement, coupled with a lot of fear of what that meant for me. Towards my graduation in November that year, I was called and informed that I had to accompany other students to a youth centre,

---

[5] Isabel Apawo Phiri, *Women, Presbyterian and Patriarchy*, Blantyre: CLAIM-Kachere, 1997, 117.

[6] Mercy A. Oduyoye, *Daughters of Anowa: African Women and Patriarchy*, Maryknoll: Orbis, 1995, 181.

where the Synod's executive committee was meeting. On the agenda was the issue of postings for the graduating students. Three of us women who had completed theological studies were waiting to be assigned congregations. However, only two of us, namely Rose Malowa (myself) and Mrs Monica Banda were assigned congregations. The process was such that we had to choose our congregations by names that were put into a basket and we were to pick one paper that had a name of a congregation. I picked mine and it read Chitoola Congregation, a rural congregation in the far eastern part of Zambia. One of the ministers chosen by the council stood up to give us words of encouragement:

> _Ichi ndicho munali kufuna ndipo takulolani tsopano pitani mukazionele nokha kaya mukakwanitsa koma muzafunika mukaonetse kukwanista kwake"_ (This is what you have been fighting for and now we have allowed you, so go and prove yourselves).

Following this kind of attitude by men, Mercy Amba Oduyoye warns that for some women asking for ordination is like asking to be co-opted into the ranks of the oppressor until the concept and purpose of ministry changes.[7] I had to choose how to handle this situation; to either be aggressive, or respond calmly with love. I decided not to be bitter but to show that God will use me to His glory.

Petronella Simango Ndlovu: Pioneer for Inclusion of Women in Ministry

In every history of women's movements there is a woman who stands out as having made a difference. In the history of the emergence of feminist theology, we read of Christine de Pizan (1365-1430) who fought for the liberation of women. Her focus was for women to be

---

[7] Ibid.

recognized as truly human and made in the image of God.[8] In this section, I wish to bring to your attention the women who played a pivotal role in the fight against the church's negative response to the ordination of women. From the onset, I must make mention that the church never allowed women to study theology. The first person that challenged the system and broke the walls of resistance to allow women to study theology was the late Petronella Simango Ndlovu who was born on the 9th March 1964. She was the seventh born daughter of the late Micheal Musiwa Simango and the late Mrs Simbisai Gumbo. Petronella trained as a teacher at Malcom Moffat Teachers Training College where she trained as a Home Economics and Christian Education teacher, as these were the most common career paths for women at tertiary level at that time.

After one year of working as a school teacher, she got married to Reverend Japhet Ndlovu and they were blessed with one son, Chitonthozo. After working as a pastor's wife and a school teacher for a while, she began to question why there were no female clergy in the church. She got so upset when she discovered that women were not even allowed to study theology. As a way of challenging the system she decided to offer herself to undertake theological education by enrolling in an entirely male dominated seminary. Through much struggle and with the help of Reverend Foston Dziko Sakala, the principal at the time, she was allowed to sit in a male dominated class which was a very courageous move. This did not mean that at the end of her studies she would be ordained but she was admitted on condition that after completion, she would use her knowledge to enhance her skills in teaching Christian Religious Education in schools. This is one of the challenges that most African women who studied theological education during this era faced. Women were enrolled for theological education to either take up the

---

[8] Annie A. Clifford, *Introducing Feminist Theology*, Maryknoll: Orbis, 2001.

teaching of Bible Knowledge in schools or as administrators in theological colleges. Petronella did her best to prove to her fellow male classmates and staff that she was the best student in all the subjects during the entire twelve semesters. At her graduation she graduated with a distinction.

Her Influence as a Female Student at the College

The very fact that there was a female theological student began to send negative shock waves about her presence in the seminary. Negative fatalism took shape as conservatives were very angry with having a female studying theology. However, amidst such negative attitude, there were some who encouraged her to stay focused on her goals. The partners of the Reformed Church in Zambia from the Netherlands partnered with the college and gave her a full scholarship to do her undergraduate degree. This partnership brought money into the college and she became the only female student who helped to bring funding into the college because of her studies. This opened a few doors for other female students who intended to study. Others that came after Petronella were Mrs Ruth Chakumika, Mrs Chipeta and Mrs Monica Banda who were all pastor's wives. Petronella never lived to see the ordination of women. She passed away in the week that the church had passed a resolution to start ordaining women (May her soul rest in peace). She provoked debates about the ordination of women and became the pioneer and a role model to those that continued to aspire to becoming ordained. She viewed scripture in the light of the Holy Spirit that was not sexiest and argued that God gives the gift of the Holy Spirit to whoever he wishes, whether male or female, and in equal measure.

My College Experience

At the age of 21 I decided to study theology and enrolled at Justo Mwale Theological College in 1998 as the first single woman student. I was a member of Chelston congregation of the Reformed Church in Zambia. When l made my application to study theology, the elders' council approved my application. During this intake, I was the only female student in a class of nine. I can remember some of the male students asking me whether there was no other career outside theology that would suit me rather than competing with the men. As we progressed with our studies, I could sense that most male students couldn't handle the fact that I was studying with them. As if that was not enough, their wives also felt insecure. There seemed to be no place where I felt I was accepted, but this did not discourage me as several lecturers encouraged me to persevere. Rev Rian Venter, the then principal of the college, would call me to his office and give me words of encouragement. He believed in me and felt that once I had completed my studies, I would be a great asset to the church. He always reminded me that I had great potential and that, if the church one day decides to ordain women, I was a deserving candidate.

Women Included and Excluded: Field Work Experience

One of the requirements to complete College studies was to do a practical field work several weeks every year in various congregations. Since the church had not yet accepted women to be ordained, women in the Reformed Church were not allowed to do practicals in their own congregations since the issue was still under discussion. As a result, we could only do our practicals in other denominations. So, I did my first practical in a congregation of the Uniting Presbyterian Church in South Africa (UPCSA). In this church, I never experienced discrimination during my time with them as they warmly welcomed me as a minister in training. But when I attended services in my church and sat in the pews, I could still hear patriarchal sermons being preached, and when I returned to the college the atmosphere always reminded me that the ordination of women was still far from happening.

In 1999, Kamwala congregation of the Reformed Church in Lusaka under the leadership of Rev Japhet Ndhlovu was the first church to open doors for female theological students to do five weeks' practical work in their congregation. This was a centenary year as the church was celebrating its 100 years of existence. I want to believe that Rev Ndhlovu had to do a lot of convincing for the elders' council to accept women to do practical work. Mrs Vainess Mwanza and I were the first women to do five weeks' practical work in our own denomination in the history of Zambia. It was memorable, and since most of the members were conservative, I always saw it as a breakthrough for us as women. This was the birth of women's entry into ordination. At the end of the practicals, we were presented with lots of gifts and we understood that we were valued by the congregation despite resistance from certain groups of the leadership.

Congregation Experience: Time for Stationing

During the stationing of ministers, I was posted to a remote area in the Eastern Part of Zambia, west of Petauke at Chitoola congregation. Before I could leave for my base, I went to see Rev Foston Dziko Sakala to get advice on life in a congregation. When he saw me, these were his words:

> "Lord, I thank you that before my death you have made it possible for me see the first woman to be ordained as minister of word and sacrament. Glory and honour be to you God who is from everlasting to everlasting."

As Mercy Amba Oduyoye states, African women theologians are welcome to men's voices in the struggle against patriarchy.[9] At this moment, I felt relieved and assured of my calling knowing that within the body of men there were some who were on our side as we fought the battle for ordination. As we sat in his office, I assured him of how prepared I was for ministry. He later said:

> "God has called you, it is not man, not the church, and not your parents, but God has called you. Depend on him and He shall use you mightily … you are a representative of God and people. Don't allow anyone to look down on you."

Men were also there: Towards a Two-winged Theology

Although the RCZ are patriarchal, especially when it comes to the ordination of women, there are some men who still fight for women. In my journey to ordination, I have mentioned a few names of men who fought alongside us to see to it that even though we operate in contested spaces we still found space to practice theology. Like women at the cross who followed from afar, some of the men in our church did just that. My journey began when I was ordained as the first female minister in the Reformed Church of Zambia on the 7th of January 2001. As Rev Foston Sakala preached at my ordination, he couldn't hide his joy as he explained how he asked God to give him more years to live so that he could see the ordination of the first woman Reverend. He spoke of how he fought for women's ordination when he was the moderator and it kept being rejected and how he kept hoping and believing that one day it would happen. He encouraged the congregants to accept the change stating that it had come from God and not from man.

While at the station, it was not easy for the elders of the Church at Chitoola to begin working with me as a woman. Many questions were

---

[9] Mercy Amba Oduyoye, *Daughters of Anowa: African Women and Patriarchy*, Maryknoll: Orbis, 1995.

raised; for instance, whether my role was any different from the roles of male reverends. They questioned if I would manage to travel long distances, and climbing mountains to visit the sick and the old. Some people made comments like climbing mountains is for men, forgetting that some women used to climb the same mountain when going to their fields. As a young female minister, unmarried and inexperienced to handle congregational matters, there were some members that doubted my capabilities. I remember at some council meeting; some elders asked questions that were not relevant to the subject being discussed, just to test my intelligence and capability.

During my time of service, many people thought I would not survive the harsh conditions of rural settings and the challenges of patriarchy in the church and society even though I served among the Nsenga people whose society is matrilineal and who are led by female chiefs. Even in these societies, men still make decisions on how things are to be administered. As Isabel Phiri puts it "it is very important to make it clear from the outset that matrilineal societies are not matriarchal, although one finds more women with power and authority and more aspects that dignify women in a matrilineal society than in a patrilineal one."[10] Therefore, in this setting, I would argue that although seeing a woman stand up to lead might be normal, when it came to the church, men still felt that they had more power than women. This encouraged me to go the extra mile to prove that God's call to ministry is wholistic and that both men and women are equipped for the ministry in the same way. I had to cycle over 40km to some congregations where I was assigned as a visiting minister. In some cases, I had to walk 22 km to go and give communion. In one of the villages, one man refused to receive communion as it was given

---

[10] Isabel Apawo Phiri, _Women, Presbyterianism and Patriarchy_, Blantyre: CLAIM-Kachere, 1997, 13.

by a female clergy. For him, to do so was sinning before God. While he had no problem being led by female chief, according to his culture, it was against his tradition and culture for a woman to be a reverend and lead a church.

Factors that led to the Resistance to the Ordination of Women

The Reformed Church of Zambia is a traditional church that took a very long time to ordain women in ministry. One of the reasons for the discrimination of women was the misinterpretation of scripture. The early church fathers saw women as sinners that brought death into the world through Eve. Rosemary Radford-Ruether notes some of the positions that are used to justify why women are seen as a danger to society.[11] Musimbi Kanyoro adds that African Christians enter the church with two worlds: "one foot in their culture and other in the culture of the Bible wrapped in the western culture. The two worlds have constructed the identity of a woman as being subordinate to a man."[12] It cannot be emphasized further that women and girls are initiated from childhood and are taught that they are lesser beings than their male counterparts.

The failure to understand the image of God brings imbalances among God's creatures. These imbalances can be seen in structures that exist in hierarchical form and do not encourage women's involvement. Many consider certain positions to be higher in status and that only men can fill these positions. Musimbi Kanyoro states:

---

[11] Rosemary Radford Ruether, *Sexism and God Talk: Towards a Feminist Theology*, Boston: Beacon Press, 1983.

[12] Musimbi Kanyoro, *Introducing Feminist Cultural Hermeneutics: An African Perspective*, New York: Sheffield Academic Press, 2002, 32.

Even if women had to rise to higher positions, the problem still remains that they have to compete with other men and it has become a game of power where everyone wants to dominate over other people.[13]

God's being is by nature relational. It is God's very essence. The true image of God is communion. "Divine nature exists as an incomprehensible mystery of relation."[14] This then strengthens the very existence of human beings to the character of relatedness with God and one another, for we are made to correspond to the gift of diversity. Men and women are to co-exist and celebrate their diversity and differences. This is true *koinonia*. Even with our fallen nature which keeps challenging the existence of humanity, the relationship is renewed through Christ.

Image of God

The definition of the image of God as given by Mercy Amba Oduyoye brings out God as the source of all life and the sustainer and controller of human evolution. "We come from God and we go back to God."[15] This supposes according to Oduyoye that the only theology is one that proposes one divine source of all beings.[16] This describes the state of the environment that exhibits relationship and unity with the creator indicating His presence. Firstly, this represents how humanity is to live with each other, being responsible for where he or she has been placed. Secondly, one feature of the image of God, which Oduyoye implores and propounds, is the act of equality.[17]

---

13 Ibid, 2002.

14 Elizabeth Johnson, *She Who Is*, New York: Cross Road Publ., 1992, 227.

15 Mercy Amba Oduyoye, *Introducing African Women's Theology*, Sheffield: Sheffield Academic Press, 2001, 45.

16 Ibid.

17 Ibid.

17 Ibid.

Oduyoye's argument lies on the ground that God is one who makes us all human and not culture, since all have been created in the same image of God. Oduyoye emphasizes, "That this is God's world, God's realm and sphere of influence has led to women's affirmation of equality before God and in the humanity community."[18] This brings to life the need for co-operation in obedience to God and not man. These factors further challenge Christian theology that has neglected to acknowledge the humanity of women in the image of God revealed in feminine terms. The image of God does not only speak of the equality of humanity, but is made more explicit as it is seen in the light of the Jesus Christ. The image of God in Christ represents the focal point for women's humanity.

Women should not find identity in man and its culture, but in God who is triune. The sacredness of life and interrelatedness are all expressed in the mutuality of relationships. Johnson notes:

> Women are equally created in the image and likeness of God, equally redeemed by Christ, equally sanctified by the Holy Spirit; women are equally involved in the ongoing tragedy of sin and the mystery of grace, equally called to mission in this world, equally destined for life with God in glory.[19]

It encourages celebration of life, especially for women. Life needs to be celebrated but we can only do so if it is free from the sin of patriarchy.

Conclusion

The history of theological education of women and thereafter ordination is one of the main issues that provoked feminist theological movements and the birth of the Circle of Concerned African Women Theologians. Within the history of the Protestant churches, women were allowed to participate in ministry; however,

---

[18] Ibid.

[19] Elizabeth Johnson, *She Who Is*, New York: Cross Road Publishing, 1992, 8.

as Christianity evolved, the ordination of women was restricted. Churches such as the Reformed Church of Zambia were also influenced by their own context and traditions that do not value women leadership. In this chapter, I have demonstrated how women have thrived in these patriarchal spaces by relating my own journey to ministry.

Chapter Eleven

We are Still Few here: An Exploration of Women's Underrepresentation in Theological Higher Education in Zambia

Nelly Mwale and
Maligelita Jofter Njobvu

Introduction

Although the underrepresentation of women in theological education has long been observed in different contexts, it is an area which has not received adequate attention in Zambian scholarship. Therefore, drawing on document analysis of women in theological higher education in Zambia and the female profiles of two Christian universities with a long history in theological education, this chapter explores female representation in theological higher education with specific reference to why women continue to be underrepresented amongst the teaching staff in Zambian theological higher education institutions. This is done by exploring the profile of women teaching theological education in selected Zambian theological higher education and relating the scenario to existing literature on women representation. This inquiry is premised on the fact that despite calls for the advancement of women through their active participation in all spheres of public and private life, including theological education, theological education continues to underrepresent women in different contexts. For example, in 2006, women represented fewer than 10% of chief executive officers in theological higher education institutions in the United States of America, despite the fact that more women were entering the ministry and religion oriented fields.[1] Similarly, Esther Mombo argues that in the African context, it has been observed that despite the overwhelming presence of African women who sustain these churches, men have filled the paid and officially recognized roles of the church and women continue to be restricted to subordinate roles, and their needs are not fully recognized.[2] Isabel Phiri further affirms that women continue to encounter numerous challenges in theological education.[3] In a survey she observed the challenges female theologians faced from 1989 to 2008. She concluded that women faced challenges such as redefining the identity of African women theologians, promoting more women to study theology, more female theologians to be appointed to permanent staff, the inclusion of African women theology in the curriculum, and collaboration with male theologians.

In view of the foregoing research, numerous interventions were made to address the challenges of women in theological education from different perspectives and in different contexts. One of these interventions was to foster women's inclusion in theological education. In Zambia, this translated into opening up theology to women in some institutions of theological education, and women started being ordained in some churches, the notable ones being those with a Reformed tradition. Theological institutions began to welcome women to study and to recruit female lecturers. The irony

---

[1] Mary E. Lowe, "Breaking the Stained-glass Ceiling: Collaborative Leadership Theory as a Model for Women in Theological Higher Education," _Journal of Women in Education Leadership_, 8(3), 2010, 123-141.

[2] Esther Mombo, "The Ordination of Women in Africa: An Historical Perspective," in I. Jones, K. Thorpe and J. Wootton (eds), _Women and Ordination in the Christian Churches: International Perspectives_, New York: T&T Clark, 2008, 123-140.

[3] Isabel Phiri, "Major Challenges for African Women Theologians in Theological Education (1989–2008)," _International Review of Mission_, 98 (1), 2009, 105-119.

was that despite these inclusive changes, women continued to be underrepresented in theological education. Additionally, scholarship of women in Zambia has been preoccupied with women's participation in politics[4] and church leadership[5] to the neglect of theological higher education, hence it became imperative to understand the persistent underrepresentation of women in theological education in post-2010 Zambia.

The chapter shows that despite strides that have been made to increase women's participation in theological education, women continue to be underrepresented, largely due to the lack of mechanisms in place to address the gender imbalance. It advocates for moving beyond women's access to theological education to the issues affecting their ability to fully participate and perform in it in ways that fully engender theological education. By doing so, the chapter hopes to contribute to existing scholarship on gender and theological education in Africa from the Zambian context where the focus had been on the history of theological education or specific programmes within theological education.[6] The chapter unfolds by

---

[4] Ilsa Schuster "Constraints and Opportunities in Political Participation: The Case of Zambian Women," *Genève-Afrique: Acta Africana*, 21(2), 1983, 7-37; Bizeck J. Phiri, "Gender and Politics: The Zambia National Women's Lobby Group in the 2001 Tripartite Elections," in *One Zambia, Many Histories*, Leiden: Brill, 2008, 259-274; Nelly Mwale, "Religion, Gender, and the Media: The Nature and Significance of a Muslim Woman – Sirre Muntanga's Contest for Mayor of Lusaka, Zambia in 2016," *The African Journal of Gender and Religion*, vol. 25(2), 2019, 1-23.

[5] Peggy Mulambya-Kabonde, "Ordination of Women: Partnership, Praxis and Experience of the United Church of Zambia," PhD, University of KwaZulu-Natal, 2014. See also: Jonathan Kangwa, "Resilience and Equality in the Household of God: Peggy Mulambya Kabonde's Search for Justice," *The Expository Times*, 131(8), 2020, 339-347.

[6] Jonathan Kangwa, "The Goodhall-Nielsen Report and the Formation of the United Church of Zambia Theological College," *Studia Historiae Ecclesiasticae*, 43(1), 2017, 1-24; Nelly Mwale and Joseph Chita "Navigating through Institutional

highlighting the approach to gender and theological education before exploring the emerging themes from the underrepresentation of women in theological higher education in Zambia

Approach to Gender and Theological Education

Gender refers to socially constructed and culturally defined differences between women and men, and it identifies the relationship between the genders in terms of power relations.[7] Engendering theological education in Africa has taken different forms, which included encouraging women to study theology, which had been the domain of men owing to the manner in which scripture was used, supported by what was conceived as African culture.[8] It also meant removing the link between theological education, ordination and churches.

Engendering theological education is based on challenging traditional assumptions that have characterized it such as western theological models, African patriarchy, or male-centered theologies, and it seeks alternatives that are inclusive.[9] Engendering theological education

---

Identity in the Context of a Transformed United Church of Zambia University College in Zambia," *HTS Theological Studies*, 73(3), 2017, 1-8; F.D. Sakala, "A Study of the History of Theological Education in the Dutch Reformed Church Mission in Zambia and its Role in the Life of Zambian Christianity," UNISA, 1996; J.M. Chizelu "Theological Education by Extension: A Missiological Analysis of the Association of Evangelicals of Africa and Madagascar TEE Programme from a Zambian Perspective," MA, UNISA, 1997.

[7] Beverly Haddad, "Engendering Theological Education for Transformation," *Journal of Theology for Southern Africa*, 116, 2003, 65-80.

[8] A Discussion with Esther Mombo - St Paul's University, Berkley Centre for Religion, Peace and World Affairs, 16 April, 2005.

[9] Beverly Haddad, "Engendering Theological Education for Transformation," *Journal of Theology for Southern Africa*, 116, 2003, 65-80.

involves the transformation of both the structures of theological education and the teaching programme.[10] Gender discrimination is manifested in the theological curriculum, in models, contents and in the structure of theological institutions, and equally so in the appointment of teaching faculty that has consequences upon the ministry of the churches.[11]

Context of Gender and Theological Education in Zambia

This inquiry on women representation among theological educators must be situated in the wider history of theological education in Zambia. Before the attainment of independence, theological education was usually aligned to the missionary groups that introduced Christianity into the country and established Bible schools. In this form of theological education, women were left out, as theological education was a domain for men only. After independence, there were shifts in theological education, especially with regards to rethinking the relevance of theological education that was inherited from Christian missionary models and contexts. This resulted in revisiting aspects such as 'recruitment, training, conditions of service for ministers, effective use of Christian ministry and the availability of theological education in most African countries.'[12] In Zambia, this translated into opening doors to women in theological education. For example, the United Church of Zambia's theological college whose origins go back to the London Missionary Society in 1949,[13] witnessed the training and ordination of female ministers

---

[10] Ibid.

[11] Limatula Longkumer, "Feminist Theological Pedagogy for Ministerial Formation," *Bulletin of the Program Area on Faith Mission and Unity*, XXII (2), 2006,1-2.

[12] Esther Mombo, "Theological Education in Africa," *Ministerial Formation* 89, 2000, 39-45.

[13] Jonathan Kangwa, "The Goodhall-Nielson Report and the Formation of the United Church of Zambia Theological College," 84; Nelly Mwale and Joseph Chita,

between 1980 and 1991. This landmark opened avenues for women not only to be admitted as students but also to become teaching staff.

Women representation in theological higher education is also situated in a changing theological higher education context in post-1990 Zambia, which raised the question of the vision and purpose of theological education.[14] In Zambia, this translated into the emerging trend of transforming Bible schools and theological colleges into universities with broadened scope of programmes on offer in a quest for survival and relevance. Thus, unlike in pre-1990 Zambia, when theological education was offered in Bible schools, seminaries and colleges, it is now offered in church-affiliated universities (often denominational in character), and also in state or public universities. In this case, theological education is being offered alongside other disciplines. This signalled that theology had become a significant marker for Christian universities.[15]

The underrepresentation of women in higher theological education is further situated in the institutional context of two Christian universities of the Reformed tradition with a long history of theological education in the country. One is rooted in evangelicalism (a post-independence establishment), the Evangelical University. The Evangelical University is a private Christian accredited university which exists as a ministry of the Evangelical Fellowship of Zambia. It was founded in 1960 by Africa Evangelical Fellowship (AEF)

"Navigating through Institutional Identity in the Context of a Transformed United Church of Zambia University College in Zambia," 1-8.

[14] Marilyn Naidoo, "Persistent Issues Impacting on the Training of Ministers in the South African Context," *Scriptura: Journal for Contextual Hermeneutics in Southern Africa*, 112(1), 2013, 1-16.

[15] Robert Benne, *Quality with Soul: How Six Premier Colleges and Universities Keep Faith with their Religious Traditions*, Grand Rapids: Eerdmans, 2001.

under the name Bible College of Central Africa (BCCA) in order to address the need for Bible taught preachers. When the Evangelical Fellowship of Zambia took up ownership of the institution in 1980, it became known as the Theological College of Central Africa (TCCA) until the college acquired university status in 2014. In 2015, the name of the institution changed to Evangelical University.[16] The second institution of interest is anchored on ecumenical liberalism (a pre-independence establishment), the United Church of Zambia University College. The history of this university has been documented.[17] These institutions both transformed into universities after 2010. They offer theology programmes from diploma to bachelor's and master's degrees, and admitted women alongside men as both students and staff. While the two institutions were purposively selected for historical reasons, this selection was not for purposes of generalization but for providing a window through which the presence of women in teaching positions in theological education could be understood.

The profile of women in theological higher education at the two institutions revealed that despite nondiscriminatory recruitment guidelines being in place, women in teaching positions in theological education were few. The United Church of Zambia University had only one female theological educator on permanent tenure, while the Evangelical University had none (women theological educators were

---

[16] For a comprehensive history of the university, see Bickson Bulanda, Mission Studies in Zambia: An Investigation of Curricula and Attitudes in Selected Bible Colleges, MA, London School of Theology and Middlesex University, 2018; www.evangelicaluniversity.ac.zm.

[17] See Jonathan Kangwa, "The Goodhall-Nielsen Report and the Formation of the United Church of Zambia Theological College," *Studia Historiae Ecclesiasticae*, 43(1), 2017, 1-24; Nelly Mwale and Joseph Chita, "Navigating through Institutional Identity in the Context of a Transformed United Church of Zambia University College in Zambia," *HTS Theological Studies*, 73(3), 2017, 1-8.

recruited on part time basis) as of April 2020. While this pointed to the inclusion of women as part of the teaching staff and the increased role for women in theological education, it also cannot be disputed that more needed to be done. Such underrepresentation could be explained from different perspectives in post-2010 Zambia that reveal the need for rethinking approaches towards women's full access to women's participation as members of the faculty in theological higher education.

Historical and Cultural Reasons

Women were underrepresented in theological education partly because of the historical cultural narratives which made them to remain behind as compared to their male counterparts, as culture deterred women from entering the field of theological education. In a study commissioned by the Jesuit Centre for Theological Reflection, it was observed that:

> Women are not given the opportunity to take up leadership positions either because they are looked down upon that they cannot do anything in leadership … cultural beliefs that men are superior to women affect women …. cultural and traditional practices continue to discourage women to take up their rightful roles and positions in both the church and society.[18]

These observations can also be related to the religio-cultural teachings that have contributed to downplaying women's potentials based on the perception that women are mere helpers and cannot lead, as opposed to men who have been sanctimoniously declared as heads in leadership. These teachings had indirect implications on women's participation as teaching staff in theological education based on the limitations imposed on women to take up leadership positions in different spheres. Gender stereotypes limit women's opportunities

---

[18] Margaret Machila and Matrine Chuulu, *Women's Participation in the Catholic Church in Zambia*, Lusaka: Jesuit Centre for Theological Reflection, 2010, 72-73.

to be appointed to senior positions exacerbated by beliefs that women are not capable, thereby creating low aspirations and limited opportunities for appointment to influential positions.[19]

Peggy Mulambya-Kabonde observed that there were qualified ordained women capable of taking up leadership positions who were nevertheless denied opportunities to perform such duties and that such well-trained women theologians were merely stationed in institutions of learning or sought employment elsewhere where they felt accepted.[20] This was evidenced by the low representation of women in theological higher education. Thus, while some theological education institutions had led the way in training both women and men for ordination, gender responsive representation of theological educators is yet to be achieved.

Other cultural reasons are linked to the social construct that theology was not for women. This made women to lag behind their male counterparts who dominated the field since the start of theological training. For example, in the Dutch Reformed Church Mission in Zambia the first group of people to be given theological education were men.[21] Women could not study theology as it was only for pastors to be, and women could not be pastors. Even in contemporary times often the role of women in churches is perceived as an extension of their home life, where a woman is associated with care and not leadership, so they should not venture into theology, based

---

[19] Lilian Kiefer, "Increasing Influence, Participation of Women in Leadership," *Daily Mail*, 16th October, 2016.

[20] Peggy Mulambya-Kabonde, "Ordination of Women: Partnership, Praxis and Experience of the United Church of Zambia," PhD, University of KwaZulu-Natal, 2014, 4.

[21] Foston Dziko Sakala, "A Study of the History of Theological Education in the Dutch Reformed Church Mission in Zambia and its Role in the Life of Zambian Christianity," PhD, UNISA, 1996.

on the notion that a woman is not to lead but to be led.[22] Similar attitudes were reported by Stellah Mungaila in her study of female pastors in which she observed that female and male pastors were perceived differently by the church community with attitudes towards male pastors being that of the head of the church, and female pastors being thought of as a helper.[23] Even today, there is a persistence of attitudes that women can play any role in the church except leadership.[24]

This attitude has not only contributed to the underrepresentation of women in theological higher education but presented the power of patriarchy. Esther Mombo, who has made a difference to African theological education, recounts that:

> It was not easy for me to be in senior management and a pioneer. I faced challenges from men who did not think that women could lead. I faced challenges from women who did not think women could lead. This was due to the stereotypical roles identified with women which were accepted as ideal.[25]

While the historical cultural realities entailed that there were only a few women from whom the female appointments in theological higher education could have been made, the few women who had progressed that far could well have been appointed to higher

---

[22] Isabel M. Hamabuyu and J. Kafumbe, "Gender Audit of Member Churches of Council in Zambia Consultancy Report," Gender Desk of Council of Churches in Zambia, Lusaka.

[23] Stellah Mungaila, "A Christian Feminist Critique of Pastors' Authority Roles: A Case of Twelve Pentecostal Churches in Lusaka, Zambia," PhD, University of Zambia, 2015, 137.

[24] Isabel M. Hamabuyu and Joyce Kafumbe, "Gender Audit of Member Churches of Council in Zambia Consultancy Report," Lusaka, 2008.

[25] C. Corman, A Discussion with Esther Mombo-St Paul's University, Berkley Centre for Religion, Peace and World Affairs, 16 April, 2005.

theological education, not only to address the historical imbalances but also to transform the structures of theological education as an aspect of engendering theological education. The fact that the historical cultural reasons continued to support the status quo also confirmed the observation by Marilyn Naidoo that theological education institutions did not have the mechanisms of redressing historical injustices and cultural prejudices against women and thus theologians were called upon to adopt liberative hermeneutical paradigms, which would enable Christians to transcend patriarchal domination. This is because the perpetuation of attitudes that have downplayed women's abilities to lead and teach reflect the entrenched patriarchal domination in both society and theological education.[26]

Institutional Reasons

Additionally, institutional structures and facilities contributed to women's low representation in theological education. For a long time, theological education was reserved for men only and so the infrastructure was designed for men, resulting in a limited space for women. For example, Peggy Mulambya-Kabonde recounted that:

> Even after the second, third and fourth women students had been accepted at different times to the UCZ seminary, the basic facilities on campus were still not women-friendly. Indeed, it took more than twenty years for the church to erect facilities that were conducive for co-educational purposes … The absence of facilities at the seminary for many years was a strategy of patriarchy as attested by women who passed through the institution.[27]

---

[26] Marilyn Naidoo, "Persistent Issues Impacting on the Training of Ministers in the South African Context," *Scriptura: Journal for Contextual Hermeneutics in Southern Africa*, 112(1), 2013, 9.

[27] Peggy Mulambya-Kabonde, "Ordination of Women: Partnership, Praxis and Experience of the United Church of Zambia," PhD, University of KwaZulu-Natal, 2014," 4.

Like the historical cultural reasons, the institutional reasons entailed that the recruitment of very few women meant that they remained behind their male counterparts in academic advancements that would enable many of them to take on leadership positions in theological higher education. In spite of this, it can be stated that times had changed and thus women in theological education needed to be afforded an opportunity to not only lead but also make a difference in theological higher education.

Gender Mainstreaming Policies

Despite the positive strides in policies that facilitated women's representation in theological education in Zambia, the scenario could not be compared with secular institutions which had clear gender mainstreaming policies, interventions and benchmarks. Thus, the lack of gender mainstreaming policies continued to contribute to women's underrepresentation in theological higher education. Marilyn Naidoo observed that the South African government has gender policies and has adopted quotas of women participating in decision making at the highest levels, but theological institutions do not have clear gender policies, neither do they have quota allocations for women in the institutional structures.[28] As such, even in the post-2010 context, narratives of institutions not having women in their top leadership and teaching staff persisted in Zambia. This scenario was contrary to the US context in which the Association of Theological Schools in the U.S. and Canada (ATS) reported that women made up about 25% of the deans and 13% of the presidents of theological schools in 2018 and that the number of faculty women in theological education had grown from 20% in 1998 to 24.8% in 2017, and the

---

[28] Marilyn Naidoo, "Persistent Issues Impacting on the Training of Ministers in the South African Context," 1-16.

greatest increase was with full-time professors.[29] The scenario signaled that despite women's advanced, the control and administration of theological higher education was still in the hands of men, and thus points to how church leadership remained male dominated.

The lack of female allocations could also be closely tied to the continued recruitment of women on a part time basis. As observed by Isabel Phiri women faced challenges in theological education which included promoting more women to study theology and be on permanent staff.[30] She observed that 'the disadvantage of not being on permanent employment was that one did not qualify to go on sabbatical leave to concentrate on research and publication, without which a staff member could not progress academically.'[31] Additionally, being appointed on a part time basis could not be detached from low retention of women as they easily opted to go for greener pastures.

Low retention was also linked to highly qualified women's search for spaces that allowed them to excel and where they felt that their contributions and abilities would be recognized. Thus, the absence of women educators in theological education in large numbers and on permanent employment terms could easily point to the fact that theological higher education spaces were yet to be engendered. There is therefore need for theological higher education to move beyond women's access to theological education to issues affecting their

---

[29] Eileen R. Campbell-Read, "Examining Trends in Theological Education for Women Part I," *Ethics Daily*, 7 March, 2019.

[30] Isabel Apawo Phiri, "Major Challenges for African Women Theologians in Theological Education (1989–2008)," *International Review of Mission*, 98 (1), 2009, 105-119; Rachel NyaGondwe Fiedler & J.W. Hofmeyr, "The Birth and Growth of the Circle of Concerned African Women Theologians in Malawi 1989-2011," *Studia Historiae Ecclesiasticae*, 37 (2), 2011, 1-9.

[31] Ibid, 8.

ability to fully participate and perform in theological education in ways that engender theological education.

While the realities surrounding women representation were closely related to conclusions that were drawn on challenges surrounding access of women to theological education, the underrepresentation of women in theological higher education signified that there is still more to be done to engender the structures (in terms of the teaching profiles of women theologians) in theological education.[32] The situation prevailing in the two Christian universities with a long history of theological education shows that contrary to what the Circle of Concerned African Women Theologians had achieved elsewhere as regards playing a major role in promoting more women to study theology and to be on permanent staff in theological institutions,[33] the struggles of women educators in theological education were yet to be addressed in the Zambian context. This would be addressed by fully engendering theological education in terms of its structure through advocacy, curriculum integration, conducive environment and collaborative networks. This would help address the retention of women educators in theological education who continue to experience hurdles in the face of historical gender biases and different emerging shades of the empire in theological higher education.

Conclusion

This chapter explored the underrepresentation of women in theological education. The chapter showed that despite non-discriminatory recruitment criteria, women continue to be underrepresented in theological education in both management and teaching positions. While this scenario was closely tied to historical factors in theological

---

[32] Ibid, 8.

[33] Ibid, 1-9.

education, the historical gender biases continue to deter women's access and full participation in theological higher education. This signifies that the structures of theological education are yet to be engendered. Given that the historical trajectory of women exclusion in theological education at inception entailed that women progression lagged behind their male counterparts and women consequently remained in the minority, including in theological education leadership positions, and that women's representation continued to be shaped by patriarchal attitudes, the chapter advocates for discourses of gender in theological education to move beyond women's access to theological education to issues affecting their ability to fully participate and perform in theological education in ways that engender theological education.

Chapter Twelve

Patriarchy in Theological Education in Zambia: Narrating my Personal Experiences at the Theological College of Central Africa and the United Church of Zambia University

Mary Zulu Mwiche

Introduction

Patriarchy is recognized as a major obstacle to attaining gender equity,[1] and many scholars have shown how systematic and endemic patriarchy is embedded in the structure of society and also in theological education. Given that patriarchy is a social system that is deeply entrenched in almost all societies, this chapter addresses the question of how theological education should be addressing this issue in contemporary society. The chapter takes the view that the foundation of patriarchy is primarily in the understanding of the Church's role to educate. Acknowledging that patriarchy is often seen as a feminist issue and discussed from a gender lens, I use the structuration approach to analyze the primary foundations of education which have perpetuated an endemic system that frowns upon women in theological education. The chapter unfolds by situating patriarchy in missionary education in Zambia, mapping the foundations of theological education, including the development of Protestant theological education (the UCZ University and the Evangelical University). The chapter further engages with my personal experiences of theological

---

1 Sarah J. Tracy, *Qualitative Research Methods*, Chichester: Wiley-Blackwell, 2013, 55.

education in Zambia and my recommendations for the structural and systemic transformation of theological education.

Patriarchy and Missionary Education in Zambia

Patriarchy is an ideology that is detrimental to having gender equality in society. An ideology is a system of ideas and values that reflects on and supports the established order, and manifests itself in everyday actions, decisions and practices, usually without our being aware of its presence.[2] Patriarchy is the best-known form of chauvinism.

> It [patriarchy] represents a system of male authority and privilege, in which men have more social power than women merely as a result of their biological identity. It is found everywhere.[3] .

Patriarchy has been and continues to be a major challenge to the progression of a just society and it is found everywhere; however, the question is, 'was it meant to be the order of society?' Certainly not! Biblical and African foundations of life lived have strong foundations in a complimentary partnership linked to power sharing. That is not to say that the Bible and African worldviews do not have patriarchal tendencies and injustices. Rather, if viewed wholistically, power sharing and partnerships are more the ideal of both worldviews. Patriarchy in education is traced back to the missionary enterprise in institutionalized education. It was a practice of the missionaries wherever they established educational facilities which included the education for women and girls, that they focused on nurturing them as potential wives. Missionaries, as well as colonial administrators, reiterated the view that there was a need to educate women in what they referred

---

[2] Stephen Brookfield, *The Power of Critical Theory: Liberating Adult Learning and Teaching*, San Francisco: Jossey-Bass, 2005, 67-68.

[3] Priya Narismulu, "Teaching Social Justice and Diversity through South African Stories that Challenge the Chauvinistic Fictions of Apartheid, Patriarchy, Class, Nationalism, Ethnocentrism," *Alternation, Interdisciplinary Journal for the Study of the Arts and Humanities in Southern Africa*, 18(2), 2011, 135-158.

to as 'receiving societies' so that they could partner with their husbands, while men were being trained to be an emerging class of 'white collar' professional men.[4] Therefore, it is not surprising that in the earliest institutionalized education offered to girls and women by the missionaries, the curriculum was tailored to focus on domestic science, a home keeping course that included cookery, sewing, home-keeping, general health and hygiene. This education was tailored to reinforce the view that a woman's role was in the kitchen and to please her husband. It assumed that all women are to be married, a view which resulted in unmarried women being frowned upon socially. A classic example of structurally reinforcing the role of women as objects of men's pleasure is evidenced in Mbereshi Girls School, initiated and administered by Mable Shaw between 1914 and 1940. It was founded as a response to the observation by the London Missionary Society (LMS) that there was a need to educate girls to become wives for the young men they were training to be teachers. Sean Morrow records that the LMS saw this need much earlier than Shaw. He records that "the L.M.S deputation that visited the Central African mission in 1913 formalized the policy to be implemented in female education. There were to be:

> 'Boarding Houses rather than Boarding Schools', accommodation on native lines and extracurricular instruction in hygiene, nursing, "native" cooking, sewing and child care, to make the students fit to be wives of Christian men.[5]

Similarly, Chipembi, a girls' school opened by the Primitive Methodist missionaries in 1927, was the first school to offer girls

---

[4] Andrew J. Kirk, *Mission Under Scrutiny: Confronting Current Challenges*, London: Darton/Longman & Todd, 2006.

[5] Sean Morrow, "No Girl Leaves School Unmarried: Mable Shaw and the Education of Girls at Mbereshi, Northern Rhodesia, 1915-1940," *International Journal of African Historical Studies*, 19(4), 1986, 601-635.

education to level 7, or standard VI, equivalent to Munali Boys government run school.[6] Chipembi girl's curriculum, apart from the academics, made domestic science and sex education compulsory, and agriculture science and carpentry skills for boys. The trend to domesticate feminism and patriarchy in the education curriculum continued until the early 1990s. It must be noted in the context of this chapter that theological education for Africans was far-fetched in the *early* missionary enterprise, as their primary concern was to get the people to first learn how to read and write.

Foundations of Theological Education

Seminary theological education has, in the history of the Christian Church, been foundational to its mission. The early Church developed what was then known as Catechetical Schools for the purpose of training an educated clergy who would be able to refute the philosophies and heresies of that age, as well as strengthen the faith of the persecuted. Alexandria was the earliest and most famous of these school.[7] It was through the Catechetical Schools that the early Church developed the Nicene Creed as early as 325 AD, which became the basis of defining the essential characteristics of a universal Christian faith. Postulating the argument that the idea of Western universities was born in Alexandria in Africa, Thomas Oden shows how the academic model of Alexandria became the basis of the European University education system,[8] and that "the unrivalled

---

[6] Peter D. Snelson, *Educational Development in Northern Rhodesia 1883-1945*, Lusaka: Zambia Educational Publishing House, 1974, 117-118.

[7] Kenneth Gangel and Warren Benson, *Christian Education: Its History and Philosophy*, Eugene, Oregon: Wipf & Stock, 1983, 110.

[8] Thomas C. Oden, *How Africa Shaped the Christian Mind: Rediscovering the African Seedbed of Western Christianity*, Centre for Early African Christianity, Downers Grove: IVP, 2010, 1.

library of Alexandria was the model for university libraries all over Europe"[9] ... and that

> it was the intellectual and religious center of the Greco-Roman world. The vast learning community of philosophers, scientists, writers, artists and educators that surrounded the Alexandrian Serapium (temple) of the third century provided the essential archetype of the University for all of medieval Europe.[10]

This shows that this early school system was modelled to educate the male gender.

On the purpose of theological education, Andrew Walls argues that theological education was initially not only intended for raising an educated clergy, but for ordinary people to be able to read and understand the faith that was entrusted to them.[11] He further argues that

> such concentrated and extensive bodies of teachings as the Epistles to the Romans and to the Hebrews were not given as lectures to Divinity students; they were written to be read in the Churches.[12]

He acknowledges Justin the Martyr to be the first theologian who used philosophy and other Greek forms to explain Christ. Justin was schooled at Alexandria, which was the first Catechetical School to become rooted in the Churches' theological education system and a place where inquirers of the Christian faith could become educated before being baptized, itself a symbol of the commitment to the

---

[9] Ibid, 1.

[10] Ibid.

[11] Andrew Walls, "Theological Education from its Earliest Jewish and African Christian Beginnings –Some Currents in the Wider History of Christianity," in I.A. Phiri and D. Werner (eds), *Handbook of Theological Education in Africa*, Oxford: Regnum, 2013, 3.

[12] Ibid, 3.

Christian faith which, in those days, was often associated with martyrdom.[13] This confirms that Church history has many patriarchs as pioneer theologians rather than matriarchs.

Male chauvinism is another manifestation of patriarchy that is almost systemic to theological education. Male chauvinism is the belief that the male gender is superior to the female.[14] For theological education, unfortunately, it is reinforced in ecclesial history and in the interpretation of the scriptures in such a way that the female gender in theological education is considered a 'taboo' in some theological doctrines. I recall an experience while in training at the then Theological College of Central Africa, of a male colleague clearly stating that they would not attend Chapel if I (or any other woman) was the one preaching. It is also my experience, which is not uncommon, to find a woman preacher or pastor being apologetic when tasked with preaching to a congregation, because of such internalized ideas that they are inferior to men.

For this reason, Isabel Phiri argues that the four main challenges women face in theological education are identity, lack of scholarship skills in women, an exclusive gender insensitive curriculum and the attitudes of male theologians. She states that the painful part for women is that the men and women, who enroll in theological education study the same content but in some cases, receive different qualifications, while others get the same qualifications but are assigned to different positions in the Church.[15] Having been trained and served as an employee in two theological institutions, the number of female theological educators was/is disproportionate to their male counterparts. In my time as Administrative Assistant to the Academic

---

[13]   Ibid.

[14]   *English Dictionary*. Scotland: Geddes & Grosset, 1999.

[15]   Isabel Apawo Phiri, "Major Challenges for African Women in Theological Education," in *International Review of Mission*, 2009, 105-119.

Dean at one of the institutions, the only female faculty member was adjunct and was a white missionary. In its curriculum, TCCA had nothing related to gender studies except having a separate programme for the wives of the men being trained, which was called the Wives' Class.[16]

This is affirmed by Priscilla Djomhoue, who observes that theological education has been projected as a right for men only, and that in most institutions in Africa, this is evident in student enrolment and staffing ratios that have very few women.[17] Citing examples from her context, Francophone Cameroon, she concludes that in "Francophone Africa, as far as theological institutions are concerned, we are not aware of writings and discussions, or consultations" that aim to have gender studies included in their curriculum.[18]

Methodological Considerations: Qualitative Structural Approach

Though patriarchy is a system that has definitely influenced the emergence of feminist theories, I use the structural approach to argue how patriarchy is systematically entrenched in theological education. According to Sara Tracy, structuration is a theory noted for its ability to examine action and structure. Among its characteristics is that it draws attention to the relationship between actions of individuals and

---

[16] Mary Zulu Mwiche, "An Evaluation of the Role and Relevance of Theological Training at the Theological College of Central Africa, in Response to the HIV/AIDS Situation in Ndola, Zambia," Honours Project, Pietermaritzburg: University of KwaZulu Natal, 2004.

[17] Priscille Djomhoue, "Mainstreaming Gender in Theological Institutions in Francophone Africa: Perspectives from Cameroon," Isabel Apawo Phiri and D. Werner (eds), *Handbook of Theological Education in Africa*, Oxford: Regnum, 2013.

[18] Ibid.

institutions as critical to the formation of cultures or organization of social systems.[19] Therefore, it "assumes that the speech and practices of individuals tend to reinforce institutional frameworks ... therefore for change or transformation to occur, there is need to consider Giddens theory of 'dialectic of control' which suggests that power of the dominant is dependent on the actions of the less powerful" as they focus on the fringe benefits they get out of the relationship.[20]

In the case of this chapter, the questions that arise are, what are the principal rules and structures that govern theological education? How do the everyday actions, that is, institutional management and administrational structure, policies, and curriculum serve to legitimize, reproduce or resist patriarchal tendencies in the process of theological education? How does the everyday language serve to strengthen or weaken patriarchy in theological education?

The chapter is also informed by my personal narrative in which I reflect on my experiences of patriarchy in theological education. This is supplemented by the thematic analysis of documents which include not only existing literature but also institutional reports, minutes of meetings and websites. To show the causal relationships of actions and practice in theological education, I give below a brief history of the two institutions that formed my theological education.

Protestant Theological Education in Zambia: Foundations of the UCZ University and the Evangelical University

The United Church of Zambia University (UCZU), was founded as a theological education institution in 1949. Jonathan Kangwa attributes its foundations to the early missionaries' conviction that "for Christian evangelization to be successful, it has to go hand in

---

[19] S.J. Tracy, *Qualitative Research Methods*, 2013, 59.

[20] Ibid.

hand with education."[21] Scholars on the history of education in Zambia amplify that the early missionaries to Zambia, then known as Northern Rhodesia, initially trained teacher-evangelists who were given the responsibility of the village schools.[22] Jonathan Kangwa observes that the London Missionary Society was among the first to train native Zambians in theological education to take up ordained ministry, at what was then called the Mbereshi Bible School between 1934 and 1937.[23] At that time, the trend of other missionary organizations was to send people to the Overtoun Institution of the Livingstonia Mission in Nyasaland, particularly those under the Church of Scotland, while those under the Methodist and Reformed traditions were trained at Epworth, either in South Africa or Zimbabwe. With the realization of the need to have a unified mission field identified at the International Missionary Conference of Edinburgh in 1910, the union talks led to the founding of the Kashinda Bible Institute in Mporokoso district of Northern Zambia 1947-1949.[24] In 1962, the college was moved to its present site, the Mindolo Ecumenical Foundation Centre, which was then known as the Mindolo Mission. The college was named the UCZ Theological College at the formation of the UCZ in 1965. In 2012, it was renamed

---

[21] Jonathan Kangwa, "The Goodhall-Nielson Report on the Formation of the United Church of Zambia Theological College," 2017, DOI: http://dx.doi-org110.1715912412-426512/201612001.[30.10.2018].

[22] Peter D. Snelson, *Educational Development in Northern Rhodesia 1883-1945*, Lusaka: Zambia Educational Publishing House, 1974; Bwalya S. Chuba, *A History of Early Christian Missions and Church Unity in Zambia*, Ndola: Mission Press, 2005.

[23] Jonathan Kangwa, "The Goodhall-Nielson Report on the Formation of the United Church of Zambia Theological College," 2017.

[24] Bwalya S. Chuba, *A History of Early Christian Missions and Church Unity in Zambia*, Ndola: Mission Press, 2005, 12.

the UCZ University College, when it registered for the first time under the higher education law of Zambia.[25]

The UCZ envisioned a university that "would provide education which is competitive, value-based and would declare a dividend to the UCZ and best serve our interest of propagating the wholistic gospel of salvation" as per UCZ Synod Minutes, 2011.[26] In its religion and code of conduct, the UCZ University states on its website that

> it is open to any member of the community regardless of their religious persuasion, notwithstanding that the University will operate on the basis of the principles and practices which underline the Christian faith of the University.[27]

The Evangelical University (hereafter EU) was initially established as the Bible College of Central Africa (BCCA) in 1960[28] and was solely used for the training of pastors for the Evangelical Church in Zambia (ECZ).[29] In 1982, the ECZ handed over the property and mandate of training its pastors to the Evangelical Fellowship of Zambia (EFZ), thereby making its theological training interdenominational and more academic. To this end, the name changed to Theological College of Central Africa (TCCA). In 1986, TCCA was accredited by the Accrediting Council for Theological Education in Africa (ACTEA), a recognition that made it offer post-secondary qualifications at

---

[25] Zambia's Higher Education Act of 2011, www.hea.org.zm.

[26] The United Church of Zambia, The UCZ Synod Minutes of the Executive Meeting held in April 2011.

[27] *The Theological College of Central Africa 2004-2005 Prospectus*, Ndola: The United Church of Zambia University (www.uczuniversity.org).

[28] Helen B. Mark, *The Wind of His Power: A Skeletal Sketch of the History of the Africa Evangelical Fellowship, formerly the South Africa General Mission*, Cape Town: AEF, 1963, 60.

[29] Mary Zulu Mwiche, "An Evaluation of the Role and Relevance of Theological Training at the Theological College of Central Africa, in Response to the HIV/AIDS Situation in Ndola, Zambia.

diploma and degree level in three main majors; missions, education and pastoral theology.

TCCA transitioned from a theological college to a university under Zambia's Higher Education Act in 2014, and changed its name to Evangelical University in 2015.[30] Despite the transition, the Evangelical University affirms its commitment to theological education based on Evangelical doctrine. This was evidenced in its prospectus, where it states that "as we transition, we remain committed to our mission to equip men and women for the ministry with academic excellence and contextual relevance."[31] The mission of the TCCA/EU is:

> to train men and women at the post-secondary level in theology and education which is Bible-based, relevant to the African context and evangelical in character, in order that they will grow in their love for God and their neighbors ... " based on 2 Timothy 2:2.[32]

From their mission statement, it can be deduced that the Evangelical University's motivation for theological education is evangelism and discipleship. It seeks to impact on the students' character with sound doctrine in order that they themselves are disciples of Jesus Christ, obedient to His commands, and equipped to serve the world. TCCA boasts that almost 100% of its alumni are serving in the Church, with

---

[30] www.evangelicaluniversity.ac.zm/about-us.

[31] *The Theological College of Central Africa 2004-2005 Prospectus*, Ndola: The United Church of Zambia University (www.uczuniversity.org).

[32] Ibid. The new mission statement (Strategic Plan 2019) reformulated this: "We are an evangelical university that exists to glorify God in providing integral transformative, Bible-based training in theology and other disciplines to serve the church and community using contextual, innovative and contemporary approaches for local and global impact."

NGOs, in education and in the mission field, with a sense of the inculcated mission of the College.

Patriarchy in Theological Education: Historical and Social Cultural Foundations

The historical foundations of theological education and the subsequent background formation of UCZU and EU indicate that patriarchy is subtly institutionalized in theological education. The historical foundations show that patriarchy was assumed in the very foundations of Church education. The school system was created for men and history shows that women were considered for education only as 'aides' to men. The missionary enterprise was blunt about it as is evidenced in the case of the LMS at Mbereshi.

Snelson observes the socio-cultural opposition to educating girls, by stating of colonial education that

> parents remained generally unconvinced of the value of or relevance of education for their daughters. The girls themselves often saw little point in going to school, and preferred to stay at home helping their mothers and preparing themselves for marriage.[33]

Furthermore, he notes that parents and grandparents genuinely feared that education would spoil their daughters for marriage purposes. First there was the fear that they might be interfered with by the teacher. Secondly, and more importantly, they might no longer be willing to accept women's traditional place in society, and prove a disruptive influence. Mable Shaw of Mbereshi highlighted some of the mistakes into which an educated girl might fall when she wrote to the director in 1933, that

> One of the finest of our girls got into trouble not too long ago because she unthinkably corrected her husband while he was reading. He was furious at

---

[33] Peter D. Snelson, *Educational Development in Northern Rhodesia 1883-1945*, 1974, 214.

being corrected by a woman. I have had a complaint from the young men that the girls do not learn respect in school; some of them when married do not kneel when giving water and food to their husbands. In school we insist on the polite form of offering and receiving in two hands. I do not feel inclined to insist on the kneeling, although I am prepared to advise girls leaving to be married to preserve this old custom if the husband wishes it.[34]

A clash of two cultures! Theology, as it is with education, has been accused of having been brought to Africa in the context of European culture. These historical foundations raise the question why the early Church fathers chose to institutionalize patriarchy in education which subsequently affected theological education. Secondly, the historical foundations help us to understand the nature of institutionalized patriarchy that we are dealing with today. In the past, human societies were embedded in cultural-traditional norms that gave them an identity and a sense of communal belonging. Communities were closed to outside influences unlike today where the world is a global village and no one culture can claim to be absolute.

Today, human societies are connected socially, culturally, economically, politically and even in the religious space. Such a connectedness, socially referred to as globalization, has brought to the fore gender inequalities that traditional social systems were not created for. However, because identity is linked to one's socialization, the gender inequalities are glaringly brought to our attention in the wake of other socialization processes, such as global institutional education. Therefore, my argument is that patriarchy in theological education is both historical and socio-cultural. However, in the view that societies have evolved into a global village, with developments that have seen the emergence of women as equal to the task of men in many industrial and social fields, the Church, as the custodians of theological education, and as an institution of social justice must be

---

[34] Ibid, 214.

seen to take the lead in promoting gender justice in the way it educates, and more so at secondary or postgraduate level of theological education.

My Personal Experience of Theological Education

Growing up in a youth fellowship at a Protestant congregation in Zambia in the early 1990s, it was strongly impressed on me that theological education was a sure way of falling from grace! In the context of the youth fellowship and the congregation of which I was a member, there was in those days an understanding that theological education was too 'secular' and that most people that had gone in for training as seminarians, came out not with the usual fervour that they had as 'theologically untrained' believers in Christ. In Zambia, where Christianity is officially recognized as the national religion,[35] there is a distinct understanding of who a believer in Christ ought to be, marked with a sense of being filled with the Holy Spirit. Furthermore, there is an understanding that theological education, which is offered in a seminary, is meant for those that seek to be ordained in the ministry of the church. It is unusual for a 'lay person' to undertake theological studies without the sense of being 'called'. However, some Protestant churches do offer basic theological education to laity through the Theological Education by Extension (TEE) programme.

With this understanding of theological education, I was not prepared to experience that this area of study is reserved for men. In my undergraduate studies (1996-1999) at the then Theological College of Central Africa (TCCA) in Ndola, Zambia, my class consisted of four ladies against nine or so men. According to the tradition of TCCA,

---

[35] Zambia constitutionalized Christianity as its official religion in 1996. The current constitution amended in 2016, states in its preamble that "We, the People of Zambia: Acknowledge the Supremacy of God Almighty; Declare the Republic a Christian Nation, while upholding a person's right to freedom of conscience, belief and religion." See www.ilo.org.docs.

we were then the largest number of female students in the regular class in the history of the institution. Gender imbalance was systematically institutionalized in that the wives of male students (for those that were married were required to come with their families) had their own class called "wives' class," where the wives were taught the basics of theological education "to prepare them to for marriage as good pastors' wives"[36] Therefore, those of us that went to study 'proper theology' (as it were), were often reminded that we could not do 'pastoral theology' as this was meant for the men (_sic_) that were being prepared to take up pastoral charges of ecclesial ministry. In those days, TCCA's curriculum had three main strands: Pastoral, Mission and Christian Education. Coming from a teaching background, I majored in Christian Education.

Looking back to my choice of major study, and with the understanding of how gender roles are shaped by society, I am convinced that my choice of majoring in Christian Education was religiously and socially constructed.

In my study of "An Evaluation of the Role and Relevance of Theological Training at the Theological College of Central Africa, in response to the HIV and AIDS situation in Ndola, Zambia", I observed that the TCCA set up was not gender sensitive.[37] In fact, to talk about gender was viewed as being liberal in thought. This conclusion was made in light of findings that TCCA had no HIV policy and that they felt it did not need to include one it in its

---

36 _TCCA Curriculum Framework_, TCCA: Ndola, 2013; see also The Council of Churches in Zambia, _Testimonies of the Women Theologians: Stories from the Heart_, Lusaka: CCZ, 2011.

37 Mary Zulu Mwiche, "An Evaluation of the Role and Relevance of Theological Training at the Theological College of Central Africa, in Response to the HIV/AIDS Situation in Ndola, Zambia."

curriculum and that such an inclusion would need to take into consideration gender for it to be implemented effectively. TCCA's doctrinal and philosophical position is shrouded in the evangelical doctrine of "women should not lead men." This belief is shaped by its institutional founders, the Evangelical Church in Zambia,[38] and the principal owners, the Evangelical Fellowship in Zambia, who hold strongly against women having authority over men or leading them. It must be noted here that the Evangelical Church in Zambia are major stakeholders in the Evangelical Fellowship of Zambia. Therefore, it can be concluded that having founded the theological training institution, the traditions and doctrines believing in the inferiority of women have continued to permeate TCCA's, now the Evangelical University's, theological education.

I came to the UCZ Theological College, as it was called then, in 2006, as a requirement for seeking to serve in the ordained ministry of the UCZ Church. Much as I was a member of the UCZ, my theological formation had been very evangelical due to my studies at TCCA as shared above. Looking back today, I must confess I had naïve expectations of the UCZ's formation ministry in that I knew that it ordained women and had seemingly no problems with accepting us into the ministry. However, in the class of 2006 and the subsequent streams, I observed that women were less than a third of the total number. The imbalanced gender ratio has been a major feature of UCZ theological education as it was observed in the study by Peggy

---

[38] Bodson Chailosi Lupyani, "The (Sub-) Ordination of Women in the Evangelical Church in Zambia. A Critical Analysis of the Ecclesiological and Hermeneutical Principles Underlying the Refusal of Women's Ordination," MA, University of KwaZulu Natal, 2009, 64-70 concludes that this tradition is informed by Scriptural interpretation and some pagan traditions from both the Roman Empire and African culture.

Mulambya-Kabonde.[39] In my time, I was accepted as a special student since I had prior theological qualifications. However, it was evident that theological studies were seen as the right of men in terms of leadership roles and ministerial formation. The UCZ theological college had class representatives and a student representative council. All the positions were held by men. The full time Faculty was all male, with three women who came in to teach as part–time lecturers. In this context, part time lecturers were appointed at congregations as full-time pastors.

Of the three-part time female lecturers, one was teaching only diaconal students, a ministry then that was only for females. In the area of ministerial formation, the female students were subtly treated as such. Lily Phiri described it better, when she concluded that ministerial formation for female students at the UCZ theological institution was "ambiguously life-denying/identity-diminishing."[40] This is because since its formation as a union church in 1965, and subsequently inheriting the theological training institution, "the UCZ's ministerial formation space remains dominated by men, thereby overtly and covertly influencing the identity of female ministers and their place and relationships within the church and the communal spaces."[41] In my observation and experience of ministerial formation, it was designed for male students, and the female students were subtly made to conform to be accepted. This was seen in

---

[39] Peggy Mulambya-Kabonde, "Ordination of Women: Partnership, Praxis, and Experience of the UCZ," PhD, University of KwaZulu Natal, 2014, 150-157.

[40] L. Phiri, "Ministerial Formation, Identity and Liturgy among the Female Ministers in the United Church of Zambia," in Roderick R. Hewitt and Lilian Cheelo Siwila (eds), *Liturgy and Identity: African Religio-cultural and Ecumenical Perspectives*, Pietermaritzburg: Cluster, 2018, 60.

[41] L. Phiri, "Ministerial Formation, Identity and Liturgy among the Female Ministers in the United Church of Zambia," 2018, 61.

wearing formal suits, preaching in almost a masculine voice, and the unwritten rule for married female students not to get pregnant while in training so they can fulfil their formation assignments with congregations.

In 2009, I joined the UCZ-TC as a part time lecturer. In 2013, I was appointed to serve as Academic Dean. It was during this time that the institution was transitioning from a theological college to a university college. The office of Academic Dean had the overall responsibility of ensuring the institution lived up to the academic rigour of being a university college. Though I found three full time female lecturers, there were four full time male lecturers as well as four male part timers. All the faculty members were ordained clergy. In an incidence where I asked a male colleague to fulfil his obligations in the management of the courses, he looked me in the face and said that I was not his supervisor and that he reported to Synod office. In the context where the Church practices hierarchical leadership,[42] I found his response very strange. Needless to say, I realized his hostile response could be because I had come in as an 'outsider' and a woman, to take up a responsibility that could have been done by an 'insider'. This was despite the fact that my predecessor had been a woman.

My experiences as student and staff in both Evangelical and Ecumenical institutions of theological education in Zambia positions this chapter's argument that patriarchy is a major hindrance to achieving gender equity in theological institutions in Zambia. There is need to restructure theological education at the institutional level by providing policy guidelines that affirm equal identity and dignity for both genders. The question of gender parity in the Church is often

---

[42] Peggy Mulambya-Kabonde, "Ordination of Women: Partnership, Praxis and Experience of the United Church of Zambia," PhD, University of KwaZulu-Natal, 2014, 69.

viewed as a secular quest as there is a general notion in Zambia that gender talk is all about women.

Towards a Structural System Transformation of Theological Education in Zambia

As much as there has been extensive talk and writing about gender equality in Zambia in general and in theological education in particular, there has been little action in terms of practice. As such, this chapter argues that gender parity in theological education can be achieved when theological institutions and its agencies consider structural transformation of the systems used in their educational practices. So, there is a need for the Church to firstly provide policy frameworks for gender education and secondly to develop theological education that is gender oriented.

Gender in Education: Zambia's Policy Framework

In Zambia the education system is governed by the 1996 National Policy of Education, *Educating Our Future*. The State recognizes the need for equity and equality in access to quality education for both genders, and highlights the commitment to remove all impediments, including those which are gender oriented.[43] As such, it provides a policy on gender in which it seeks to achieve four strategic goals: (1) attain gender balance in access to education at all levels; (2) integrate female students as equal beneficiaries and participants to males in education; (3) eliminate factors that impede access, progression and accomplishment of females, and (4) to encourage females to study perceived male dominated subjects such as the

---

[43] Government of Zambia, *Educating our Future: National Policy on Education*, Lusaka, Ministry of Education, 1996, 3-4.

sciences.[44] The policies on gender in education show that the state has taken strides to ensure gender parity in its entire education system. What about the Church in its theological education considering that it has a prophetic role in the world? It is obvious in this chapter that both the Evangelical and Protestant theological education institutions do not have a definite policy for gender education though the nation has a policy for it. In the absence of such a policy, the institutions could also align gender inclusion in theological education to the existing national educational policies which aim to achieve gender equality in the education system.

Gender in Theological Education

The literature surveyed makes it clear that the Church, as the custodian of theological education, has no policy framework to ensure gender parity, despite the theological principle of human dignity which is based on the *Imago Dei* (Image of God) concept in Gen 1:27.[45] *Imago Dei* essentially points to a non-gender-discriminatory God. The principle of Christ's redemption too is non-discriminatory, a factor Paul recognizes in Gal 3:22. It is worth observing that the majority of members in almost all churches in Zambia are women, yet when it comes to theological education, very few women have access to it due to lack of policy frameworks that address all ecclesial impediments that account for it. The UCZ has no gender policy despite the fact that it ordains women, which, in effect, means they have been theologically trained. However, due to

---

[44] Ibid, 65.

[45] "So God created mankind in his own image, in the image of God he created them; male and female he created them." (NIV)

lack of policy, only a few women are seen enrolling to study theology, where for every one female student there are ten male students.[46]

It is equally true that the Evangelical University (formerly TCCA), though it recognizes its mission to train men and women in theological education, has no policy to encourage women's access and participation. Policy development is necessary for the Church to increase access for women in theological education.

Need for Gender Education Inclusion in Theological Training

Zambia is a signatory to many international protocols on gender parity. In its Vision 2030, which Zambia recognizes as critical to achieving sustainable development, is the need for gender equality which aims to "reduce and ultimately eliminate gender imbalances and inadequacies associated with the provision of education, training and development."[47] The Ministry of General Education has since implemented gender education in its curriculum framework.[48] The Church, as custodians of theological education in Zambia, has no excuse for not implementing gendered education that ensures the fulfilment of equity and equality and contributes to the goals of sustainable development.

Conclusion

This chapter explored how patriarchy is deeply entrenched in theological education using my personal experiences at two

---

[46] Peggy Mulambya-Kabonde, "Ordination of Women: Partnership, Praxis and Experience of the United Church of Zambia," PhD, University of KwaZulu-Natal, 2014, 69.

[47] Zambia's Higher Education Act of 2011, www.hea.org.zm.

[48] Ibid.

Protestant institutions of theological education. It showed that patriarchy in theological education is an extension of the early missionary education that neglected girls' and women's education and the nature of early theological education that perpetuated gender inequality. The chapter concludes that patriarchy remains entrenched in the two Protestant theological institutions where I trained and worked in ways that reflect the ongoing struggles of women in theological spaces in the country. Based on the findings I suggest that theological educators need to consider systematic and structural reforms for implementing gender transformation. My findings call for the development and implementation of policies that foster transformed education which truly liberates the less powerful to reclaim their rightful identity and social standing in society. Patriarchy dehumanizes women and makes them vulnerable to the powerful structures of society.

Theological education, as has been experienced by the author, and from the literature surveyed, tends to inculcate a male chauvinistic theology and the perpetuation of patriarchy rather than an equitable society in which both genders are upheld in the *Imago Dei*. The danger of theological education in its current form is that it is streamlined on secularism more than on sacredness. As such, the chapter agrees with John Pobee's observation of the creeping of secularism into theological education, which began during the time of the Enlightenment:

> under the canopy of the Enlightenment culture and ideology, a relic of the Cartesian mind-set, theological education in Africa has been ensouled with the scientific method. Fundamental to it is rationality (ratio), with its undergirding of *fact, theory,* and *objectivity*. In the process, the link between epistemology and ontology has been short-changed. Besides, the ultimate goal of theological education, namely creating men and women who have a commitment to the mission of the church in a plural world, has, time and again, been short-changed. Consequently, it has been said that the *seminary,*

the place for germinating the seeds of true religion and mission, has become the *cemetery* for faith and commitment.[49]

The dearth of seminary and theological education lies in the failure to recognize the equal worth of both genders as being called, and therefore both need to be trained adequately to be able to faithfully carry out God's mission.

---

[49] John Pobee, "Good News Twined by Native Hands: Twined by Native Hatchet and Tended with Native Earth," Isabel Apawo Phiri and Dietrich Werner (eds), *Handbook of Theological Education in Africa*, Oxford: Regnum, 2013.

Chapter Thirteen

Jezebel the Female Empire: Hermeneutic Reflections on 1 Kings 21

Charity Mulalami

Introduction

After the world conference on equality, development and peace convened by the United Nations in 1995, commonly known as the "Beijing Conference,"[1] there has been a tremendous improvement on women's empowerment both in academics and in secular society. Zambia is no exception in this, which was vividly seen when the late President Mr Michael Chilufya Sata announced publicly in 2011 that he was set on developing women's empowerment. This presidential vision saw several women in the government offices being appointed to higher positions. This signified the recognition of women and the implementation of the international protocols championing equal opportunities for men and women, to which Zambia is a signatory. This decision was greatly celebrated by Women for Change and the Non-Governmental Organizations Coordinating Committee (NGOCC). The narrative in 1 Kings 21 on Naboth's vineyard involving the female character of Jezebel will be used as a theological framework to analyze the spirit of empire in women leadership in the 21st century. Experience will be used as a research methodology to analyze women's leadership in Biblical times with regards to 1 Kings 21 and the present scenario. This analysis is intended to show how women have fared and whether they have set a good precedence as

---

[1] United Nations, "Fourth World Conference on Women Beijing Declaration," 1995, www.un.org/womenwatch/daw/beijing/platform/declar. htm.[15.4.2020].

ambassadors for other women to be trusted with the mantle of leadership in positions of influence.

Definition of Leadership

Leadership, according to Karin Klenke, can be defined in terms of traits, behaviours, influence, processes, power, politics, authority, change, goals, achievement, management, and transformation among other concepts.[2] John Maxwell defines leadership as the art of influencing and directing people as a way that will win their obedience, confidence, respect, and loyal cooperation in achieving common objectives.[3]

Leadership and Gender

Since time immemorial (the biblical times included), leadership has always carried a gendered face in that it has been male-dominated. One cannot talk about gendered leadership without talking about leadership and context, because context plays a significant role in leadership. Deborah Rhode observes that "women's unequal representation in leadership positions poses concerns."[4] Patriarchy

---

[2] Karin Klenke, *Women and Leadership: A Contextual Perspective*, New York: Springer, 1996, 6.

[3] John C. Maxwell, *The Maxwell Leadership Bible (NKJV)*, (2nd ed), Nashville: Thomson Nelson, 2007. Analysing Maxwell's definition of leadership from the empire's point of view, royal cooperation in achieving the common objectives is not so much in the empire as they ride on the wings of others to achieve their goals. In other words, the empire is more self-centred than others-centred like in the narrative of Naboth's vineyard. King Ahab and Jezebel, the female empire, did not consider royal cooperation in achieving the common objectives, but rather stood for their selfish desires. Jezebel used the unity of command to order around their subordinates in the kingdom.

[4] Deborah L. Rhode, *Women and Leadership*, Oxford University Press, 2017, 3.

continues to pose the most significant barrier to women who are outside the structures of decision making and power as well as to those who are elected as Members of Parliament or appointed as Ministers. Building on this line of argument, Rosemary Radford-Ruether concludes that these are traits of sexism and she describes sexism as an act of gender privilege of males over females.[5] Ursula King also observes that sexism is the exclusive ordering of life through the use of gender.[6]

Africa is home to gendered leadership as evidenced in many countries where men have dominated leadership positions, whether in church or in secular spaces. However, a few countries such as Liberia, the first African country to have a female president and South Africa, Malawi, Tanzania and Zambia, just to mention a few, have given women the second-highest position of vice president. Munroe contends that the United Nations Convention on the Elimination of All Forms of Discrimination Against Women, referred to as 'The International Bill of Rights for Women' suggests the cause of the problem.[7] She further maintains that it targets culture and tradition as influential forces shaping gender roles and family relations.[8]

I agree with Munroe and maintain that from an African perspective, this experience is due in part to the cultural context that has very much embraced the patriarchal system in leadership. Authors such as J. Poltera argue that initiatives such as Africa's Agenda 2063, the African Union's Women's Decade, Women and the UN Sustainable

---

[5] Rosemary Radford Ruether, *Sexism and God-talk: Towards a Feminist Theology*, London: SPCK, 1983, 165.

[6] Ursula King, *Women and Spirituality: Voices of Protest and Promise*, London: Macmillan, 1989, 28.

[7] Miles Munroe, *Understanding the Purpose and Power of Women*, New Kensington: Whitaker House, 2001, 12.

[8] Ibid.

Development Goals, and the UN's Commission on the Status of Women, come as a recognition of the need to redress longstanding gender inequality and inequity, oppression of women, power imbalances, and patriarchal norms and systems.[9] Although women have been embraced to lead at different levels of society in recent times, gendered leadership still remains an issue in Africa.[10] Karin Klenke maintains that "when examining, analyzing and evaluating female and male leaders, gender operates as the first of a series of prisms."[11] She further states that gender refers to the historical, social and cultural construction of biological sex, and is mostly defined "by default."[12] Given this line of argument, that we are gendered human beings from birth, gender should, however, not be conceived as a fixed aspect of individuals, but as part of an ongoing process by which women and men are defined, usually in confounding ways.[13]

Raewyn Connell observes that gender order begins with the assumption that gender is better thought of as a process than a "thing" that people have.[14] Deborah Rhode agrees with Raewyn Connell and maintains that the point is not that there is some single "woman's point of view," or "women's leadership," but rather that gender differences matter in ways that should be registered in leadership

---

[9] J. Poltera, "Exploring Examples of Women's Leadership in African Context," *Agenda*, 33:1, 2019, 3-8.

[10] Ibid.

[11] Karin Klenke, *Women and Leadership: A Contextual Perspective*, New York: Springer, 1996.

[12] Ibid.

[13] Liesbet van Zoonen, *Feminist Media Studies*, London, Sage, 1994.

[14] Raewyn Connell, *Gender and Power: Society, the Person, and Sexual Politics*, Stanford, CA: Stanford University Press, 1987, 3.

positions.[15] In looking at leadership and context, since every kind of leadership operates from a certain context, Karin Klenke contends that context influences what leaders must do and how they can do it, bearing in mind that context can either be historical or situational.[16] For her, context simply refers to the setting in which leadership is exercised.[17] I agree with Karin Klenke's statement, and I want to conclude that in Jezebel's portrayal of the empire mentality of leadership, the situation she was in influenced her actions against Naboth. I also want to argue that the setting of the palace where she was as the queen, influenced the way she usurped authority over Naboth's vineyard.

In this chapter the term 'Empire' will be defined as a way to name powers at work in our world which are not located in one country under one government, but in many places, locally, nationally and globally. It is a concept which helps us see manifestations of power and their connections in history and today. Empire is a way to speak about these powers and how they operate.

A Brief Hermeneutic Reflection on the Life of Jezebel

The biblical story of Jezebel in is found in 1 Kings 16:30 – 2 Kings 9:37 as part of the Elija/Ahab story. Queen Jezebel was the daughter of the Phoenician king Ethbaal of Sidon and the wife of Ahab, king of Israel. As a Phoenician princess she would have naturally worshipped Baal, and Asherah, the goddess of the Sidonians.[18] Jezebel's first appearance is in 1 Kings 16:31 where a note on her marriage to Ahab, King of Israel, is included in an introductory

---

[15] Deborah L. Rhode, *Women and Leadership*, Oxford University Press, 2017, 3.

[16] Karin Klenke, *Women and Leadership: A Contextual Perspective*, 18.

[17] Ibid, 18.

[18] Carol A. Newsom and Sharon H. Ringe, *Women's Bible Commentary*, Louisville: Westminster/John Knox Press, 109.

summary of the king's evil ways, as it led to Ahab worshiping her gods.[19] In 1 Kings 18:4 there is the parenthetical reference to her efforts to "cut off" the prophets of Yahweh. Jezebel's concerns were probably not first and foremost religious, but as a Phoenician princess she was accustomed to royal prerogatives and not used to the democratic impulse in Israelite culture that regarded land as Yahweh's gift to each Israelite family rather than as property at the command of the king.[20] Furthermore, her brutal response to Naboth's refusal to sell his vineyard might be understood, from her point of view, as an appropriate royal response to insubordination, in contrast to Ahab's unconscionable weakness as a leader.[21]

The Characteristics of Empire Portrayed by Jezebel

In my view, the empire is a system that can be operated anywhere and by anyone, male or female; just like patriarchy, it includes:

1. Power and authority
2. Exploitation
3. Manipulation
4. Intimidation
5. Negative aggressiveness
6. Control and domination
7. Negative masculinity
8. Patriarchy
9. Abuse of power
10. Negative courage
11. The demand for obedience and control

---

19   Ibid.

20   Ibid, 110.

21   Ibid.

12. Divide and rule tactics

Unmasking the Hidden Spirit of Empire in Jezebel

In many instances it is difficult to detect the hidden acts of the spirit of empire in people. Looking at many African countries today concerning the colonial masters, the truth of the matter is that the empire has not left Africa but has just changed its way of operating. In the face of the Coronavirus [Covid 19] that has hit the world with Western countries being so adversely affected, two French doctors have publicly discussed that Africa should be the centre for vaccine trials.

Tedros Ghebreyesus replied that the WHO "condemns this in the strongest terms possible" and said, "We assure you that this will not happen in Africa."[22] The response from the WHO Director-General demonstrates the unmasking of the spirit of empire in medical operations that Africa has been subjected to for centuries, and a colonial presence of power is still evident in some areas of influence such as control of the economy, family, education and health.[23] Given this line of argument, I want to stress that things cannot change until Africans themselves realize this to the fullest and begin to unmask this hidden empire still functioning in the medical, educational, political and economic sectors of Africa, to mention just a few. The empire spirit in female leadership remains undetected too as empire is linked more to men than women as is the case with patriarchy. The observation from experience, both past and present, is that the church and secular society have become spaces where traits of Jezebel, the female empire, have not been easily detected. In the

---

[22] Tedros Ghebreyesus, "What French Doctors and the WHO Really Said about Africa and Vaccine Testing," *Euronews*, 2020.

[23] Walter D. Mignolo, "Introduction: Coloniality of Power and De-Colonial Thinking," *Cultural Studies* 21(2&3), 2007, 155-167.

character of Jezebel, domination and intimidation and lack of leadership charisma (not being others-centred) are observed as the traits of empire. The Council for World Mission presents the following on how to detect the empire:

> Asking questions becomes an important way to identify the culture of the Empire around us, whether it is in our communities or our churches. Questions like: 'In whose interests is this being done?' 'In whose interests is money being spent?' 'How is difference treated?' 'How is dissent treated?' Answers to questions like these will begin to identify how Empire is present, assuming you can even ask such questions.[24]

Another way to unmask the spirit of empire is to look at the characteristics as guiding principles to detect this spirit of empire in someone, whether in the church or in secular spaces. Unmasking the empire in Jezebel is a job half-done, only if the empire is exposed, the job will be complete. I want to articulate further that it is important to understand that the empire will not and cannot do anything for the benefit of others, it only knows its own benefit. The questions then are: Which empire have you been serving? What benefits have you reaped in serving that empire? The fact is that the empire spirit of Jezebel is the act of using and dumping people after the oppressor's intended goals have been achieved. In 1 Kings 21:8-14 we find Jezebel (the female empire) engaged in her mission to eliminate Naboth, using the concept of *"use and dump."*

The Vulnerability of Naboth to the Empire

The empire is better placed than its subjects, therefore, it uses its position of influence to manipulate and abuse others. In other words, there is an element of vulnerability on the part of those who fall prey to the empire, so that "the experience of vulnerability presents us

---

24 Council for World Mission [CWM], *Unmasking the Empire*, Singapore: CWM Publications, 2018, 3.

with the reality of fallibility, mutability, unpredictability, and uncontrollability."[25] Besides, the experiences of vulnerability can also prompt fear, defensiveness, avoidance, and disavowal.[26] "The leading men of Jezreel obviously feared Jezebel more than they feared God because they carried out her orders exactly according to the instructions she gave them (1 Kings 21:11-16)."[27] When Naboth and his sons (2 Kings 9:26) were dead, the scoundrels dutifully reported that the job was done.[28] Notable aspects in the vulnerability of subjects to the empire as observed from Jezebel are as follows:

- She used her royal position to manipulate the leaders in the kingdom to execute Naboth.
- She used her superiority to oppress and suppress those who were below her – an empire is always suppressive and oppressive.
- As an empire, Jezebel did not easily give up until her agenda was fulfilled. Empires have a tendency of pushing their way through – not for the benefit of others but for selfish gains – thereby making their subjects more vulnerable.

Naboth was vulnerable to Jezebel the female empire, and there are great lessons to learn from him: Naboth's refusal to sell the vineyard shows that he understood the Mosaic law over land and he also vowed not to be a puppet to the empire. Anyone who does not bend to fit into the demands of the empire falls out of favour with the empire; however, this did not bother Naboth.

---

[25] Erinn Gilson, *The Ethics of Vulnerability: A Feminist Analysis of Social Life and Practice*, New York: Routledge, 2014, 3.

[26] Ibid.

[27] John Walvoord and Roy B. Zuck (eds), *The Bible Knowledge Commentary: An Exposition of the Scriptures*, Colorado Springs: David C. Cook, 1983, 532.

[28] Ibid.

The empire is comfortable in interacting with the "_inde bwana_"[29] type of people, those who easily say yes to everything that the empire wants, never objecting to anything that is detrimental to others. Naboth refused to be an _inde bwana_ and unfortunately, those who executed him, feared that their lives would be destroyed by Jezebel – the empire has a tendency of creating fear in its subordinates.

The empire has a tendency of riding on the wings of others to achieve its goals – Jezebel used the leaders in the kingdom to execute Naboth so that she and the king could have Naboth's vineyard.

At the point where our vulnerability is exposed to others who seek to do us harm, it becomes a condition that precipitates violence,[30] and "recognizing vulnerability in oneself and in others can further lead to unmasking privileged positions of the past that the former political dispensation has produced."[31] This is true of the vulnerability of those who are victims of the empire. However, others do not realize their vulnerability to the empire as they see it as a favour.

The Theology of Leadership: A Comparison of Two Female Royals

This section analyzes the narratives of two female royals in the Old Testament regarding the topic at hand. Jezebel in 1 Kings 21 and

---

[29] _Inde bwana_ mostly used among military people/service men and women as a way of responding to the commands of their superiors. However, in the Zambian context it has come to be used to refer to those who easily say to everything from those who are above them and cannot object by any means even when it isn't not helpful.

[30] Erinn Gilson, _The Ethics of Vulnerability: A Feminist Analysis of Social Life and Practice_, New York: Routledge, 2014, 4.

[31] Gerrie Snyman, "Empire and a Hermeneutics of Vulnerability," _Studia Historiae Ecclesiasticae_, 37 – Supplement, 2011, 1-20

Esther in Esther 5 were both foreign queens but with different means of executing their authority. In 1 Kings 21 we find the story of Naboth's vineyard and how Jezebel demonstrated her authority and influence in a brutally patriarchal and exploitative manner, leading to the death of Naboth and his sons in Jezreel. The characteristics of empire as mentioned above are seen in Jezebel as she takes over the issue from King Ahab, her husband, to handle it all by herself. Deborah Rhode maintains that, essentially, women are more likely than men to engage in transformational leadership which emphasizes inspiring and encouraging their followers to contribute to their organization,[32] but this was not so for Jezebel, the female empire. Jezebel's leadership was not transformational but destructive, as she used her power to order her men to kill Naboth over his vineyard. In contrast, Esther's leadership can be considered transformational, inspiring and encouraging her followers to contribute to the well-being of the Israelites:

> Jezebel, on one hand, eagerly uses her royal power for apostasy and exploitation, while Esther, on the other hand, heroically saves the people of Israel from destruction in a foreign land. She is portrayed as charming yet humble, reluctant yet courageous.[33]

Jezebel and Esther were both courageous in executing their plans, although with different intentions in that one was life-affirming, while the other one was not. Although Jezebel was a woman, she enforced patriarchal beliefs and traits of hegemonic masculinity, while Naboth and the leading men in the execution mission were subjected to some kind of subordinate masculinity. Rosemary Radford-Ruether defines patriarchy as "a social system that promotes hierarchies and awards

---

[32] Deborah L. Rhode, *Women and Leadership*, Oxford University Press, 2017, 6.

[33] Cameron B.R. Howard, "When Esther and Jezebel Write: A Feminist Biblical Theology of Authority," in P.K. Tull and J.E. Lapsley (eds), *After Exegesis: Feminist Biblical Theology: Essays in Honor of Carol A. Newsom*, Waco, TX: Baylor University Press, 2015, 110-111.

economic, political and social power to one group over others."[34] In addition, patriarchy is fundamentally androcentric and hierarchical in nature. By patriarchy, we mean not only the subordination of females to males, but the "whole structure of father ruled society: aristocracy over serfs, masters over slaves, kings over subjects, racial overlords over colonized people."[35] This can be summed up in the definition of empire as highlighted by the Council for World Mission, as "manifestations of power and their connections in history and today; empire is a way to speak about these powers and operations of power."[36]

Patriarchy does not mean the subordination of females to males only, but the whole structure of a "father ruled society" as exhibited by Jezebel in the manifestation of power over Naboth. The observation is that patriarchy also refers to structures and ideologies which engender the domination and exploitation of the weak and the powerless amongst us. Jezebel used her position for personal gain, while Esther portrayed feminine attributes, using her position to help others while risking her own life.

Ahab and Jezebel lacked charisma in leadership, hence they used manipulation, selfishness and scheming to get what they wanted.[37] Charisma may be defined as:

---

[34] Rosemary Radford Ruether, _Sexism and God-talk: Towards a Feminist Theology_, London: SPCK, 1983, 61.

[35] Ibid.

[36] Council for World Mission [CWM], _Unmasking the Empire_, Singapore: CWM Publications, 2018, 3.

[37] John C. Maxwell, _The Maxwell Leadership Bible (NKJV)_, 2nd ed., Nashville: Thomson Nelson, 2007, 452. – Maxwell, articulating on selfishness, contends that Ahab and Jezebel felt no incentive to develop charisma because their position allowed them to use people. Nevertheless, people can tell if you are using them

A magnetic personal attraction that draws others to the leader, making them feel better about themselves. Therefore, effective leaders do well to develop some level of charisma. However, leaders are to give it away to others; charismatic people are others-centred.[38]

Following this line of thought concerning leadership charisma, I want to affirm that having had an opportunity to work in the church, the observation is that most leaders, once they ascend to top positions, lack charisma as they become more self-centred than others-centred in running the church's affairs. Furthermore, church politics are often just like secular politics where people operate more around how they will benefit from certain positions than around what they can do for others. Esther demonstrates leadership charisma as she makes use of her royal position to help others, giving us hope that there are still a few leaders who are others-centred. King Ahab and Jezebel used patriarchal leadership to force their way into Naboth's vineyard. Therefore, patriarchy can rightly be described as an empire, a spirit of lawless domination, created by humankind.[39]

The Council for World Mission [CWM] affirms this and highlights that empire is built on hierarchies and dominates by keeping diversity in check.[40] Another notable aspect is that value, rank and position are ascribed in a society based on patriarchal attitudes to gender, race, ethnicity, class, caste and sexual identity. Patriarchy is the way empire

---

merely to reach your own goals. Maxwell's point gives an overview of the leadership crisis that this 21st century is facing both in the church and the secular spaces, in which leadership charisma is significantly lacking to a greater extent.

[38] John C. Maxwell, *The Maxwell Leadership Bible (NKJV)*, 2007, 452.

[39] Attie van Niekerk, "Dreaming a Different World: Globalisation and Justice for Humanity and the Earth—The Challenge of the Accra Confession for the Churches," *International Journal of Public Theology*, vol. 5, Issue 1, 2011, 2, https://doi.org/10.1163/156973211X543869.

[40] Council for World Mission [CWM], *Unmasking the Empire*, Singapore: CWM Publications, 2018, 11.

operates to domesticate as well as to socially control others.[41] I agree with this line of argument and maintain that even with Jezebel as a female empire, hierarchy and domination were strongly at play in 1 Kings 21. Moreover, though female, Jezebel operated in a patriarchal manner as patriarchy is not about the domination of males over females but rather a system of oppression. Due to the patriarchal system in operation in many institutions and nations, the traits of empire in female leaders can be observed.

Deconstructing the Spirit of an Empire in Leadership

The most important thing that needs to be done after unmasking and exposing the empire is to deconstruct the spirit of the empire in leadership to create an environment that promotes the well-being of everyone. In discussing the "law of addition," John Maxwell remarks that leaders add value by serving others,[42] and Blanchard and Broadwell affirm that servant leaders lead by serving their people, not by exalting themselves.[43] Although the empire often *seems* to be serving the people, there is always a hidden agenda for selfish gain and fame. The hidden effects of the empire on others are that the identity of a person is challenged when under the influence and manipulation of the empire. The leaders who had been instructed to kill Naboth did not function under free will but by the empire of Queen Jezebel. Therefore, in the process of deconstructing the empire in leadership, there is also a reconstruction of the personal or self-identity of those who fall prey to empire. It becomes necessary

---

[41] Ibid.

[42] John Maxwell, *The 21 Irrefutable Laws of Leadership*, 10th ed., Nashville, Tennessee: Thomson Nelson, 2007, 47.

[43] Ken Blanchard and Renee Broadwell (eds), *Servant Leadership in Action: How you can Achieve Great Relationships and Results*, Oakland: Berrett-Koehler, 2018.

to investigate the possibility of a non-imperial political practice that begins to develop even within the environment of empire to produce its alternatives to generate the conditions of its modification, and to form the anthropological ethos that allows the overcoming of the subjectivity generated in the imperial space.[44]

Conclusion

This chapter sought to reflect on Jezebel the female empire as a hermeneutic reflection of 1 Kings 21. In doing this, leadership and gender was analyzed on how leadership has been gendered in Africa due to the African culture of embracing a patriarchal system of leadership. Therefore, although some women have risen to positions of influence in recent times, the challenge of patriarchy remains. From biblical times to the present time, women have risen to leadership with greater challenges than men. Queens Jezebel and Esther were in similar positions of influence in foreign lands. However, a comparison of the two reveals that Jezebel became an empire who dominated and manipulated her authority against Naboth leading to his death. Jezebel shows that the empire lacks leadership charisma and reveals its self-centredness. In other words, they ride on the wings of others to achieve their goals. For this reason, there is need to unmask the empire, otherwise those who fall prey to it will always be vulnerable. Lastly, deconstructing the empire in leadership is another factor that needs to be dealt with if those who fall prey to the empire must reconstruct their personal identity lost in the process of being under the empire's domination, exploitation and manipulation.

---

[44] Néstor Miguez, Joerg Rieger and Jung Mo Sung, *Beyond the Spirit of Empire: Theology and Politics in a New Key*, London: SCM, 2009, 172.

Chapter Fourteen

Participation of Women in the *'Kuomboka kwa Likomu'* Ceremony in Munyama Area in Kalabo District

Lungowe Sinjwala &
Judith Lubasi Ilubala-Ziwa

Introduction

This chapter explores women's participation in the seemingly male dominated *Kuomboka kwa Likomu* (KKL) ceremony in Munyama area of Kalabo district in Western Zambia. This ceremony is characterized by the movement of cattle from the flood plains to the flood free upper land. This movement of cattle is marked by the colourful *Kuomboka kwa Likomu* (KKL) ceremony, flavoured with perform-ances of rituals, upholding traditional beliefs, and the adherence to stringent taboos. The chapter seeks to complement studies on indigenous religious beliefs and practices in Zambia in general by scholars such as, Lumbwe,[1] Mwale[2], Kanene,[3] Masaiti and Ngabwa,[4]

---

[1] Kapambwe Lumbwe, "Kuomboka Ceremony, Nc'wala Traditional Ceremony, Lwindi Gonde Traditional Ceremony," *Journal of the Musical Arts in Africa*, 9(1), 2012, 86-89.

[2] Nelly Mwale, "African Traditional Religion in the Context of Climate Change: A Zambian Perspective," *Journal of Humanities*, *13*, 2014, 1-14.

[3] M. Kanene Kennedy, "The Environmentality of Shrines: Case of Gonde Malende (Shrine) of the Tonga People of Southern Zambia," *Asian Journal of Social Sciences & Humanities*, vol. 4, 2015, 2.

[4] Gift Masaiti and Dorothy Ngabwa, "Religious, Cultural and Social Changes in the Chibwelamushi Harvest Ceremony of the Lala-Swaka People of Serenje and Mkushi Districts," *Zambia Journal of Religion and Contemporary Issues*, 1/1 (2018).

and those foregrounded in women studies such as Jonathan Kangwa,[5] and Lilian Siwila.[6] These are male dominated traditional ceremonies which have not been static but changed over time as evidenced by the participation of women in one such ceremony (*Kuomboka kwa Likomu*) among the Lozi speaking people of Western Zambia. This chapter is informed by an empirical study of the ceremony that involved the thematic analysis of interviews, observations and document review. The chapter argues that, while the shifts in women's participation point to growing women's emancipation and involvement in conserving the religious practices embedded in the ceremony, there is a need for the on-going reconstruction of women's identities as some traditional beliefs and taboos still exclude women from participating fully in the KKL rituals. The chapter unfolds by giving a brief context of the ceremony, the theoretical framework and a literature review, before highlighting the emerging themes from the study on which the chapter is anchored.

Brief Historical Overview of the *Kuomboka kwa Likomu* Ceremony

Cattle (*Likomu*) rearing is the mainstay of the Lozi people of the Western Province and it dates as far back as the 17th century. Apart from providing economic safety, the activity has religious significance, as cattle are considered a "magical gift from God."[7] This is also supported by their oral traditions which hold that Nyambe (the

---

[5] Jonathan Kangwa, "In Search of Indigenous Knowledge Systems for Ecological Justice: A Gendered Ecological Reading of Genesis 1-3 in the Context of the Tonga People in Zambia," PhD, University of KwaZulu Natal, 2014.

[6] Lilian Cheelo Siwila, "An Encroachment of Ecological Sacred Sites and its Threat to the Interconnectedness of Sacred Rituals: A Case Study of the Tonga People in the Gwembe Valley," *Journal for the Study of Religion*, 28(2), 2015, 138-153.

[7] Ernest Brown, *The Heritage Library of African People: Lozi*, New York: Rosen Publishing Group, 1998, 24.

Lozi God) created many wives including Mwambwa, the ancestor and queen of the true Lozi, from whom all members of the Lozi royal family descended. Mwambwa's daughter, Mbuywamwambwa, also became one of Nyambe's wives and gave birth to both human babies and calves, thus giving a common mythical origin for both the cattle and the Lozi.[8] This myth portrays the special place of cattle in the lives of the Lozi people. The myth explains the social importance attached to cattle in the Lozi culture and the existence of personal names like Mwanangombe (cow's offspring). Furthermore, this also conveys the maternal affection associated with the cow in Lozi traditions.[9] Economically, ownership of cattle is often the deciding factor of a family's socio-economic position in the community because a herd of cattle may be the only practical way of accumulating wealth. Even among family members, the number of cattle credited to an individual determines his or her worth.

Additionally, religious and social importance linked to cattle rearing among the Lozi explains their choice of settlement, in this case, the Munyama area positioned within the Zambezi floodplain. The area was strategically identified by the Lozi to provide large grazing land with abundant water for their cattle. Unfortunately, between the months of January and June every year, the plain gets flooded. This implies that the cattle have to 'omboka' (get out of floods), to a flood free upper land.[10] The movement of cattle is marked by the colourful *Kuomboka kwa Likomu* (KKL) ceremony, flavoured with performances of rituals, upholding of traditional beliefs and adherence of stringent taboos.

---

[8] S. Paul, *An Introduction to the Lozi Culture*, Unpublished Booklet, 1996, 4.

[9] Ibid, 12.

[10] Daphne Johnson, *Research Methods in Education Management*, London: Pearson Education, 1994.

Up until recent times, issues of cattle and cattle caring were dominated by men. If a couple owned cattle, the man assumed full custody of them. If some cattle were to be given to children, only male children were eligible. It also followed that in religious practices aligned with cattle rearing such as KKL, men were the main participants whereas women contributed only by performing simple domestic work such as preparing beer and other food used during the ceremony in addition to singing and dancing. This tendency also contributed to women accepting their inferior position in Lozi society. However, with changing times and forces, Lozi women became key participants in KKL ceremonies despite negative attention from the society. To us as Lozi women and female scholars, this marked an important milestone towards the emancipation of women. It was, however, not clear whether women participated at every level of the ceremony, and their general experience in a historically male dominated activity was equally difficult to tell. In this context the study ,which informs this chapter, was undertaken, seeking to understand women's participation in a seemingly male dominated KKL ceremony.

Theoretical Framework

The discussion in this chapter is guided by Theodore Brameld's (1904-1987) social reconstruction theory which is anchored in the idea that education has the responsibility to mould human beings into a cohesive and compassionate society.[11] The theory has been

---

[11] Bart Sobel, "A Reconstructionist Perspective of the Teaching of Social Studies," *The High School Journal*, 60(8), 1977, 353-364, www.jstor.org/stable/403 65469.[11.7.2020]

extended to explain the changing behaviour of people in societies in response to changes taking place around the globe.[12]

The basic assumption is that the survival of societies is threatened by many problems. These problems include, but are not limited to, poverty, food and energy shortage, illiteracy, and unemployment (often relative to a given place at a given time). Underlying many of these problems are deep social structures of which many are based on conceptions of knowledge, of culture and of values and beliefs. In response to internal and external forces, some beliefs and cultural values naturally undergo reconstruction or deconstruction.[13]

On feminist forums, social reconstruction and gender is talked about when discussing how changing internal and external forces have expedited paradigm shifts in the way women's roles are defined and redefined in their communities at any given time. Such reconstruction of knowledge has influenced policy and actions affecting the lives of women.[14] In this chapter, the theory is used to discuss the participation of women in the '*Kuomboka kwa Likomu*' ceremony which was initially completely dominated by men but has now changed to include women.

---

[12]   Stephen R. White, "Theodore Brameld's Thought Infused in Higher Education Global Studies Curriculum," *Journal of Education and Learning*, Canadian Center of Science and Education, 2016.

[13]   Ibid.

[14]   Jane L. Parpart. "Where is Your Mother? Gender, Urban Marriage and Colonial Discourses on the Zambian Copperbelt, 1924-1945," *International Journal of Historical Studies*, 27(2), 2000, 241-271.

Literature Review: Situating Women's Participation in the *Kuomboka kwa Likomu* (KKL) Ceremony in Scholarship

Like in any other African country, Zambian women have had to wrestle with engendered traditional norms deeply embedded in various activities (including the KKL ceremony) in their quest to secure proper representation in society. This has presented a challenge to the government in realizing the frequently talked about gender equality in that even when policies are introduced at national level, the status of most women is still determined by traditional beliefs and practices at the community level.

Claire Jones,[15] Carol Minton and Knottnerus,[16] Funmi Para-Mallam,[17] and Linda Mujuru,[18] have shown that women have endured and negotiated with traditional gender stereotypes in their endeavour to upgrade their social and economic status in society. For example, a study carried out in Nigeria by Funmi Para-Mallam showed that gender biased cultural practices which influenced the lifestyle of most women were a main factor that restrained women from taking up seemingly male dominated privileges, specifically prioritized for them

---

[15] Claire Jones, "Shona Women Mbira Players: Gender, Tradition and Nation in Zimbabwe," *Ethnomusicology Forum*, 17, 2008, 125-149.

[16] Carol A. Minton and J. David Knottnerus, "Ritualised Duties: The Social Construction of Gender Inequality in Malawi," *International Review of Modern Sociology*, 34(2), 2008, 181-210, www.jstor.org/stable/41421678.[10.7.2020].

[17] Funmi J. Para-Mallam, "Promoting Gender Equality in the Context of Nigerian Cultural and Religious Expression: Beyond Increasing Female Access to Education," *A Journal of Comparative and International Education*, 40(4), 2010, 459-477.

[18] Linda Mujuru, "Breaking with Tradition: Zimbabwean Women Perform on the Mbira," *Global Press Journal*, 2018, https://globalpressjournal.com/ africa/Zimba-bwe/breaking-tradition-zimbabwean-women-perform-mbira [9.7.2020]

by the government.[19] Funmi Para-Mallam argued that merely increasing female access to education is an incomplete strategy for reducing gender inequality.[20] She adds that stakeholders needed to equally overcome pervasive patriarchal cultural practices that restrain women from participating in programmes meant to enhance their social status.[21]

Other scholars have demonstrated how Asante women in modern day Ghana practically challenged cultural perceptions which justified men exercising authority over the money women earned through cocoa farming. Instead of withdrawing into themselves and seeking solace in patriarchal beliefs, Asante women courageously withdrew their labour and created their own cocoa farms while others went to court to challenge the rules of matrilineal inheritance that excluded them from the benefits of their labour.[22]

In Zimbabwe, Claire Jones noted that due to gendered traditional beliefs, women who pioneered participation in playing in public the _mbira dzabvadzimu_ (an instrument closely associated with traditional religious practices of spirit possession) suffered ridicule, discrimination, and misjudgment by the society.[23] Quoting Impley,[24] Claire

---

[19] Funmi J. Para-Mallam, "Promoting Gender Equality in the Context of Nigerian Cultural and Religious Expression," 2010, 459-477.

[20] Ibid.

[21] Ibid.

[22] Gareth Austin, _Labour, Land and Capital in Ghana: From Slavery to Free Labour in Asante, 1807-1956_, Rochester: University of Rochester Press, 2005.

[23] Claire Jones, "Shona Women Mbira Players: Gender, Tradition and Nation in Zimbabwe," _Ethnomusicology Forum_, 17, 2008, 178., doi: 10.1080/1741191-0801972982.[8.7.2020].

[24] A. Impley, "They Want us with Salt and Onions: Women in the Zimbabwean Music Industry," PhD, Indiana University, 1992.

Jones asserts that Beauler Dyoko, the first Zimbabwean woman to make a commercial recording of Shona *mbira* music in 1962, testified to being called 'mad' and a 'joker' in addition to being a laughing stock for both society and family members. A woman such as Beauler Dyoko taking part in *mbira* was perceived as taboo, since tradition holds that playing *mbira* summons the spirits of dead ancestors and that a woman should not play the *mbira* to do so.[25] This perception seems to have stubbornly resisted state and non-state actors' reformation schemes. For example, a recent report by Linda Mujuru featured the following comments and reactions towards female *mbira* players in Zimbabwe:[26]

> I have faced a lot of discrimination. I am usually associated with traditional healers and evil spirits.

> I desired for years to play the *mbira*, but I was discouraged by my family. They took me to a pastor, thinking that I had some evil spirits possessing me. The first time I began playing the *mbira* was in 2015.[27]

Another study carried out in Malawi by Carol Minton and David Knottnerus established that traditional beliefs worked antagonistically against legal, political, and economic reforms meant for the emancipation of women.[28] Despite using different efforts to reach a balanced level, gender inequality continued to be a problem among women and men. For Minton and Knottnerus, gender inequality was incubated and reproduced by everyday social interaction and

---

[25] Claire Jones, "Shona Women Mbira Players: Gender, Tradition and Nation in Zimbabwe,", 2008, 178.

[26] Linda Mujuru, "Breaking with Tradition: Zimbabwean Women Perform on the Mbira," *Global Press Journal*, 2008, 1, https://globalpressjournal.com/Africa /-zimbabwe/breaking-tradition-zimbabwean-women-perform-mbira/.[9.7.2020]

[27] Ibid.

[28] Carol A. Minton and J. David Knottnerus, "Ritualised Duties: The Social Construction of Gender Inequality in Malawi," *International Review of Modern Sociology*, 34(2), 2008, 181-210, www.jstor.org/stable/41421678.[10.7.2020].

behaviour and was largely influenced by traditional beliefs and practices that characterized the daily lives of women and men.[29] In simple yet clear terms, calls against gender inequality in this case went off target. Minton and Knottnerus further argued that seemingly minor behaviours such as the way women and men were greeted, where women sat after welcoming visitors (on a far corner of a mat), and women's lack of participation in conversations (when their husbands were present) had a bearing on the status of women.[30]

From the Zambian context, women's experiences of patriarchy also abound. For example, in rural Serenje District, women suffered patriarchal stereotypes upon their early attempts to participate in growing cash crops, an agricultural activity initially associated with men. As noted by Han Seur, women cash crop growers were the subjects of envy and hostility by society.[31] Some were even accused of practicing sorcery, all as a result of society's failure to accept and legitimize women's success in entrepreneurship. With changing times, however, society has accommodated this practice by women. Later on, female pioneers in cash crop growing were admired by men who even consulted them for advice. Han Seur equally observed that there was increasing participation of women in funeral discussions, previously dominated by men. This marked an erosion of traditional beliefs that kept women marginalized in Lalaland of Serenje District.[32]

---

[29] Ibid.

[30] Ibid.

[31] Han Seur, *Sowing the Good Seed: The Interweaving of Agricultural Change, Gender Relations and Religion in Serenje District, Zambia*, Wageningen: Landbouwuniversiteit Wageningen, 1992.

[32] Ibid.

Additionally, Lilian Siwila in her article *"Reconstructing the Distorted Image of Women as Reproductive Labour on the Copperbelt Mines in Zambia (1920-1954)"* discusses how traditional beliefs attempted to block women from going to the Copperbelt towns in the colonial era.[33] She asserts that traditional patriarchal beliefs created an understanding that women belonged to the village performing domestic work, while men had rights to go and do mining work in town. In this way, women who acted above such beliefs and moved to town to equally work and pursue an improved life were perceived as uncultured deviants and prostitutes.[34] However, due to external forces, society gradually accepted women staying in town and that they contributed positively towards the development of the Copperbelt towns; however, their contributions were mis-documented.[35] Thus, in Lilian Siwila's view, this traditional trend had a bearing on how women were treated in the modern global market economy, where, despite their massive contributions, the system kept them peripheral.[36]

Similarly, Judith Lubala-Ziwa reports how women in Chongwe District acted above their socially constructed inferior status concerning economic activities. Women took part in digging,

---

[33] Lilian Cheelo Siwila, "Reconstructing the Distorted Image of Women as Reproductive Labour on the Copperbelt Mines in Zambia (1920-1954)," *Journal for the Study of Religion*, 30(2), 2017, 75–89, http://dx.doi.org/10.17159/ 2413-3027/2017/v30n2a3 [11.4.2020].

[34] Ibid.

[35] Karen Tranberg Hansen, "Negotiating Sex and Gender in Urban Zambia," *Journal of Southern African Studies*, 10(2), 1984, 219-238. J. Parpart, "Where is Your Mother? Gender, Urban Marriage and Colonial Discourses on the Zambian Copperbelt, 1924-1945," *International Journal of Historical Studies*, 27(2), 1994, 241-271.

[36] Lilian Cheelo Siwila, "Reconstructing the Distorted Image of Women as Reproductive Labour on the Copperbelt Mines in Zambia (1920-1954)," *Journal for the Study of Religion* 30, 2, 2017 75–89, http://dx.doi.org/10.17159 /2413-3027/2017/v30n2a3.[11.4.2020].

heaping, and selling of building sand. Selling of building sand in Chongwe was considered the domain of men.[37] Their activities initially attracted all sorts of negative comments with some being uttered by fellow women. However, they persisted and, supported by the church, consequently society considered it a norm.[38]

In general, this section has demonstrated how traditional beliefs, practices and myths legitimized women's lower status and made them accept their perceived insignificance. Interestingly, literature also demonstrates how some women looked at themselves from outside the box and acted above societal expectations, thereby orchestrating a reconstruction of gender roles within society. Though we did not find scholarly works pertaining to participation of women in the '*Kuomboka kwa Likomu*' ceremony, the above literature provides a suitable context within which the findings of this study can be discussed.

Findings of the Study

The study established that the ancestors (*balimu*) were key players in the organization and successful holding of the KKL ceremony. Historically, traditional beliefs and stringent taboos related to KKL ceremonies have had regrettable consequences for non-adherence and confined women to their household tasks. It was taboo for women to even get near a kraal on the day of the ceremony. Even though a woman owned a herd of cattle, she had no close contact with them. She had no say about their care and she had no right to

---

[37] Judith Lubasi Ilubala-Ziwa, "Community Based Theological Education for Social Transformation of Women in Chongwe District, Zambia," in J. Amanze, M. Masango, E. Chitando and L. Siwila (eds), *Religion and Development in Southern and Central Africa*, vol 1, 2019, 143-164, Mzuzu: Mzuni Press.

[38] Ibid.

make decisions concerning them. During the ceremony, a woman's role was simply ululating by the edge of a village to excite both the men and the cattle as they embarked on *'kuomboka'*.

Women Participation in Kuomboka Kwa Likomu Ceremony

With regard to women's participation in KKL ceremonies at the time of the study, the participants indicated that compared to the period before the mid-1980s, women are currently allowed to participate in the ceremony. However, they were quick to say that the level of participation was not as much as those of men, as women were only allowed to perform less important roles in the event. As cited by participants, women were, unlike in the olden days, allowed to paddle their canoes behind the KKL ceremony procession up to the place where the hand-over was conducted—a thing that was never heard of in the past.

Generally, the findings suggested an improvement with respect to the involvement of women in the affairs of cattle, including their participation in the ceremony. However, women's dissatisfaction with the purported improvement regarding their involvement in the affairs of their cattle and the KKL ceremony could not be detached from the women's perspectives. For example, one female participant stated:

> We are not involved in the organization aspect. We are not involved in drawing contractual agreements with the caretakers.

Seemingly, the non-involvement of women in the drawing of contractual agreements robbed them of the opportunity to decide the conditions on which their cattle would be taken care of.

Also, the ceremony involved rituals such as *kupailela, kuolelisa likomu, kuolela* and *kufundula likomu*. All of them are still only performed by men. Initial socialization into gender may have been responsible, and to some extent, this takes away women's self-worth. The exclusion robs them of an influential social standing which is cardinal to emancipation and empowerment. To a large extent, women are being deprived of the opportunity to decide their own destiny.

Despite the foregoing, and compared to the historical times, women's 'voices' are gradually gaining men's attention. Nonetheless, the presence of open dissatisfaction among women is enough indication of the need to still improve the situation.

Factors Restraining Women's Full Participation in the Kuomboka kwa Likomu Ceremony

Participants mentioned do's and don'ts in the form of taboos associated with women's biological make-up. For example, women were not allowed to go near the kraal because they were believed to be unclean due to their menstrual cycle. It was traditionally believed that the menstrual cycle had the potential to dissolve the magical power of the charms used in cattle protection. In this manner, going against this taboo was perceived as a traditional blunder, in fact a sin against *Nyambe* who was thought of repaying such a woman by causing her death, or at least loss of her marriage. One participant lamented:

> Getting nearer a kraal was a taboo. You would even lose your marriage if you defied this restriction. But now, we can join the menfolk in the ceremony.

In addition, women were not allowed to take part in rituals associated with cattle rearing as well as the actual KKL ceremony. This is evident in this submission:

> As a woman, taboos prohibit me from performing any rituals, I do not even know the protective medicines and sometimes I keep items such as the medicinal necklace that is surrounded by a lot of taboos, even life-threatening consequences. In the olden days, Kuomboka kwa Likomu ceremony was a male event. Taboos stopped us from full participation.

Going by the above, it can be rightly put that traditional do's and don'ts such as the one narrated above were a tool which kept women in their subordinate position. These restrictions permeated different levels of interaction and socialization in society and were accepted as such. Hence, any change was judged as abnormal, this is one area which has worked against women's empowerment. It was further learnt that even with current adjustments that have allowed women to participate, their history still affected implementation.

Gender Analysis on the Participation of Women in Kuomboka kwa Likomu

This section engages with the themes that emerged from the study in relation to women's participation in KKL and factors that determined their level of participation from a gendered perspective and the social reconstruction and theoretical orientation.

Women Participation in the Kuomboka kwa Likomu Ceremony

The study showed that in the past, the people of Munyama depended largely on ancestors (*balimu*) for the success of the ceremony and that the ancestors required that the living keep the ancestral relationships alive and harmonious. There was no distinction related to gender. Men and women who owned cattle were expected to carry out their duties regarding the KKL in line with the expected relationship with the *balimu*. Regardless of the *balimus'* expectations, society did not see the value of women taking part in the rituals meant to appease the ancestors. This was due to deep rooted beliefs and practices which marginalized women from participating in societal activities.

However, at the beginning of this study it was established that there was a perceived change in levels of participation of women in KKL. Unlike in the old times, women could participate. Nevertheless, due to socially constructed beliefs and myths which had kept women away from participating, their growing involvement raised eyebrows in society. It is not surprising that some women also regarded their participation as something strange. So, while the ancestors favoured women's participation, society negated their full participation. The experiences of the Lozi women in this case were not different from what other women elsewhere experienced. For example, women in Zimbabwe were prevented from taking part in a _mbira_ performance because it called the spirits, and only men were traditionally allowed to perform the _mbira_.[39] To some extent, however, and in line with Stephen White's application of the social reconstruction theory, women have currently used different means to participate. This is a result of changing times and circumstances which have compelled women to take up new roles such as heading families and caring for relatives.[40]

Factors Restraining Women's Participation in Kuomboka kwa Likomu Ceremony

An equally important point to discuss here is how men and society at large strategically used women's biological make-up to justify men's domination of wealth. For example, the link between the menstrual blood of a woman and her drawing closer to the kraal technically marginalized all energetic women from exercising full custodianship of their cattle; yet the activity was a key source of livelihood. It is put in this manner since men were the only ones to closely monitor the cattle by being able to be close to the kraal thereby prioritizing their preferences in terms of how family cattle were managed and used.

---

[39] Claire Jones. "Shona Women Mbira Players: Gender, Tradition and Nation in Zimbabwe, _Ethnomusicology Forum_ 17, 2008, 125-149.

[40] Stephen R.R.S. White, "Theodore Brameld's Thought Infused in Higher Education Global Studies Curriculum," _Journal of Education and Learning_, North Carolina: Canadian Center of Science and Education, 2016.

This was compounded by the tradition that women were considered unclean due to their menstrual cycle. It was held among the people that menstrual blood is unclean and associated with pain and death. Therefore, women who touched the paddling stick made it lose its powers. This was affirmed by traditional leadership (headmen) who recounted that in the past, women never used to accompany men as they drove the cattle to the Luanginga River as is the case currently. In the past women were not even allowed to reach the kraal. Although stringent taboos continue to exist towards women, in the past, taboos barred them from participating altogether as it was alleged that women were unclean because of their monthly periods. The consequence of breaching this taboo was the death of cattle and people during the ceremony. This taboo resulted in women not participating in the ceremony altogether.

The situation was even more severe due to another cultural practice that forbids women from attending crucial discussions involving the transfer of temporary ownership of cattle to a custodian or caretakers during KKL ceremonies. A woman cattle owner, by virtue of her biological makeup, could not be involved in negotiating the welfare of her property. She had to appoint a male (even if he was younger than her) to make decisions on her behalf.

This type of women's socialization was also observed by scholars such as Lilian Siwila among the Lamba people of the Copperbelt,[41] Han Seur among the Lala people of Serenje,[42] and Gareth Austin

---

[41] Lilian Cheelo Siwila, "Reconstructing the Distorted Image of Women as Reproductive Labour on the Copperbelt Mines in Zambia (1920-1954)," *Journal for the Study of Religion* 30, 2, 2017 75–89, http://dx.doi.org/10.17159/ 2413-3027/2017/v30n2a3.[11.4.2020].

[42] Han Seur, *Sowing the Good Seed: The Interweaving of Agricultural Change, Gender Relations and Religion in Serenje District, Zambia,* 1992.

among the Asante people of Ghana.[43] For example, Asante women worked hard to commercialize cocoa growing in Ghana, yet men wanted to keep the money in their own pockets. Lala women were even accused of practicing sorcery, all because they took part in entrepreneurship activities, and women who moved to the Copperbelt in search of an improved lifestyle were labelled immoral, especially if they were not married.

What is worth noting, however, is how society has gradually been accepting women as key partners in development resulting in the decline of patriarchal belief systems. As the social reconstruction theory shows, this change of gender roles has been attributed to factors such as economic pressure and the declining trend of women to depend on men for material support. As a result of these changes, there has been a change in women's participation during the KKL ceremonies. Similar factors have also influenced Shona women's participation in a field that was previously dominated by men. Beauler Dyoko was the first women who made a commercial recording of Shona Mbira music.

Additionally, given the beliefs surrounding uncleanliness of women due to their menstrual cycle (feared to have detrimental consequences on the KKL as it was thought to negatively affect the charms used to protect the cattle), it can be stated that the shift towards allowing women to participate fully in the ceremony was facilitated by factors such as a growing flexibility in culture, an improved acceptance of women as partners in cattle rearing, the realization that women's involvement added colour to the ceremony, the evolutionary changes aimed at conforming to modernity, socio-economic and family dynamics (or circumstances related to gender) of the Lozi people of

---

[43] Gareth Austin, *Labour, Land and Capital in Ghana: From Slavery to Free Labour in Asante, 1807-1956.* Rochester: University of Rochester Press, 2005.

Munyama Area that compelled women to be responsible for their well-being and that of their families. Currently, the women join the men in the procession, right from the kraal to the handover point, something which was unheard of in the past.

Conclusion

Using the context of the *Kuomboka kwa Likomu* ceremony in Western Zambia, this chapter explored the participation of women in this male dominated ceremony. Acknowledging the shifts in women's participation in the ceremony, the chapter concludes that although there is an international call for gender equality in facilitating social and economic transformation, gender inequalities still remain a challenge to women participating in different ceremonies as demonstrated in KKL. Although changes have been made that allow women to participate in KKL, their full participation continues to be hindered by the ritualistic taboos that regard them as being unfit due to their biological make up.

Kuomboka kwa Likomu as a social ceremony describes roles, both social and religious, to be taken by individual men and women; the chapter calls for the need of ongoing reconstruction of gender identities to facilitate the full emancipation of women which starts with societies' recognition of the importance of women as participants in the traditional ceremony. As such, the people of Munyama area have the power to fully legitimize change by allowing women to participate in KKL without discrimination, as is the case with their male folk. The notion that gender is an emancipatory tool for women's participation in societal activities should not be undermined, especially in the 21st century when development demands a collective female-male effort.

Bibliography

"Betty Kaunda: Mother of Zambia, Heroine of the Struggle," *The Herald*, 2020, 2, www.herald.co.zw/betty-kaunda-mother-of-zambia-heroine-of-the-struggle/.[9.4.2020].

"Human Rights and Mental Health in Zambia" *Mental Disability*, September 4, 2014.

"Prophet Sued for Swindling Widow on Pretext that he would Raise her Husband from the Dead," *Muvi TV News*, 15 July 2017.

"Thursdays in Black," "Towards a World without Rape and Violence," World Council of Churches, 2013, www.oikoumene.org>get-involved [6.10.2020].

"Thursdays in Black," "World Federation of Methodist and Uniting Church Women," 2020, www.lutheranworld.org [28.5.2020]

"Thursdays in Black," Christian Aid, 2020, https//christianaid.org.uk [28.5.2020].

Pobee, John, "Good News Twined by Native Hands: Twined by Native Hatchet and Tended with Native Earth," Isabel Apawo Phiri & Dietrich Werner (eds), *Handbook of Theological Education in Africa*, Oxford: Regnum, 2013.

2004_02_27_John_Jay_Main_Report_Optimized.pdf.

Abang, Theresa B., "Disablement, Disability, and the Nigerian Society," *Disability, Handicap & Society*, 3(1), 1988, 71-77.

Adams, G. & Phia S. Salter, "Health Psychology in African Settings: A Cultural-Psychological Analysis," *Journal of Health Psychology*, 12(3), 2007, 539-551.

Adiibokah, Edward & S. Nyame, "Local Suffering and the Global Discourse of Mental Health and Human Rights: An Ethnographic Study of Responses to Mental Illness in Rural Ghana," *Global Health*, Oct 14, 2009, doi: 10.1186/1744-8603-5-13.

Agazue, Chima, "'He Told me that my Waist and Private Parts have been Ravaged by Demons': Sexual Exploitation of Female Church Members by 'Prophets' in Nigeria." *Dignity: A Journal on Sexual Exploitation and Violence*, 1(1), 2016, 9-10.

Agazue, Chima, *The Role of a Culture of Superstition in the Proliferation of Religio-Commercial Pastors in Nigeria*, Bloomington: AuthorHouse, 2015.

Aina, Olabisi I., "Women, Culture and Society," in Sesay Amadu and Odebiyi Adetanwa (eds), *Nigerian Women in Society & Development*, Ibadan: Dokun Publishing House, 1998, 6.

Akintunde, Olubanke D., "Partnership and the Exercise of Power, in the Christ Apostolic Church, Nigeria," in Isabel Phiri & Sarojini Nadar (eds), *On Being Church: African Women's Voices and Visions*, Geneva: WCC, 2005.

Akyeampong, Emmanuel & Hippolite Fofack, *The Contribution of African Women to Economic Growth and Development: Historical Perspectives and Policy Implications Part I: The Pre-colonial and Colonial Periods*, Policy Research Working Papers, April 2012, doi: 10.1596/1813-9450-6051.

Alida, Gersie, *Story Making in Bereavement. Dragons Fight in the Meadow*, London: Jessica Kingsley, 1992.

Allende, Isabel, "Violence against Women: The Health Sector Responds," World Bank, http://web.worldbank.org/archive/website01213/web/images/vaw_heal. pdf [30.11.2019].

Allman, Jean Marie, "Rounding up Spinsters: Gender Chaos and Unmarried Women in Colonial Asante," *Journal of African History*, 1996, 37(2), 195-214.

Alves, Rubem, *Tomorrow's Child: Imagination, Creativity, and the Rebirth of Culture*, London: SCM Press, 1972.

Amanze, James & Fidelis Nkomazana (eds), *Disability is not Inability. A Quest for Inclusion and Participation of People with Disability in Society*, Mzuzu: Mzuni Press, 2020.

Amanze, Janes, Maake Masango, Ezra Chitando & Lilian Siwila (eds), *Religion and Development in Southern and Central Africa*, vol 1, 2019, Mzuzu: Mzuni Press.

Anthonia, Essien, "Proliferation of Churches: A Leeway to Commercialisation of Religion," *European Journal of Scientific Research*, 45, 2010, 649-657.

Arboleda-Flórez, Julio & N. Sartorius, *Understanding the Stigma of Mental Illness: Theory and Interventions*, Chichester: John Wiley & Sons, 2008.

Asante, Molefi Kete, *The Afrocentric Idea*, Philadelphia: Temple University Press, 1986.

Austin, Gareth, *Labour, Land and Capital in Ghana: From Slavery to Free Labour in Asante, 1807-1956*, Rochester: University of Rochester Press, 2005.

Axelrod, Julie, "The Five Stages of Grief and Loss," 2016, https://pyshecentral.-com/hb/the-5-stages-of-loss-and-grief [1.6.2017]).

Bailey, C., *The Priest. A Bridge to God*, Huntington: Our Sunday Visitor Publishing Press, 2012, 108-110.

Bam, Brigalia, "Women and the Church in (South) Africa: Women are the Church in (South) Africa," in Isabel Phiri & Sarojini Nadar (eds), *On Being Church: African Women's Voices and Visions*, Geneva: WCC, 2005, 8.

Banda [Fiedler], Rachel NyaGondwe, *Women of Bible and Culture: Baptist Convention Women in Southern Malawi*, Zomba: Kachere, 2005.

Bank of Zambia, Summary Exchange Rate Data Bank of Zambia Mid-Rates, accessed from https://boz.zm/StatisticsFortnightly2017Vol25No3.pdf.

Battle, Michael, *Reconciliation: The Ubuntu Theology of Desmond Tutu*, Cleveland: Pilgrim Press, 1997, 39-43.

Belleville, Linda L., *Women Leaders and the Church. Three Crucial Questions*, Baker, 2000.

Benne, Robert, *Quality with Soul: How Six Premier Colleges and Universities Keep Faith with their Religious Traditions*, Grand Rapids: Eerdmans, 2001.

Bentley, Sarah, "The New Feminism in the USA," in *Sexism in the 1970s: Discrimination against Women: A Report of a World Council of Churches Consultation West Berlin 1974*, Geneva: WCC, 1975, 20-23.

Berger, Peter & Thomas Luckman, *The Social Construction of Reality a Treatise in the Sociology of Knowledge*, New York: Open Road Media, 2011.

Berk, James R. & Craig L. Blomberg, *Two Views on Women in Ministry*, Grand Rapids: Zondervan, 2001.

Besa, Mwansa, "The Curious Case of the Prophets," *Lusaka Voice*, 22.5.2017.

Beynon, John, *Masculinities and Culture*, Celtic Court: Open University Press, 2002, 27; www.openup.co.uk.[20.6.2020].

Black, Kathy, *A Healing Homiletic: Preaching and Disability*, Nashville: Abingdon, 1996.

Blanchard, Ken & Renee Broadwell (eds), *Servant Leadership in Action: How you can Achieve Great Relationships and Results*, Oakland: Berrett-Koehler, 2018.

Boa, Kenneth, "Perspectives on Parenthood," 2016, https://bible.org/ article/perspectives-parenthood [18.2.2018].

Botswana Daily News, 3rd July, 2019, www.dailynews.gov.bw/news-details.php?-nid=50159.[4.4.2020].

Bradbury, Ray, "The Greatest Leadership Principle," in Pockell Leslie & Avila Adrienne (eds), *The 100 Greatest Leadership Principles of All Time*, New York: Warner Books, 2007, 70.

Brookfield, Stephen, *The Power of Critical Theory: Liberating Adult Learning and Teaching*, San Francisco: Jossey-Bass, 2005.

Brown, Ernest, *The Heritage Library of African People: Lozi*, New York: Rosen Publishing Group, 1998.

Bruce, P.F., "The Mother's Cow: A Study of the Old Testament References to Virginity in the Context of HIV/AIDS," in Isabel Phiri, Beverly Haddad & Madipoane Masenya (eds), *African Women, HIV/AIDS and Faith Communities*, 2003, 44-70.

Burns, Lisa M., *First Ladies as Political Women: Press Framing of Presidential Wives 1900-2001*, Maryland: University of Maryland, 2004.

Burr, Vivian, *An Introduction to Social Constructionism*, London: Routledge, 1995.

Byrne, Lavinia, *Women before God*, London: SPCK, 1988.

Cahill, Desmond & Peter Wilkinson, *Child Sexual Abuse in the Catholic Church: An Interpretive Review of the Literature and Public Inquiry Reports*, Melbourne: RMIT University, 2017.

Campbell-Read, Eileen R., "Examining Trends in Theological Education for Women Part I," *Ethics Daily*, 7 March, 2019.

Central Statistical Office, *Zambia National Disability Survey*, 2015.

Cheyeka, Austin, "Toward a History of the Charismatic Churches in Post-colonial Zambia," in J. Gewald et al (eds), *One Zambia, Many Histories: Towards a History of Post-colonial Zambia*, Leiden: E.J. Brill, 2008;

Cheyeka, Austin, *Church, State and Political Ethics in a Post-colonial State. The Case of Zambia*, Zomba: Kachere, 2005.

Cheyeka, Austin, *The Politics and Christianity of Chilubaism, 1991-2011*, Ndola: Mission Press, 2014.

Chidoori, Rumbidzai Elizabeth, "Putting Women First – Zambia's Anti Gender based Violence Act of (2011)," https://au.int/sites/default/files/ documents /31520-ocputting_women_first__zambias_anti_gender_based _violence_act _of_2011_by_chidoori_rumbidzai_elizabeth.pdf.[20.5.2019].

Chilenje, Lazarus, *Paul's Gender Theology and the Ordained Women's Ministry in the CCAP in Zambia*, Mzuzu: Mzuni Press, 2021.

Chileshe, Alderman Habbock, *A Tribute to (the Man), His Life and History*, Ndola: Mission Press, 1998.

Chirongoma, Sophie, "Karanga-Shona Rural Women's Agency in Dressing Mother Earth: A Contribution towards an Indigenous Ecofeminist Theology," *Journal of Theology for Southern Africa*, 142, 2012, 120.

Chitando, Ezra & Sophie Chirongoma (eds), *Redemptive Masculinities: Men, HIV and Religion*, Geneva: WCC, 2012.

Chitando, Ezra, "A New Man for a New Era? Zimbabwean Pentecostalism Masculinities and the HIV Epidemic," *Missionalia*, 35(3), 2007, 112-127.

Chitando, Ezra, "Religion and Masculinities in Africa: An Opportunity for Africanisation," in Afe Adegame, Bolaiji Bayete & Ezra Chitando (eds), *African Traditions in the Study of Religion, Diaspora and Gendered Societies*, Farnham: Ashgate, 2013, 145.

Chuba, Bwalya S., *A History of Early Christian Missions and Church Unity in Zambia*, Ndola: Mission Press, 2005.

Chuba, Bwalya S., *Choosing a Life Partner for a Christian Marriage and a Christian Home*, Mansa: Book & Stationary Centre, 2005.

Churchill, Winston, "The Greatest Leadership Principles," in Leslie Pockell & Adrienne Avila (eds), *The 100 Greatest Leadership Principles of All Time*, New York: Warner Books, 2007.

Clifford, Annie, *Introducing Feminist Theology*, Maryknoll: Orbis, 2001.

Connell, Raewyn, *Gender and Power: Society, the Person, and Sexual Politics*, Stanford, CA: Stanford University Press, 1987, 3.

Conrad, Peter & Kristin K. Barker, "The Social Construction of Illness: Key Insights and Policy Implications," *Journal of Health and Social Behaviour*, 51(1_suppl), 2010, S67-S79.

Cook, Skinner A. & Daniel S. Dworkin, *Helping the Bereaved, Therapeutic Interventions for Children, Adolescents and Adults*, Harper Collins, Basic Books, 1992.

Council for World Mission [CWM], *Unmasking the Empire*, Singapore: CWM Publications, 2018.

Council of Churches in Zambia: *Women of the Collar*, 2015.

Covey, Stephen R., "The Greatest Leadership Principles," in Leslie Pockell & Adrienne Avila (eds), *The 100 Greatest Leadership Principles of all Times*, New York: Warner Books, 2007, 16.

Creswell, J.W., *Qualitative Inquiry and Research Design*, London: Sage, 2007.

Cullingford, Elizabeth, "Evil, Sin or Doubt? The Dramas of Clerical Child Abuse," 2010, 4-6, www.jostor.org/stable/40660605 [13.3.2019].

Dahlschen, Edith, *Women in Zambia*, Lusaka: Kenneth Kaunda Foundation, 1970.

Damon, Rose, "Stop Trying to 'Heal' me," *British Broadcasting Corporation News*, 28 April, 2019, www.bbc.com/news/uk-48054113 [7.9.2019].

Danziger, Kurt., "The Varieties of Social Construction," *Theory & Psychology*, 7(3), 1997, 399-416.

Darwin, John, *After Tamerlane: The Global History of Empire since 1405*, London: Bloomsbury, 2008.

Davies, Kathy, "Intersectionality as Buzzword: A Sociology of Science Perspective on What Makes a Feminist Theory Successful," in *Journal of Feminist Theory*, vol. 9(1), 2008, 67-85.

Deetman, Wim, "Sexual Abuse of Minors in the Roman Catholic Church," 2010, www.onderzoekrk.nl/fileadmin/commissiedeetman/data/downloads/eind rapport/20111216/Samenvatting_eindrapport_Engelstalig.pdf [29.3.2019].

Devandas-Aguilar, Catalina, "Report of the Special Rapporteur on the Rights of Persons with Disabilities on her Visit to Zambia," 2016, www.med box.org.[20.10.2019].

Devine, M.A., "Inclusive Leisure Services and Research: A Consideration of the Use of Social Construction Theory," *Journal of Leisurability*, 24(2), 1997, 1-9.

Devlieger, Patrick, "Why Disabled? The Cultural Understanding of Physical Disability in an African Society," in Susan Whyte & Benedicte Ingstal (eds), *Disability and Culture*. Los Angeles: University of California Press, 1995, 93.

Djomhoue, Priscille, "Mainstreaming Gender in Theological Institutions in Francophone Africa: Perspectives from Cameroon," Isabel Apawo Phiri & D. Werner (eds), *Handbook of Theological Education in Africa*, Oxford: Regnum, 2013.

Doyle, Michael, *Empires*, New York: Cornell University Press, 1986.

Doyle, Thomas P. & Marianne Benkert, *Clericalism, Religious Duress and its Psychological Impact on Victims of Clergy Sexual Abuse*, New York: Spring Science + Business Media, 2009.

Doyle, Thomas P., "Roman Catholic Clericalism, Religious Duress and Clergy Sexual Abuse," 2003, 223, www.researchgate.net/publications/251344247 [18.3.2019].

Drum, Charles E., Gloria L. Krahn & Hank Bersani, *Disability and Public Health: American Association on Intellectual and Developmental Disabilities*, Washington, D.C.: APHA Press, 2009, 1.

Dube, Musa, "Grant Me Justice: Towards Gender Sensitive Multisectoral HIV/AIDS Reading of the Bible," in Musa Dube & Musimbi Kanyoro (eds),

Grant Me Justice: HIV/AIDS and Gender Readings of the Bible, Pietermaritzburg: Cluster, 2004, 3-27.

Dube, Musa, "John 4:1-42, The Five Husbands at the Well of Living Waters: The Samaritan Woman and African Women," Nyambura Njoroge & Musa Dube (eds), *Talita Cum! Theologies of African Women,* Pietermaritzburg: Cluster, 2001, 48.

Dzokoto, Vivian Afi and Glenn Adams, *Understanding Genital-Shrinking Epidemics in West-Africa: Koro, Juju or Mass Psychogenic Illness, Culture, Medicine and Psychiatry,* 2005, 29, 53-78.

Eskay, M. et al, "Disability within the African Culture," *Contemporary Voices from the Margin: African Educators on African and American Education,* 2012.

Etieyibo, Edwin & Odirin Omiegbe, "Religion, Culture, and Discrimination against Persons with Disabilities in Nigeria, *African Journal of Disability,* 5(1) 2016.

Fast, Jonathan, *Beyond Bullying, Breaking the Cycle of Shame Bullying and Violence,* New York: Oxford University Press, 2016.

Fee, Gordon, "The New Testament and Kenosis Christology," in C.E. Evans (ed), *Exploring Kenotic Christology – The Self-Emptying of God,* New York: Oxford University Press, 2006, 25-44.

Fergus, Lara and Rogier van 't Rood, *Unlocking the Potential for Change; Education and Prevention of Gender Based Violence,* London: Rochester Publications, 2013.

Fernau, Sandra, "Sexual Abuse by Catholic Clergy: Patterns of Interpretation and Coping Strategies of Victims, in the Light of a Religious Socialization," 2016, 8, www.jostor.org/stable/j.ctvsz3.12 [13.5.2019].

Fiedler, Rachel NyaGondwe & Johannes W. Hofmeyr, "The Birth and Growth of the Circle of Concerned African Women Theologians in Malawi 1989-2011," *Studia Historiae Ecclesiasticae,* 37 (2), 2011, 1-9.

Fiedler, Rachel NyaGondwe, *Coming of Age. A Christianized Initiation among Women in Southern Malawi,* Zomba: Kachere, 2005

Fiedler, Rachel NyaGondwe, Johannes W. Hofmeyr & Klaus Fiedler, *African Feminist Hermeneutics. An Evangelical Reflection,* Mzuzu: Mzuni Press, 2016.

Fiedler, Rachel NyaGondwe, *The History of the Circle of Concerned African Women Theologians, 1989-2007,* Mzuzu: Mzuni Press, 2016.

Fisk, Bruce N., "The Odyssey of Christ: A Novel Context for Philippians 2: 6-11," in C.E. Evans (ed), *Exploring Kenotic Christology - The Self-Emptying of God,* New York: Oxford University Press, 2006, 45-73.

Fitzgerald, Jennifer, "Reclaiming the Whole: Self, Spirit, and Society," *Journal of Disability and Rehabilitation,* Vol. 19, no. 10, 1997.

Flannery, Austin (ed), *Vatican Council II: The Conciliar and Post-conciliar Documents.* Collegeville, MN: Liturgical Press, 2014.

Freeman, Donald B., "Survival Strategy or Business Training Ground? The Significance of Urban Agriculture of the Advancement of Women in African Cities," *African Studies Review,* 36/3, 1993.

Gangel, Kenneth and Warren Benson, *Christian Education: Its History and Philosophy*, Eugene, Oregon: Wipf & Stock, 1983.

Geisler, Gisela, "Sisters under the Skin: Women and the Women's League in Zambia," *The Journal of Modern African Studies*, *25*(1), 1987, 43-66 [11.4.2020], www.jstor.org/stable/160966.

Ghebreyesus, Tedros, "What French Doctors and the WHO Really Said about Africa and Vaccine Testing," *Euronews*, 2020.

Gherard, Marta D., "What is Empathy," 2012, www.counselling.org.uk [26.2.2018].

Gilbert, Paula R., *Violence and the Female Imagination: Quebec Women Writers Reframe Gender in North American Cultures*, Montreal: McGill-Queen's University Press, 2006.

Gilson, Erinn, *The Ethics of Vulnerability: A Feminist Analysis of Social Life and Practice*, New York: Routledge, 2014.

Glasgow, Arnold H., "Greatest Leadership Principle," in Pockell Leslie and Adrienne Avila (eds), *The 100 Greatest Leadership Principles of All Time*, New York: Warner Books, 2007, 17.

Gould, Lewis L., "First Ladies," *American Scholar*, 55, 1986, 529.

Government of Zambia, *Educating our Future: National Policy on Education*, Lusaka, Ministry of Education, 1996.

Gribaudo, Jeanmarie, *A Holy Yet Sinful Church: Three Twentieth-Century Moments in a Developing Theology*. Collegeville: Liturgical Press, 2015.

Gupton, Sandra Lee and Gloria Appelt Slick, *Highly Successful Women Administrators: The Inside Stories of how they got there*, Thousand Oaks: Corwin, 1996.

Guzmán Bouvard, Marguerite, *Speaking Truth to Power. Madres of the Plaza de Mayo*, 1994, www.womeninworldhistory.com.

Hackett, Rosalind, A. Melice, S.V. Wolputte & K. Pype, "Interview: Rosalind Hackett Reflects on Religious Media in Africa," *Social Compass*, 61(1), 2014, 67-72.

Haddad, Beverley, "Choosing to Remain Silent: Links between Gender Violence, HIV/AIDS and the South African Church," in Isabel Phiri, Beverly Haddad & Madipoane Masenya (eds), *African Women, HIV/AIDS and Faith Communities*, Pietermaritzburg: Cluster, 2003.

Haddad, Beverly, "Engendering Theological Education for Transformation," *Journal of Theology for Southern Africa*, 116, 2003, 65-80.

Hamabuyu, Isabel M. and J. Kafumbe, "Gender Audit of Member Churches of Council in Zambia Consultancy Report," Gender Desk of Council of Churches in Zambia, Lusaka, 2008.

Hamilton, "Marci, The Waterloo for the So-Called Church Autonomy Theory: Widespread Clergy Abuse and Institutional Cover-Up," www.researchgate.net /publication /228160852, 2007, 12-13.

Hanmer, Jalna, "Men, Power and the Exploitation of Women," _Women's Studies International Forum_, 13(5), 1990, 443-456.

Haralambos, M. and M. Holborn, _Themes and Perspectives_, London: Harper Collins, 1995.

Haron, Muhammed, "Religion and the Media: Reflections on their Position and Relationship in Southern Africa," _Global Media Journal_, 4, no. 1, 2010, 28-50.

Haslam, Molly C., _A Constructive Theology of Intellectual Disability: Human Being as Mutuality and Response_, New York: Fordham University Press, 2012.

Haynes, Naomi, "Why Can't a Pastor Be President of a 'Christian Nation?'" 2016.

Heise, L., "A Global Overview of Gender Based Violence," _International Journal of Gynecology and Obstetrics_, vol. 78, supplement 1, 1998, 262-290. www.oikoumene.org/en/get-involved/thursdays-in-black [4.4.2020].

Heitink, Gerben, _Practical Theology: History, Theory, Action Domains, Manual for Practical Theology_, Grand Rapids: Eerdmans, 1993.

Hermans, Chris et al (eds), _Social Constructionism and Theology_, Leiden: Brill, 2002, xvi.

Hill, Polly, _The Migrant Cocoa Farmers of Southern Ghana_, Cambridge: Cambridge University Press, 1963.

Hjarvard, Stig, "The Mediatisation of Religion: A Theory of the Media as Agents of Religious Change," _Northern Lights: Film and Media Studies Yearbook_, 6(1), 2008, 9-26.

Howard, Cameron B.R., "When Esther and Jezebel Write: A Feminist Biblical Theology of Authority," in P.K. Tull and J.E. Lapsley (eds), _After Exegesis: Feminist Biblical Theology: Essays in Honor of Carol A. Newsom_, Waco, TX: Baylor University Press, 2015, 110-111.

Ilubala-Ziwa, Judith Lubasi, "Community Based Theological Education for Social Transformation of Women in Chongwe District, Zambia," in James Amanze, M. Masango, Ezra Chitando and Lilian Siwila (eds), _Religion and Development in Southern and Central Africa_, vol 1, 2019, 143-164, Mzuzu: Mzuni Press.

Isabel Apawo Phiri, Devakarsham Betty Govinden & Sarojini Nadar (eds), _Her-Stories: Hidden Histories of Women of Faith in Africa_, Pietermaritzburg: Cluster, 2002.

Jackson, Lynette, _Surfacing Up: Psychiatry and Social Order in Colonial Zimbabwe, 1908-1968 – the Birth of Asylum in Africa_, Ithaca: Cornell University Press, 2005.

Jacobsson, Lars, "The Roots of Stigmatization," _Journal of the World Psychiatric Association_ (WPA), 1(1), 2002, 25.

Jay, Anthony, "The Greatest Leadership Principles," in Leslie Pockell and Adrienne Avila (eds), _The 100 Greatest Leadership Principles of All Time_, New York: Warner Books, 2007.

Jennings, M., "Communities in Development: The Theory and Practice of Gender," in Mary van Lieshout (ed), _A Woman's World beyond the Headlines_, Dublin: Attic Press, 1996, 107-117.

Jewkes, R., "Intimate Partner Violence: Causation and Primary Prevention," *Lancet*, 2002, 1423-1429.

Johnson, Daphne, *Research Methods in Education Management*, London: Pearson Education, 1994.

Johnson, Elizabeth, *She Who Is*, New York: Cross Road Publishing, 1992.

Jones, Claire "Shona Women Mbira Players: Gender, Tradition and Nation in Zimbabwe," *Ethnomusicology Forum*, 17, 2008, 125-149. doi: 10.1080/1741191-0801972982 [8.7.2020].

Kamga, Djoyou, "Call for the Protocol to the African Charter on Human and Peoples' Rights on the Rights of Persons with Disabilities in Africa," *African Journal of International and Comparative Law*, 21(2), 2013, 219.

Kanene, Kennedy M., "The Environmentality of Shrines: Case of Gonde Malende [Shrine] of the Tonga People of Southern Zambia," *Asian Journal of Social Sciences & Humanities*, vol. 4, 2015, 2.

Kangwa, Jonathan, "Resilience and Equality in the Household of God: Peggy Mulambya Kabonde's Search for Justice," *The Expository Times*, 131(8), 2020, 339-347.

Kangwa, Jonathan, "The Goodhall-Nielsen Report and the Formation of the United Church of Zambia Theological College," *Studia Historiae Ecclesiasticae*, 43(1), 2017, 1-24.

Kangwa, Jonathan, "The Goodhall-Nielson Report on the Formation of the United Church of Zambia Theological College," 2017, DOI: http://dx.doi-org 110.1715912412-426512/201612001.[30.10.2018].

Kangwa, Jonathan, *Gender, Christianity and African Culture*, Texas: St Paul Press, 2017.

Kanyoro, Musimbi, "Engendering Communal Theology," in Nyambura Njoroge & Musa Dube (eds), *"Talitha Cum! Theologies of African Women,"* Pietermaritzburg: Cluster, 2001, 158-180.

Kanyoro, Musimbi, "Introducing Feminist Cultural Hermeneutics: An African Perspective," *Introductions in Feminist Theology,"* Cleveland: Pilgrim Press, 2002.

Kanyoro, Musimbi, "Introduction," in Musimbi Kanyoro and Mercy Amba Oduyoye (eds), *The Will to Arise: Women, Tradition and the Church in Africa*, Maryknoll: Orbis, 1995, 1-8.

Kanyoro, Musimbi, *Introducing Feminist Cultural Hermeneutics: An African Perspective*, New York: Sheffield Academic Press, 2002.

Kasongo, Micheline Kamba, "Mission to Persons with Disabilities: A Transforming Love for Justice in 1 Samuel 9: 1-11," *International Review of Mission*, 108(1), 2019, 18-24.

Kaunda, Betty and Stephen A. Mpashi, *Betty Kaunda: Wife of the President of the Republic of Zambia*, Lusaka: Longman, 1969.

Kaunda, Chammah J., 'Christianising Edgar Chagwa Lungu: The Christian Nation, Social Media Presidential Photography and 2016 Election Campaign.' *Stellenbosch Theological Journal* 4 (1), 2018, 215-245.

Kaunda, Chammah J., "From Fools for Christ to Fools for Politicians: A Critique of Zambian Pentecostal Theopolitical Imagination," *International Bulletin of Mission Research*, 41(4), 2017, 296-311.

Kaunda, Kenneth, *Letter to my Children*, Lusaka: Longman, 1973.

Kaunda, M.M. & C.J. Kaunda, "Pentecostalism, Female Spirit-Filled Politicians and Populism in Zambia," *International Review of Mission*, 107(1), 2018, 23-32.

Kelly, Liz, "Wars against Women: Sexual Violence, Sexual Politics and the Militarized State," in Susie M. Jacobs, Ruth Jacobson and Jen March Bank (eds), *State of Conflict, Gender, Violence and Resistance*, New York: Zed Books, 2000.

Kiefer, Lilian, "Increasing Influence, Participation of Women in Leadership," *Daily Mail*, 16th October, 2016.

King, Ursula, *Introduction: Gender in the Study of Religion*, Oxford: Blackwell, 1995.

King, Ursula, *Women and Spirituality: Voices of Protest and Promise*, London: Macmillan, 1989.

Kirk, Andrew J., *Mission under Scrutiny: Confronting Current Challenges*, London: Darton, Longman & Todd, 2006.

Kirwen, Michael C., *African Widows*, Maryknoll: Orbis, 1979.

Kisitu, Gyaviira and Lilian Cheelo Siwila, "Whose Body, Whose Language? A Feminist Critique of the Construction of Discourses on a Woman's Body in African Religious Spaces and its Effect on Well-being," in *Alternation* 23(2), 2016, 185–200.

Kiura, F.M., *Unwed Teenage Mothers*, Oxford University Press, 1999.

Klenke, Karin, *Women and Leadership: A Contextual Perspective*, New York: Springer, 1996.

Koszela, Kelsey, "The Stigmatization of Disabilities in Africa and the Develop mental Effects," *Independent Study Project (ISP) Collection 1639*, 2013, 2, https:// digitalcollections.sit.edu/isp_collection/1639 [20.6.2019].

Kouzes, James M. & Barry Z. Posner, *The Leadership Challenges Book*, San Francisco: Jossey-Bass/A Wiley Company, 2003, 11-12.

Kramarae, Cheris, "The Condition of Patriarchy," in Cheris Kramarae and Spender Dale (eds), *The Knowledge Explosion: Generations of Feminist Scholarship*, London: Athan Series, Teachers College Press, 1992.

Kretzschmar, Louise, *The Church and Disability*, Pietermaritzburg: Cluster, 2018.

Kriger, Colleen, *Cloth in West African History*, Lanham: AltaMira Press, 2006.

Kroesbergen, Hermen, "The Prosperity Gospel: A Way to Reclaim Dignity?" *Word and Context*, 2003, 78-88.

Kübler-Ross, Elizabeth, *Death the Final Stages of Growth*, Hoboken: Prentice Hall, 1975.

Landman, Christina, "The Implementation of Biblical Hermeneutics," in Nyambura Njoroge & Musa Dube (eds), *Talita Cum! Theologies of African Women*, Pietermaritzburg: Cluster, 2001.

Lartey, Emmanuel, "Practical Theology as a Theological Form," in David Willows and John Swinton (eds), *Spiritual Dimension of Pastoral Care, Practical Theology in a Multidisciplinary Context*, London: Jessica Kinsley, 2000, 74.

le Deouff, Michelle, "Women and Philosophy," in T. Moi (ed), *French Feminist Thought: A Reader*, Oxford: Basil Blackwell, 1987, 182.

Lester, Andrew D., *Hope in Pastoral Care and Counselling*, London/Louisville: Westminster/John Knox, 1995.

Lips, Hilary M., *Women, Men and Power*, Toronto: Hayfield Publishing, 1991.

Loeb, M.E., A.H. Eide, and D. Mont, "Approaching the Measurement of Disability Prevalence: The Case of Zambia," *Alter*, vol. 2, no. 1, 2008, 32-43.

Longkumer, Limatula, "Feminist Theological Pedagogy for Ministerial Formation," *Bulletin of the Program Area on Faith Mission and Unity*, XXII (2), 2006,1-2.

Longwe, Molly, *African Feminist Theology and Baptist Pastors' Wives*, Mzuzu: Luviri Press, 2019.

Longwell, S., *Gender and the Media: Issues for Media Personnel*, Lusaka: ZARD, 1993; Natalie Watson, *Introducing Feminist Ecclesiology*, Sheffield: Sheffield Academic Press, 2002.

Loseke, Donilen and Joel Best, *Social Problems: Constructionist Readings*, London: Routledge, 2017.

Lounibos, John B., *Self-Emptying of Christ and the Christian: Three Essays on Kenosis*, Eugene: Wipf & Stock, 2011.

Louw, D., "From Phenomenology to Ontology in the Gender Debate," in S. Pillay, S. Nadar and Le Bruyns (eds), *Rag Bag Theologies: Essays in Honour of Denise M. Ackermann: A Feminist Theologian of Praxis*, Stellenbosch: SUN Press, 2009, 95-102.

Lowe, Mary E., "Breaking the Stained-glass Ceiling: Collaborative Leadership Theory as a Model for Women in Theological Higher Education," *Journal of Women in Education Leadership*, 8(3), 2010, 123-141.

Luis, Martin, "Radical Justice: Spain and the Southern Cone beyond Market and State," Lewisburg: Bucknell University Press, 2011, http://epaper.daily-mail.co.zm [3.5.2020].

Lumbwe, Kapambwe, "Kuomboka Ceremony, Nc'wala Traditional Ceremony, Lwindi Gonde Traditional Ceremony," *Journal of the Musical Arts in Africa*, 9(1), 2012, 86-89.

Lusaka Voice Opinion, "Women Stop Being Naïve, Prophets and Pastors won't Solve your Problems," *Lusaka Voice*, 1 May, 2015.

Machila, Margaret and Matrine Chuulu, *Women's Participation in the Catholic Church in Zambia*, Lusaka: Jesuit Centre for Theological Reflection, 2010.

Magesa, Laurent, *African Religion: The Moral Traditions of Abundant Life*, New York: Orbis, 1997.

Mahatma Ghandi, "The Greatest Leadership Principles," in Leslie Pockell and Adrienne Avila (eds), *The 100 Greatest Leadership Principles of All Time*, New York: Warner Books, 2007, 25.

Maluleke, Tinyiko S., "The 'Smoke Screens' Called Black and African Liberation Theologies – The Challenge of African Women Theology," in *Journal of Constructive Theology*, 3:2, 1997, 39-63.

Mama, Amina, "Sheroes and Villains: Conceptualizing Colonial and Contemporary Violence against Women in Africa," in M. Jacqui Alexander and Chandra Talpade Mohanty (eds), *Feminist Genealogies, Colonial Legacies, Democratic Futures*, New York: Routledge, 1997.

Mama, Amina, *Women's Studies and Studies of Women in Africa during the 1990s*, Dakar: CODESRIA, 1996.

Mark, Helen B., *The Wind of His Power: A Skeletal Sketch of the History of the Africa Evangelical Fellowship, formerly the South Africa General Mission*, Cape Town: AEF, 1963.

Masaiti, Gift and Dorothy Ngabwa, "Religious, Cultural and Social Changes in the Chibwelamushi Harvest Ceremony of the Lala-Swaka People of Serenje and Mkushi Districts," *Zambia Journal of Religion and Contemporary Issues*, 1/1 (2018).

Masenya, Madipoane, "Trapped between Two 'Canons': African-South African Christian Women in the HIV/AIDS Era," in Isabel Phiri, Beverly Haddad & Madipoane Masenya (eds), *African Women, HIV/AIDS and Faith Communities*, Pietermaritzburg: Cluster, 2003, 113-127.

Mason, Gail, *The Spectacle of Violence: Homophobia, Gender and Knowledge*, London: Routledge, 2002, 117-126.

Mathabane, Mark, *African Women, Three Generations*, London: Penguin, 1994.

Matsebula, Sebenzile, "Inclusion and Participation: A Success Story and Convictions of a Person with a Disability," in James Amanze & Fidelis Nkomazana (eds), *Disability is not Inability. A Quest for Inclusion and Participation of People with Disability in Society*, Mzuzu: Mzuni Press, 2020, 171-178.

Maxwell, John C., *The 21 Irrefutable Laws of Leadership*, 10th ed., Nashville, Tennessee: Thomson Nelson, 2007.

Maxwell, John C., *The Maxwell Leadership Bible (NKJV)*, (2nd ed), Nashville: Thomson Nelson, 2007.

Mbeki, Tabo, "The Deputy President's Statement, on Behalf of the African National Congress," At the adoption of South Africa's 1996 Constitution Bill, Cape Town, 8 May 1996, on the theme "I am an African."

Mbiti, John S., *African Religions and Philosophy*, 2nd ed, London: Heinemann, 1969; also, Nairobi: East African Educational Publishers, 1999.

Mcbrien, Richard, "I Believe in the Holy Spirit: The Role of Pneumatology in Yves Congar's Theology," in G. Flynn (ed), *Yves Congar: Theologian of the Church*, Leuven: Peeters Press, 2005, 303-327.

Mental Disability Advocacy Center and Mental Health Users Network of Zambia, *British Colonial Mental Disorder Act*, 2014, www.mdac.org/sites/mdac-.info/files/zambia_layout_web4.pdf [7.2.2019].

Mental Disability Advocacy Centre and Mental Health Users Network of Zambia, "Human Rights and Mental Health in Zambia – Mental Disability," September 4, 2014, www.mdac.org/sites/mdac.info/files/zambia_layout_web4.pdf [7.2. 2019].

Mignolo, Walter D., "Introduction: Coloniality of Power and De-Colonial Thinking," *Cultural Studies* 21(2&3), 2007, 155-167.

Miguez, Néstor, Joerg Rieger and Jung Mo Sung, *Beyond the Spirit of Empire: Theology and Politics in a New Key*, London: SCM, 2009.

Mikell, Gwendolyn, *Cocoa and Chaos in Ghana*, New York: Paragon House, 1989.

Ministry of Community Development and Social Welfare, "National Policy on Disability Launched," 2016, www.mcdsw.gov.zm/?page_id=5266 [25.10.2019].

Ministry of Women's Affairs, *Restoring Soul: Effective Interventions for Adult Victims/Survivors of Sexual Violence*, Wellington: MWA, Google Scholar, 2009.

Minton, Carol A. and J. David Knottnerus, "Ritualised Duties: The Social Construction of Gender Inequality in Malawi," *International Review of Modern Sociology*, 34(2), 2008, 181-210, www.jstor.org/stable/41421678 [10.7.2020].

Mombo, Esther, "The Ordination of Women in Africa: An Historical Perspective," in I. Jones, K. Thorpe and J. Wootton (eds), *Women and Ordination in the Christian Churches: International Perspectives*, New York: T&T Clark, 2008, 123-140.

Mombo, Esther, "Theological Education in Africa," *Ministerial Formation* 89, 2000, 39-45.

Moore, Henrietta L., "Gender and Status: Explaining the Position of Women," in Henrietta L. Moore (ed), *Feminism and Anthropology*, Cambridge: Polity Press, 1988, 12-30.

Morrel, Robert, *Journal of Southern African Studies*, vol. 24, no. 4, December 1998, 607, www.tandfonline.com/loi/cjss20 [22.6.2020].

Morris, Madeleine, "In War and Peace: Rape, War, and Military Culture," in Ann Llewellyn Barstow (ed), *War's Dirty Secret, Rape, Prostitution, and Other Crimes against Women*, Barstow, Cleveland OH: Pilgrim Press, 2000.

Morrison, Andrew R. and M.B. Orlando, "The Socio-economic Costs of Domestic Violence: Chile and Nicaragua," in Andrew R. Morrison and Mariah L. Biehl (eds), *Too Close to Home: Domestic Violence in the Americas*, Washington DC: Inter-American Development Bank, 1999, 3.

Morrow, Sean, "No Girl Leaves School Unmarried: Mable Shaw and the Education of Girls at Mbereshi, Northern Rhodesia, 1915-1940," *International Journal of African Historical Studies*, 19(4), 1986, 601-635.

Moyo, Fulata Lusungu, "Sex Gender, Power and HIV/AIDS in Malawi: Threats and Challenges to Women Being Church," in Isabel Phiri & Sarojini Nadar (eds), *On Being Church: African Women's' Visions*, Geneva: WCC, 2005, 127-146.

Moyo, Fulata Lusungu, "Singing and Dancing Women's Liberation: My Story of Faith," in Isabel Apawo Phiri, Devakarsham Betty Govinden & Sarojini Nadar (eds), *Her-Stories: Hidden Histories of Women of Faith in Africa*, Pietermaritzburg: Cluster, 2002, 398.

Moyo, Herbert (ed), *Pastoral Care in a Globalized World: African and European Perspectives*, Pietermaritzburg: Cluster, 2015.

Moyo, Herbert, "The Pastor and the Embryonic Pastoral Identities in Southern Africa in the 21st Century," in Herbert Moyo (ed), *Pastoral Care in a Globalized World: African and European Perspectives*, Pietermaritzburg: Cluster, 2015.

Mudimbe, Harrow K., "The Power of the Word," in Stephen Arnold (ed), *African Literature Studies: The Present State*, Washington DC: Three Continents Press/African Literature Association, 1985, 91-100.

Mujuru, Linda, "Breaking with Tradition: Zimbabwean Women Perform on the Mbira," *Global Press Journal*, 2008, 1, https://globalpressjournal.com/africa/-zimbabwe/breaking-tradition-zimbabwean-women-perform-mbira [9.7.2020]

Mukwita, Anthony, *Against All Odds: Zambia's President Edgar Chagwa Lungu's Rough Journey to State House*, South Africa: Partridge Africa, 2017.

Mung'omba, James, "Comparative Policy Brief: Status of Intellectual Disabilities in the Republic of Zambia," *Journal of Policy and Practice in Intellectual Disabilities*, 5(2), 2008, 142-144.

Munroe, Miles, *Understanding the Purpose and Power of Women*, New Kensington: Whitaker House, 2001.

Munshya wa Munshya, "In the Name of God: Miracles in Zambia's Pentecostal Movement," *Daily Nation*, 26.6.2015.

Murray, Christopher and Alan Lopez, *The Global Burden of Disease: A Comprehensive Assessment of Mortality and Disability from Diseases, Injuries and Risk Factors in 1990 and Projected to 2020*, Global Burden of Disease and Injury Series, vol. I, Cambridge, 1996.

Musonda, Emelda, "False Prophets Thriving on Ignorance," *Daily Mail*, 25.8.2017.

Muthoni, Muriithi, Chioma Ukuwagu, Saskia van Venn & Anneli Verkade, *Breaking a Culture of Silence: Social Norms that Perpetuate Violence against Women and Girls in Nigeria*, Oxford: Oxfam, 2018.

Muzenda, Mako, "The Invisible Trauma of Women in Zimbabwe's Liberation Struggle," 2019, https://thisisafrica.me/politics-and-society/the-invisible-trauma-of-women-in-zimbabwes-liberation-struggle [11.4.2020].

Mveng, Engelbert, "Third World Theology – What Theology? What Third World? Evaluation by an African Delegate," in Virginia M.M. Fabella and Sergio Torres (eds), *Irruption of the Third World: Challenge to Theology*, Maryknoll: Orbis, 1983, 201-221.

Mwaanga, Vernon, *The Long Sunset: My Reflections*, Lusaka: Fleetfoot, 2008.

Mwaba, Sydney O., "Gender Based Violence: The Zambian Situation. Studies in Social Sciences and Humanities," *Research Academy of Social Sciences*, vol. I, 4(2) 2020, 105-118, ideas.repec.org [23.5.2020].

Mwale, Nelly & Joseph Chita "Navigating through Institutional Identity in the Context of a Transformed United Church of Zambia University College in Zambia," *HTS Theological Studies*, 73(3), 2017, 1-8.

Mwale, Nelly & Joseph Chita, "Religious Pluralism and Disability in Zambia: Approaches and Healing in Selected Pentecostal Churches," *Studia Historiae Ecclesiasticae*, 42(2), 2016, 53-57.

Mwale, Nelly & Joseph Chita, "Pentecostalising the Voice in Zambian Charismatic Church History: Men of God's Expression of Spiritual Identities, 1990 to Present," *Studia Historiae Ecclesiasticae*, 44(3), 2018, 1-13.

Mwale, Nelly, "Religion, Gender, and the Media: The Nature and Significance of a Muslim Woman – Sirre Muntanga's Contest for Mayor of Lusaka, Zambia in 2016," *The African Journal of Gender and Religion*, vol. 25(2), 2019, 1-23.

Mwale, Nelly, "African Traditional Religion in the Context of Climate Change: A Zambian Perspective," *Journal of Humanities*, 13, 2014, 1-14.

Mwansa, George, *Women and Marriage: Why Marriage Means Everything to a Woman*, Lusaka: Zambia Adventist Press, 2012.

Nadar, Sarojini, "On Being the Pentecostal Church: Pentecostal Women's Voices and Visions," in Isabel Apawo Phiri and Sarojini Nadar (eds), *On Being Church: African Women's Voices and Visions*, Geneva: WCC, 2005, 18.

Nadar, Sarojini, "On Being the Pentecostal Church: Pentecostal Women's Voices and Visions," *Ecumenical Review*, 2004, 56/3, 354-367.

Nadar, Sarojini, "Stories are Data with Soul: Lessons from Black Feminist Epistemology," *Agenda*, 28(1), 2014, 18-28.

Naidoo, Marilyn, "Persistent Issues Impacting on the Training of Ministers in the South African Context," *Scriptura: Journal for Contextual Hermeneutics in Southern Africa*, 112(1), 2013, 1-16.

Nalumango, Mbuyu and Monde Sifuniso (eds), *Women Power in Politics*, Lusaka: Zambia Women Writers Association, 1988.

Narismulu, Priya, "Teaching Social Justice and Diversity through South/African Stories that Challenge the Chauvinistic Fictions of Apartheid, Patriarchy, Class, Nationalism, Ethnocentrism," *Alternation. Interdisciplinary Journal for the Study of the Arts and Humanities in Southern Africa*, 18(2), 2011, 135-158.

Ndlovu, Hebron, "African Beliefs Concerning People with Disabilities: Implications for Theological Education," *Journal of Disability & Religion*, 20(1-2), 2016, 29-39.

Newsom, Carol A. and Sharon H. Ringe, *Women's Bible Commentary*, Louisville: Westminster/John Knox Press, 109.

Ng'uni, Chambo, "Be Wary of False Prophets who Promise Marriage," *Daily Mail*, 10 January 2018.

NGOCC, http://ngocc.org.zm/2019/09/13/zambia-unite-end-sexual-gender-ba sed-violence [14.9.2019].

Nieves, Rico, "Gender Based Violence: A Human Rights Issue," *Women and Development Unit, Mujer Y. Desarrallo*, 1997, 13-16.

Njoroge, Nyambura, "A Spirituality of Resistance and Transformation," in Nyambura Njoroge & Musa Dube (eds), *Talitha Cum! Theologies of African Women*, Pietermaritzburg: Cluster, 2001, 66-68.

Oden, Thomas C., *How Africa Shaped the Christian Mind: Rediscovering the African Seedbed of Western Christianity*, Downers Grove: IVP, 2010, 1.

Oduyoye, Mercy Amba, "African Culture and the Gospel: Inculturation from an African Woman's Perspective," In Mercy Amba Oduyoye & H.M. Vroom (eds), *One Gospel—Many Cultures: Case Studies and Reflections on Cross-Cultural Theology*, Amsterdam/New York: Editions Rodopi, 2003.

Oduyoye, Mercy Amba, "Reflections from a Third World Women's Perspective Women's Experience and Liberation Theologies," In Virginia Fabella & Sergio Torres, *Irruption of the Third World: Challenge to Theology*, Maryknoll: Orbis, 1983, 244-250.

Oduyoye, Mercy Amba, "The Search for a Two-winged Theology," in Mercy Amba Oduyoye & Musimbi Kanyoro (eds), *Talitha Cum! Proceedings of the Convocation of African Women Theologians*, 1989, Ibadan: Daystar, 53.

Oduyoye, Mercy Amba, *Daughters of Anowa: African Women and Patriarchy*, Maryknoll: Orbis, 1995.

Oduyoye, Mercy Amba, *Hearing and Knowing: Theological Reflections on Christianity in Africa*, Maryknoll: Orbis, 1986.

Oduyoye, Mercy Amba, *Introducing African Women's Theology*, Sheffield: Sheffield Academic Press, 2001.

Ogundipe-Leslie, Omolara, *Re-claiming Ourselves: African Women and Critical Transformation*, Trenton, New Jersey: Africa World Press, 1994.

Okali, Christine, *Cocoa and Kinship in Ghana: The Matrilineal Akan of Ghana*, London: Kegan Paul, 1983.

Oliver, Mike, "A New Model of the Social Work Role in Relation to Disability," In Jo Campling (ed), *The Handicapped Person: A New Perspective for Social Workers*, London: Radar, 1981, 19–32.

Onukwugha, Gerald Onyewuchi, "Death and Dying in the African Context, Chicken Bones," *Journal for Literary and Artistic African American Themes*, 2016, www.nathanielturner.com/deathanddyingafrican.htm [17.2.2018].

Opare-Henaku, Annabelle & S.O. Utsey, "Culturally Prescribed Beliefs about Mental Illness among the Akan of Ghana," *Transcultural Psychiatry*, 54(4), 2017, 502-522.

Para-Mallam, Funmi J., "Promoting Gender Equality in the Context of Nigerian Cultural and Religious Expression: Beyond Increasing Female Access to Education," *A Journal of Comparative and International Education*, 40(4), 2010, 459-477.

Parkes, Colin M., "The First Year of Bereavement: A Longitudinal Study of the Reaction of London Widows to the Death of their Husbands," London, 1970, *Psychiatry: Journal for the Study of Interpersonal Processes*, 33(4), 444–467.

Parpart, Jane L., "'Where Is Your Mother?': Gender, Urban Marriage, and Colonial Discourse on the Zambian Copperbelt, 1924-1945." *International Journal of African Historical Studies*, 27/2, 1994:241–71. https://doi. org/10.2307/221025.

Pattison, Stephen, *The Challenges of Practical Theology. Selected Essays*, London: Jessica Kingsley Publishers, 2007.

Payne, Sheila, Sandra Horn & Marilyn Relf (eds), *Health Psychology. Loss and Bereavement*, Buckingham: Open University Press, 2000.

Phiri, Bizeck J., "Gender and Politics: The Zambia National Women's Lobby Group in the 2001 Tripartite Elections," in *One Zambia, Many Histories*, Leiden: Brill, 2008, 259-274.

Phiri, Elizabeth, "Minister Bemoans Rise in GBV Cases," *Lusaka Times*, September 11, 2019, www.lusakatimes.com/2019/09/11/gender-minister-bemoans-rise-in-gbv-cases [11.9.2019].

Phiri, Isabel Apawo "Why does God Allow our Husbands to Hurt us? Overcoming Violence against Women," *Journal of Theology for Southern Africa*, 114, Nov 2002, 19-30.

Phiri, Isabel Apawo *Women, Presbyterian and Patriarchy*, Blantyre: CLAIM-Kachere, 1997, 117.

Phiri, Isabel Apawo, "Called at Twenty-Seven and Ordained at Seventy-Three! The Story of Rev. Victory Nomvete Mbanjwa in the United Congregational Church in Southern Africa," in Isabel Apawo Phiri et al (eds), *Her Stories. Hidden Stories of Women of Faith in Africa*, Pietermaritzburg: Cluster, 2002, 119-138.

Phiri, Isabel Apawo, "Doing Theology in Community: The Case of African Women Theologians in the 1990s," *Journal of Theology for Southern Africa*, 99, 1997, 68-76.

Phiri, Isabel Apawo, "Major Challenges for African Women Theologians in Theological Education (1989–2008)," *International Review of Mission*, 98 (1), 2009, 105-119.

Phiri, Isabel Apawo, "President Frederick J.T. Chiluba of Zambia: The Christian Nation and Democracy," *Journal of Religion in Africa*, 33(4), 2003, 401-428.

Phiri, Isabel Apawo, Devakarsham Betty Govinden & Sarojini Nadar (eds), *Her-Stories: Hidden Histories of Women of Faith in Africa*, Pietermaritzburg: Cluster, 2002, 3-12.

Phiri, L., "Ministerial Formation, Identity and Liturgy among the Female Ministers in the United Church of Zambia," in Roderick R. Hewitt and Lilian Cheelo Siwila (eds), *Liturgy and Identity: African Religio-cultural and Ecumenical Perspectives*, Pietermaritzburg: Cluster, 2018, 60.

Phiri, Prudence, "Zambia Begins Crackdown on Self-Proclaimed Prophets," *Global Press Journal*, 21 June, 2017.

Phiri, Sam, "Anointed Pants on SALE!" *Times of Zambia Newspaper*, 3.10.2015.

Pockell, Leslie and Adrienne Avila (eds), *The 100 Greatest Leadership Principles of All Time*, New York: Warner Books, 2007.

Poling, James N., *The Abuse of Power: A Theological Problem*, Nashville: Abingdon, 1991.

Polkinghorne, Donald E., "Narrative Configuration in Qualitative Analysis," *Qualitative Studies in Education*, 8, 1995, 5-23.

Poltera, J., "Exploring Examples of Women's Leadership in African Context," *Agenda*, 33:1, 2019, 3-8.

Pope Francis, "A Letter to the People of God," 2018, 2, http://w2.vati can.va/content/francesco/en/letters/2018/documents/papa-francesco_2018 0820_lettera-popolo-didio.html [14.4.2019].

Pope Francis, "Address at the End of the Eucharistic Celebration," 2019, 9. http:// w2.vatican.va/content/francesco/en/speeches/2019/february/documents /papa francesco_20190224_incontro-protezioneminori-chiusura.html.[14.4. 2019].

Pope Francis, "Letter to the Bishops of Chile," 2018, 4-5, www.vaticannews.va-/en/pope/news/2018-05/letter-of-pope-francis-to-the-chileanbishops.html. [14.4.2019].

Pope Francis, "Letter to the People of God," 2018, 1, http://w2.vatican. va/content/francesco/en/letters/2018/documents/papa-francesco_201808 20_lettera-popolo-didio.html.[14.4.2019].

Pope Francis, http://w2.vatican.va/content/francesco/en/speeches/2019/Febru ary/documents/papafrancesco_20190224_incontro-protezione minori-chiusu ra.html.[14.4.2019].

Prokopenko, Lyubov Y., "Development of the Institution of the First Ladyship in Africa," *Journal of Globalisation Studies*, vol, 12/1, 2021, 38-60.

Radford Ruether, Rosemary, *Sexism and God Talk: Towards a Feminist Theology*, Boston: Beacon Press, 1983.

Radford Ruether, Rosemary, *Women-Church. Theology and Practice of Feminist Liturgical Communities*, Eugene: Wipf & Stock, 1985.

Rakoczy, Susan, "Living Life to the Full: Reflections on Feminist Spirituality," in Celia Ellen Teresa Kourie and Louise Kretzschmar (eds), *Christian Spirituality in South Africa*, Pietermaritzburg: Cluster, 2000, 69-91.

Rakoczy, Susan, *In Her Name: Women Doing Theology*, Pietermaritzburg: Cluster, 2004.

Ratele, Kopano, "Analysing Males in Africa: Certain Useful Elements in Considering Ruling Masculinities," *African and Asian Studies* 7, 2008, 515-536, www.brill.nl/aas.

Retief, Marno & Rantoa Letšosa, "Models of Disability: A Brief Overview," *HTS Teologiese Studies/Theological Studies*, 2018, 74(1), 2.

Reynolds, Thomas E., *Vulnerable Communion: A Theology of Disability and Hospitality*. Grand Rapids: Brazos Press, 2008, 25.

Rhode, Deborah L., *Women and Leadership*, Oxford University Press, 2017.

Robinson, Lillian, "Feminist Criticism – How do we Know when we've Won?" In S. Benston (ed), *Feminist Issues in Literary Scholarship*, Bloomington and Indianapolis: Indiana University Press, 1987.

Romito, Patrizia, *A Deafening Silence. Hidden Violence against Women and Children*, Bristol, UK: Policy Press, 2008.

Rowan, John, *The Horned God, Feminism and Men as Wounding and Healing*, New York: Routledge and Kegan Paul, 1987.

Said, Edward W., *Orientalism*, New York: Vintage, 1978.

Sande, Nomatter, "Pastoral Ministry and Persons with Disabilities: The Case of the Apostolic Faith Mission in Zimbabwe," *African Journal of Disability* (Online), 2019/8, 1-8.

Scharnick-Udemans, Lee-Shae Salma, "A Historical and Critical Overview of Religion and Public Broadcasting in South Africa," *Journal for the Study of Religion*, 30(2), 2017, 257-280.

Schüssler-Fiorenza, Elisabeth, *Discipleship of Equals*, New York: Crossroad, 1993.

Schuster, Ilsa, "Constraints and Opportunities in Political Participation: The Case of Zambian Women," *Genève-Afrique: Acta Africana*, 21(2), 1983, 7-37.

Schuster, Ilsa, "Zambian Women in Politics, Constraints and Opportunities in Political Participation: The Case of Zambian Women," vol. xxi, no. 2, 2000.

Schwarzkopf, Norman, "The Greatest Leadership Principles," In Leslie Pockell and Adrienne Avila (eds), *The 100 Greatest Leadership Principles of All Time*, New York: Warner Books, 2007, 51.

Scott, James C., *Domination and the Arts of Resistance: Hidden Transcripts*, New Haven: Yale University Press, 1990.

Semple, Rhoda, "Missionary Manhood: Professionalism, Belief and Masculinity in the Nineteenth-Century British Imperial Field," *The Journal of Imperial and Commonwealth History*, 36:3, 397-415 [1.4.2020].

Servant Church: The Programme for Adult Formation, Hinckley: St Peters Community, 2013-2014.

Setume, Sensokhuhle Doreen, "Myths and Beliefs about Disabilities: Implications for Educators and Counsellors," *Journal of Disability & Religion*, 20(1-2), 2016, 62-76.

Seur, Han, *Sowing the Good Seed: The Interweaving of Agricultural Change, Gender Relations and Religion in Serenje District, Zambia*, Wageningen: Landbouwuniversiteit Wageningen, 1992.

Shea, Diane J., "Effects of Sexual Abuse by Catholic Priests on Adults Victimized as Children: Sexual Addictions and Compulsivity," *Research Gate* 15, vol. 3, 2008, 250-268, www.researchgate.net/publication/232959291 [13.3.2019].

Siebers, Tobin, "Disability in Theory: From Social Constructionism to the New Realism of the Body," *American Literary History*, 13(4), 2001, 737-754.

Simpson, Graeme and Gerald Kraak "The Illusions of Sanctuary and the Weight of the Past: Notes on Violence and Gender in South Africa," in *Development Update 2: The Right to be: Sexuality and Sexual Rights in Southern Africa*, 1998, 1-10.

Siwila, Lilian Cheelo, "An Encroachment of Ecological Sacred Sites and its Threat to the Interconnectedness of Sacred Rituals: A Case Study of the Tonga People in the Gwembe Valley," *Journal for the Study of Religion*, 28(2), 2015, 138-153.

Siwila, Lilian Cheelo, "Feminist Critique of the Education Model of Mabel Shaw Girls' Boarding Mission School in Zambia 1915-1940 and its Effect on the Education of Girls," *Scriptura 116*, 2017, 1-12, http://scriptura.journals.ac.za [11.4.2020].

Siwila, Lilian Cheelo, "Gender Trouble: Navigating Distorted Gender Discourses in Faith Communities," in Herbert Moyo (ed), *Pastoral Care in a Globalised World: African and European Perspectives*, Pietermaritzburg: Cluster, 2015, 243-256.

Siwila, Lilian Cheelo, "In Search of a Feminist Cultural Analysis Model for Effective Dialogue on Harmful Cultural Practices," in Isabel Apawo Phiri and Sarojini Nadar (eds), *Journal of Gender and Religion in Africa, Publication Information*, vol. 18, no. Special Issue, 2012, 106-112.

Siwila, Lilian Cheelo, "Problematizing a Norm: A Religio-cultural Gender Analysis of Child Marriage in the Context of HIV and AIDS," *Journal of Gender & Religion in Africa*, (17)1, 2011, 27-49.

Siwila, Lilian Cheelo, "Reconstructing the Distorted Image of Women as Reproductive Labour on the Copperbelt Mines in Zambia (1920-1954)," *Journal for the Study of Religion* 30, 2, 2017 75–89, http://dx.doi.org/10.17159/2413-3027/2017/v30n2a3.[11.4.2020].

Siwila, Lillian Cheelo, "In Search of a Feminist Cultural Analysis Model for Effective Dialogue on Harmful Cultural Practices," in Isabel Apawo Phiri and Sarojini Nadar (eds), *Journal of Gender and Religion in Africa*, vol. 18, Special Issue, 2012, 106-112.

Snelson, Peter D., *Educational Development in Northern Rhodesia 1883-1945*, Lusaka: Zambia Educational Publishing House, 1974, 117-118.

Snyman, Gerrie, "Empire and a Hermeneutics of Vulnerability," *Studia Historiae Ecclesiasticae*, 37 – Supplement, 2011, 1-20

Sobel, Bart, "A Reconstructionist Perspective of the Teaching of Social Studies," *The High School Journal*, 60(8), 1977, 353-364, www.jstor.org/stable/40365469 [11.7.2020]

Soko, Lucas, "Zambia Dziko la Chonde," *Word and Context Journal*, 2013, 90-99.

Steinmetz, George, "The Sociology of Empires, Colonies and Post-colonialism," *Annual Review of Sociology*, 40, 2014, 77-103.

Sullivan, Francis, *The Church we Believe in*, New York: Pauline Press, 1988.

Swinton, John, "Friendship in Community, Creating a Space for Love," in David Willows and John Swinton (eds), *Spiritual Dimension of Pastoral Care. Practical Theology in a Multidisciplinary Context*, London: Jessica Kinsley, 2000, 74.

Talle, Aud, "A Child is a Child: Disability and Equality among the Kenya Maasai," in Susan Whyte and Benedicte Ingstal (eds), *Disability and Culture*, Los Angeles: University of California Press, 1995, 67.

TCCA Curriculum Framework, TCCA: Ndola, 2013.

The Council of Churches in Zambia, *Testimonies of the Women Theologians: Stories from the Heart*, Lusaka: CCZ, 2011.

The Theological College of Central Africa 2004-2005 Prospectus, Ndola: The United Church of Zambia University (www.uczuniversity.org).

Thornicroft, G., E. Brohan, & A. Kassam, "Public Attitudes and the Challenge of Stigma," in Michael Gelder, Juan López-Ibor, and Nancy Andreasen (eds), *New Oxford Textbook of Psychiatry*, Oxford University Press, 2009.

Torjesen, Karen Jo, "Reconstruction of Women's Early Christian History in Searching the Scriptures," in Elisabeth Schüssler Fiorenza (ed), *A Feminist Introduction*, vol. 1, New York: Crossroads, 1993, 291.

Tracy, Sarah J., *Qualitative Research Methods*, Chichester: Wiley–Blackwell, 2013.

Tranberg Hansen, Karen, "Negotiating Sex and Gender in Urban Zambia," *Journal of Southern African Studies*, 10(2), 1984, 219-238.

Udelhoven, Bernhard, *The Changing Face of Christianity in Zambia*, Fenza documents. https://fenza. org/docs/ben/changing_face.pdf.

Ukah, Asonzeh, "Banishing Miracles: Politics and Policies of Religious Broadcasting in Nigeria," *African Sociological Review*, 5, 2011, 39-60.

UN Women, "Patriarchal Culture," 2019, https://eca.unwomen.org [29.5. 2020].

Union for the Physically Impaired Against Segregation, *Fundamental Principles of Disability*, London: The Union of Physically Impaired Against Segregation, 1976.

United Church of Canada, "Gender Justice and Partnership Guidelines," February, 1998, www.ucc.home.page [20.3.2020].

United Nations Population Fund (UNFPA), _Ending Widespread Violence against Women_, 1998, www.unfpa.org/gender/violence.htm [29.2.2020].

United Nations, "Fourth World Conference on Women. Beijing Declaration," 1995, www.un.org/womenwatch/daw/beijing/platform/declar.htm. [15.4. 2020].

United Nations, _Declaration on the Elimination of Violence against Women_. United Nations General Assembly Resolution 48/104, New York: United Nations, 1993.

van Binsbergen, Wim, "Chiefs and the State in Independent Zambia: Exploring the Zambian National Press," _Journal of Legal Pluralism and Unofficial Law_, 10, 1987, https://openaccess.leidenuniv.nl/search.[11.4.2020].

van Klinken, Adriaan S., "Theology, Gender Ideology and Masculinity Politics: A Discussion on the Transformation of Masculinities as Envisioned by African Theologians and a Local Pentecostal Church," _Journal of Theology for Southern Africa_, 138, 2.11.1985, 2-18.

van Klinken, Adriaan S., _Transforming Masculinities in African Christianity: Gender Controversies in Times of AIDS_, Farnham: Ashgate, 2013.

van Niekerk, Attie, "Dreaming a Different World: Globalisation and Justice for Humanity and the Earth–The Challenge of the Accra Confession for the Churches," _International Journal of Public Theology_, vol. 5, Issue 1, 2011, 2, https://doi.org/10.1163/156973211X543869.

van Zoonen, Liesbet, _Feminist Media Studies_, London: Sage, 1994.

Villa-Vicencio, Charles, "Difference and Belonging," in J. Witte and van der Vyer (eds), _Religious Human Rights in Global Perspectives_, The Hague/Boston/London: Martinus Nijhoff, 1994, 517-553.

von Balthasar, Hans Urs, _Who is a Christian?_ San Francisco: Ignatius Press, 2014, 122.

von Clausewitz, Karl, "The Greatest Leadership Principle," in Pockell and Avila Adrienne (eds), _The 100 Greatest Leadership Principles of all Time_, New York: Warner Books, 2007, 72.

Waldo, Emerson Ralph, "The Greatest Leadership Principles," in Leslie Pockell and Adrienne Avila (eds), _The 100 Leadership Principles of All Time_, New York: Warner Books, 2007, 8.

Walker, Trish, "Anger in Bereavement: How Counselling Can Help," 2012, www.counselling-directory.org.uk.counseeling-can-help [1.6.2017].

Walls, Andrew, "Theological Education from its Earliest Jewish and African Christian Beginnings –Some Currents in the Wider History of Christianity," in Isabel Apawo Phiri and Dietrich Werner (eds), _Handbook of Theological Education in Africa_, Oxford: Regnum, 2013, 3.

Walvoord, John and Roy B. Zuck (eds), _The Bible Knowledge Commentary: An Exposition of the Scriptures_, Colorado Springs: David C. Cook, 1983.

Warren, Rick, _Purpose Driven Life: What on Earth am I Here for_, Grand Rapids: Zondervan, 2014.

Watson, Natalie K., _Introducing Feminist Ecclesiology_, Sheffield: Sheffield Academic Press, 2002.

Wendell, Susan, _The Rejected Body: Feminist Philosophical Reflections on Disability_, New York: Routledge, 1996.

White, Stephen R., "Theodore Brameld's Thought Infused in Higher Education Global Studies Curriculum," _Journal of Education and Learning_, North Carolina: Canadian Center of Science and Education, 2016.

Winfield, Betty H., "The First Lady's Relations with the Mass Media," in Laura Bush (ed), _The Report to the First Lady_, New York: Nova History Publications, 2001.

Winn, Harriet, "Thursdays in Black: Localized Responses to Rape Culture and Gender Violence in Aotearoa New Zealand," in: C. Blyth, E. Colgan & K. Edwards K. (eds) _Rape Culture, Gender Violence, and Religion. Religion and Radicalism_. Palgrave Macmillan, Cham. https://doi.org/10.1007/978-3-319-72224-5_4, (2018).

Wiredu, Kwasi (ed), _A Companion to African Philosophy_, Oxford: Blackwell, 2005.

www.evangelicaluniversity.ac.zm.

www.evangelicaluniversity.ac.zm/about-us.

www.ilo.org.docs.

Yong, Amos, _The Bible, Disability, and the Church: A New Vision of the People of God_, Grand Rapids: Eerdmans, 2011.

Young, Pamela D., _Feminist Theology/Christian Theology: in Search of Method_, Minneapolis: Fortress, 1990.

Zambia's Higher Education Act of 2011, www.hea.org.zm.

Zulu, E., "'Fipelwa na ba Yahweh': A Critical Examination of Prosperity Theology in the Old Testament from a Zambian Perspective," _Word and Context_, 2013, 27-35.

Unpublished

Bulanda, Bickson, "Mission Studies in Zambia: An Investigation of Curricula and Attitudes in Selected Bible Colleges," MA, London School of Theology and Middlesex University, 2018.

Chilapula, Mercy, "A Cry for Inclusion – Experiences of Women Clergy in the Church of Central Africa Presbyterian (CCAP) Blantyre Synod," PhD [submitted], Mzuzu University, 2021.

Chilcote, Paul Wesley, "John Wesley and the Women Preachers of Early Methodism," PhD, Duke University, 1984.

Chizelu, J.M., "Theological Education by Extension: A Missiological Analysis of the Association of Evangelicals of Africa and Madagascar TEE Programme from a Zambian Perspective," MA, UNISA, 1997.

Franzen, Bjorn, "Attitudes Towards People with Disabilities in Kenya and Zimbabwe," MA module, School for International Training, Nybro, 1990.

Haynes, N., "Why can't a Pastor be President of a Christian Nation? Mapping the Diverse Political Theologies of Zambia's Pentecostals," 2016 (unpublished).

Impley, A., "They Want us with Salt and Onions: Women in the Zimbabwean Music Industry," PhD, Indiana University, 1992.

Kangwa, Jonathan, "In Search of Indigenous Knowledge Systems for Ecological Justice: A Gendered Ecological Reading of Genesis 1-3 in the Context of the Tonga People in Zambia," PhD, University of KwaZulu Natal, 2014.

Krishna, K. and F.E. Mulenga, "Contribution of Zambian Women and Indian Women to the Struggle for Freedom: A Legend of Courage and Compassion," Paper presented at the *African Renewal, African Renaissance': New Perspectives on Africa's Past and Africa's Present, The African Studies Association of Australia and the Pacific (AFSAAP) Annual Conference*, 26-28 November 2004, University of Western Australia.

Limann, Hasila Leda, "Womanhood Rites and the Rites of Women in Africa, The Ugandan Experience," LLM (Human Rights and Democratization in Africa), Makerere University, Kampala, 2003, 27-30.

Lupyani, Bodson Chailosi, "The (Sub-) Ordination of Women in the Evangelical Church in Zambia. A Critical Analysis of the Ecclesiological and Hermeneutical Principles Underlying the Refusal of Women's Ordination," MA, University of KwaZulu Natal, 2009.

Mbano-Moyo, Fulata Lusungu, "A Quest for Women's Sexual Empowerment through Education in an HIV and AIDS Context," PhD, University of KwaZulu-Natal, 2009.

Micheline Kamba Kasongo, "Developing a Holistic Educational Programme through Contextual Bible Study with People with Disabilities in Kinshasa, Democratic Republic of Congo: Iman'enda as a Case Study," PhD, University of KwaZulu-Natal, Pietermaritzburg, 2013.

Mukuka, Sylvia, "A Critical Comparative Study of Experiences of Bereavement in the Western and African Contexts with Implications for Pastoral Care," MA, University of Aberdeen, 2001, 4-10.

Mukuka, Sylvia, "The Quest for Embracing Indigenous Knowledge Systems in The United Church of Zambia; Pastoral Care and the Imbusa," PhD, University of KwaZulu Natal, 2019.

Mulalami, Charity, "A Feminist Critique of Ecumenical Bodies' Silence to the Sexual Abuse of the Women with Mental Disability in Zambia', MA, University of KwaZulu Natal, 2020.

Mulambya-Kabonde, Peggy, "Ordination of Women: Partnership, Praxis and Experience of the United Church of Zambia," PhD, University of KwaZulu-Natal, 2014.

Mulambya-Kabonde, Peggy, "Ordination of Women: Partnership, Praxis, and Experience of the UCZ," PhD, University of KwaZulu Natal, 2014.

Mungaila, Stellah, "A Christian Feminist Critique of Pastors' Authority Roles: A Case of Twelve Pentecostal Churches in Lusaka, Zambia," PhD, University of Zambia, 2015.

Mushibwe, Christine, "What are the Effects of Cultural Traditions on the Education of Women (The Study of the Tumbuka People of Zambia)," PhD, University of Huddersfield, 2009, 109;

Mwiche, Mary Zulu, "An Evaluation of the Role and Relevance of Theological Training at the Theological College of Central Africa, in Response to the HIV/AIDS Situation in Ndola, Zambia," Honours Project, University of KwaZulu-Natal, 2004.

Ntuli, Thandi, "Ubuntombi – A Zulu Religio-cultural Heritage and Identity: A Path to Adulthood and Sex Education Practices," PhD, University of KwaZulu-Natal, 2018.

Oliello, J.K., "The Gospel and African Culture: Polygamy as a Challenge to the Anglican Church of Tanzania – Diocese of Mara," MTh, University of KwaZulu-Natal, 2005.

Paul, S., *An Introduction to the Lozi Culture*, Unpublished Booklet, 1996.

Sakala, Foston Dziko, "A Study of the History of Theological Education in the Dutch Reformed Church Mission in Zambia and its Role in the Life of Zambian Christianity," PhD, UNISA, 1996.

Siwila, Lilian Cheelo, "African Women, Hospitality and HIV/AIDS: The Case of the Mothers' Union of St. Margaret's United Church of Zambia," MA, University of KwaZulu Natal.

Siwila, Lilian Cheelo, "Gender, Culture and HIV and AIDS: United Church of Zambia's Response to Traditional Marriage Practice," PhD, University of KwaZulu Natal, 2011.